A THOUSAND FACES

LON CHANEY'S
UNIQUE ARTISTRY
IN MOTION PICTURES

LON CHANEY-Metro Goldwyn-Mayer

4C-1

A THOUSAND FACES

LON CHANEY'S UNIQUE ARTISTRY IN MOTION PICTURES

Michael F. Blake

Lanham ◆ New York ◆ Oxford

VESTAL PRESS, Inc.

Published in the United States of America
by Vestal Press, Inc.
4720 Boston Way
Lanham, Maryland 20706

British Library Cataloguing in Publication Information Available

Library of Congress Cataloging-in-Publication Data

Blake, Michael F. (Michael Francis), 1957–
    A thousand faces : Lon Chaney's unique artistry in motion pictures /
Michael F. Blake. —1st ed.
      p.   cm.
    Includes bibliographical references and index.
    ISBN 1-879511-20-7 (cloth : alk. paper) — ISBN 1-879511-21-5
(pbk. : alk. paper)
    1. Chaney, Lon, 1883–1930. I. Title.
PN2287.C48B59   1995
791.43'028'092—dc20   95-44639

ISBN: 978-1-879511-21-7
ISBN 1-879511-21-5 (pbk. : alk. paper)

⊖™ The paper used in this publication meets the minimum requirements of
American National Standard for Information Sciences—Permanence of
Paper for Printed Library Materials, ANSI Z39.48–1984.
Manufactured in the United States of America.

For Linda,
whose support is endless

Autographed picture to Joseph De Grasse and his screenwriter/director wife, Ida May Park. Chaney appeared in 67 pictures for the husband-and-wife team during his early years at Universal.

Table of Contents

Preface ix

Acknowledgements xiii

An Actor Beyond Greasepaint 1

A Theatrical Education (1883 - 1913) 11

A Fledgling Career at Universal (1913 - 1918)..................................21

From Freelancing to Stardom (1919 - 1923) 39

A Hunchback Becomes an International Star (1923) 102

A Phantom Before Stardom at M-G-M (1924 - 1928) 147

The Actor's Actor (1928 - 1930) 229

Chaney's Life on Film: Man of a Thousand Faces (1957) 309

Appendix...331

Endnotes 349

Bibliography 377

Index 383

About the Author...397

Lon Chaney
*The Man of 1000 faces
and 100 million fans*

Chaney's popularity at its peak: a page from an M-G-M exhibitors book.

Preface

I was thirteen years old when I saw my first Lon Chaney film. It was not the often-shown *The Hunchback of Notre Dame* or *Phantom of the Opera*, nor was it one of the many films he made at M-G-M studios. No, my introduction to the world of Lon Chaney movies was the 1922 independent film *Shadows*, which was being shown on a local PBS station. Although the print was less than pristine, I found myself fascinated with Chaney's performance, and from then on I was hooked. I had first become interested in Chaney three years earlier when I watched his film biography starring James Cagney. But until I saw that scratched and faded print of *Shadows*, my exposure to Lon Chaney had been limited to brief clips I'd seen from *The Hunchback of Notre Dame* and *Phantom of the Opera*, which had served only to whet my appetite. At that time, Chaney's other films were merely vague images that I saw in books, so scarce were the opportunities to actually see a Chaney film on the screen. I had no idea what any of these films held in store for me, and only the anticipation of Chaney's masterful performances kept my interest piqued until the time when I would be lucky enough to see them.

Admittedly, *Shadows* is probably not a good first choice for an aspiring Chaney fan. While Lon's performance is excellent, the pace of the film is unmercifully slow for a thirteen-year-old. Yet Chaney's exceptional talent was able to reach out and grab my attention so forcefully that I walked around my house mimicking his performance long after the movie was over. When I finally was able to view *The Hunchback of Notre Dame* and *Phantom of the Opera* in their entirety, they further ignited my passion and, like the person who can't eat just one potato chip, my appetite became insatiable for more Chaney films. Since that time, I have had the good luck to view 36 of the 41 existing films from his 156 known screen performances. While the remaining 115 pictures are considered forever lost, I

A Thousand Faces

remain hopeful that more of his work will eventually surface so that the legion of his admirers might be able to see yet other facets of Lon's talent.

I must confess that I never planned to pen a second volume on Lon Chaney, and after six and a half years of research, I honestly thought I had unearthed every possible piece of information available on him. Then, to my dismay, every biographer's nightmare came true — I uncovered some material that had *never* been available before. At first I was terribly depressed, lamenting, "Where was this stuff three years ago?" But I wanted to see this material published. I considered including it in a magazine article, yet if I had done that, much of it would have had to be either condensed or simply omitted altogether. Over the years, several film historians have expressed the desire to author books relating to Chaney's performances but, for whatever reasons, the projects never came to fruition. Realizing that there was a literary void and that a text of this nature was definitely needed, I made the decision to write this book. Besides, a book is the best forum in which to present new material of this magnitude.

I never would have given a thought to authoring this book, however, if it hadn't been for the introduction by Connie Chaney to the relatives of Alfred Grasso (Chaney's business manager from 1920 to 1924). They generously shared their wealth of material with me, enabling another dimly lit passage of Chaney's life and the history of that era to see the light of day. Chaney's admirers owe a debt of gratitude to Lillian Broadbent, Mary Clark, and her daughter Tina Rainey for saving this amazing material.

In *Lon Chaney: The Man Behind the Thousand Faces*, my biography of Chaney, I deliberately avoided analysis of his numerous performances because, in my opinion, it is not the place of a biographer to assay his subject's work. Instead, I wanted to give the reader a sense of what the man was like away from the camera. In this volume, though, I do indeed endeavor to give the reader a sense of what Chaney was trying to convey through his performances. Other writers attempting to analyze an actor's performances tend to integrate their own opinions into their analyses. Some may have little or no idea of what it takes to give a character life on the stage or on the screen. But having grown up with a father who was a film actor for over 40 years, having worked as a child actor myself for 18 years, and having spent the past 16 years as a make-up artist for motion pictures and television, I feel I have a fairly good idea of what it takes for an actor to create a role. This background, combined with the fact that I have studied Lon Chaney's life both on and off the screen for the last 28 years and have viewed his pictures numerous times (for which I could possibly set a Guinness world record!), gives me some additional insight into his performances, which I hope to be able to convey to you. Of course, some readers may disagree with my opinions. This is, of course, both expected and welcomed. My father once said that acting was simply a matter of opinion. Some think John Wayne was a great actor, while others strongly take the opposite opinion. The purpose of this book, aside from passing on the new-found information, is to stimulate the thinking of those who have seen Lon Chaney's work. You may not agree with my opinions, but if this book gives you a better understanding and some insight into the depth of this truly gifted artist, then the book has accomplished one of its purposes.

Most books dealing with the performances of an actor are fairly cut and dried (i.e., boring). I hope that with the infusion of the newly discovered material and my discussions regarding Chaney's performances, you will not only find this book to be of interest but also will discover another piece of the puzzle that is Lon Chaney, the actor and the man. I have included photographs of several deleted scenes from many of his pictures. These photos are by no means a complete record because 115 of his films are lost, and there is no way of telling what may have been cut from these films when they were originally released. However, this just serves to illustrate that before the phrase "your work is on the cutting room floor" became part of the Hollywood vernacular, an actor's best performance could indeed end up on that ill-fated floor.

With the advent of videotapes, laser discs, and classic movie channels on cable television, Lon's admirers are finally able to see some of his performances that just a few years ago were generally difficult to find unless one was fortunate enough to live near a revival theatre or metropolitan library. These new medias are allowing a whole new generation to see why Lon Chaney and his contemporaries were considered screen legends. This was made clear to me recently, when I observed the reaction of a certain twelve-year-old boy who was seeing Chaney's *The Unknown* for the first time. Throughout the film, the young boy (without ever taking his eyes from the screen) would pull his foot up to his face, mimicking Lon as the armless knife thrower. With a sense of déjà vu, I realized that Lon Chaney had once again reached out and touched someone with his unique talent.

Michael F. Blake

Acknowledgements

A book such as this cannot be accomplished by just one person. I am greatly indebted to the following people for sharing their knowledge and advice.

Robert G. Anderson

Larry Austin

Larry J. Blake

Teresa A. Blake

Mary Bourne

Lillian Broadbent

Harry Carey, Jr.

Harold Casselton

Cinema and Television Library,
University of Southern California,
Los Angeles, California

Connie Chaney

George Chaney

Keith Chaney

Lon R. Chaney, Jr.

Mary and Bert Clark

Ned Comstock

Jackie Coogan

James Curtis

Vincent D'Onofrio

William N. Dunphy

Larry Edmonds Bookshop

Barry L. Friedman

Michael Germain

Sam Gill

Loren Harbert

Mike Hawks

Michael Holland

Margaret Herrick Library,
Academy of Motion Picture
Arts and Sciences
Beverly Hills, California

Roger Hurlburt

Robert Israel

Kevin Joy

Carla Laemmle

Dr. Burton J. Lee III

Los Angeles Public Library
Los Angeles, California

Scott MacQueen

Bob McChesney

Leonard McSherry

Leonard Maltin

Lisa Mitchell

Joseph Newman

Cheryl Pappas

Vance Pollock

James Peers III

Harvey Perry

Joseph Pevney

Vincent Price

Tina Rainey

The Silent Movie Theatre,   Steve Tanner

    Hollywood, California   Takashi Teshigawa

Malcolm Sabiston   Mitch Trimboli

Leonard Schrader   Charles Van Enger, A.S.C.

David J. Skal   Herbert Voight

Willard Sheldon   George Wagner

David C. Smith   Bret Wood

Lamar D. Tabb   Patrick Wood

I would also like to thank Elaine Stuart at The Vestal Press
for her help and unwavering support.

One of the many publicity pictures M-G-M designed to illustrate Chaney's varied talents.

An Actor
Beyond Greasepaint

———————————

This is an extremely rare picture showing Chaney applying make-up to his face, in this case fake blood. The blood was actually chocolate syrup, which photographed with greater accuracy than red with orthochromatic film stock. Note the man to the left holding the mirror for Chaney. (Taken on the set of *Tell It to the Marines* [1927].)

L on Chaney was *not* a "horror actor."

This inaccurate and misleading designation has been applied to Chaney for over fifty years, primarily because his son, Creighton, better known as Lon Chaney, Jr., found moderate success in the horror films produced by Universal Studios in the 1940s. Unfortunately, the adage "like father, like son" doesn't apply in this case, but Hollywood producers were quick to capitalize on Creighton's family name, and they placed him in numerous horror films under layers of make-up. Because Lon's most often-viewed pictures, *The Hunchback of Notre Dame* and *Phantom of the Opera*, have been seen so many times on television, while his work at M-G-M has been limited to screenings at universities and museums, his persona as a horror actor has been embedded in the mind of the public.

This appellation has also been derived from numerous monster magazines beginning in the 1950s. While many younger fans of Lon Chaney cite these periodicals (along with the Chaney film biography, *Man of a Thousand Faces*) as sparking their interest in the actor, the magazine coverage has proved to be a double-edged sword. Editors have indeed printed pictures and stories about Chaney, as well as other actors who might have been forgotten by a new generation, but for the monster-genre magazines. Unfortunately they have also helped to stereotype Chaney as an actor who supposedly appeared in numerous horror films and they have perpetuated the many inaccurate myths that have surrounded Chaney since his death. Even though many of the actor's coworkers were still alive during the 1950s and 1960s, these magazines never attempted to interview any of these people. Such interviews could have put to rest the fabricated stories and given us a more factual interpretation of Chaney's life and career. These magazines rarely published pictures or stories relating to Chaney's non-made up roles, such as in *Tell It to the Marines* or *While the City Sleeps*. Instead, editors preferred to play up Chaney's more elaborate make-ups, some of which were not even part of a horror film! Consequently, these magazines have served only to promote Chaney as a horror actor and have done little to present him as he truly was, a serious actor with a wide appeal.

The monster magazines were not the only medium to give the wrong impression of Chaney. Most of Chaney's films, until the recent advent of cable television and videotapes, were not readily available to his many admirers. Unless you lived near a major city where libraries or revival theaters provided screenings (especially the M-G-M pictures), the only films shown with any frequency were *The Hunchback of Notre Dame* and *Phantom of the Opera*, and even then they were usually billed as a Halloween special. People have come away with the preconceived idea that these two titles are horror films when, in truth, they are variations on the Beauty and the Beast theme. The limited screenings of Chaney's work (as well as the movies of many other stars of the silent era) have, until recently, left film buffs with a restricted knowledge of the vast range of Chaney's performance capabilities.

As other Chaney films have become available for viewing, however, people have begun to realize that there was more to his talent than a few vivid portrayals or elaborate make-ups. Lon never used make-up as a crutch for his acting, nor was it something he merely slapped on because the script said the character wore a beard or had a large nose. He put a great deal of thought into each of his roles, often analyzing his character or making a study of someone on the street, preparation that would later become part of his interpretation on the screen. Lon felt that make-up could show at a glance the kind of person he was portraying. He wanted to get into the mind and heart of a role, "but, as a man's face reveals much that is in his mind and heart, I attempt to show this by the make-up I use, and the make-up is merely the prologue." [1]

Chaney's complete absorption of a character extended not only to make-up but to the character's wardrobe and gestures, as well. A character's wardrobe, not just the clothing itself but its tailoring, is important to the overall portrayal. Chaney's attention to the minute details in his wardrobe is clearly evident, whether it was the food-stained vest of the detective in *While the City Sleeps* or the oversized coat he wore to hide his bent-up legs in *The Penalty*. Equally important were the gestures and body movements of his characters. For instance, Lon felt that if a woman were to play a mother, she must know how to handle a baby properly or she would not be believed. [2] Before he ever set foot in front of the camera, Chaney thought out every gesture of his character, how he might use his hands and body, how he would walk, even how he might talk. A tremendous amount of thought and preparation went into each role, so that on the screen, everything he did appeared to be second nature — a true compliment to Chaney's talent. Despite the use of greasepaint, or the lack of it, Chaney always brought a certain chemistry to his characters that can best be described by that often abused word "charisma." No matter how grotesque some of his characters were, Chaney had that magical quality that the camera inevitably picked up and audiences responded to. As one reviewer said of Chaney, "This star is the only film luminary who can play dumb gents minus sex appeal and ring the gong at the box office." [3]

A Thousand Faces

Chaney was highly respected by his fellow actors, and they looked upon him as the consummate artist. The impression that emerges from these professionals who either worked with him or knew him personally is that he was considered the actor's actor of his time. Critics, for the most part, admired his work, although there were a few who occasionally found fault with some of his performances. The volume of Lon's fan mail had increased to 10,000 letters a week by the late 1920s, yet Lon judged his popularity only by the box office receipts. Had Chaney been under contract to any other studio, his popularity might not have been so great. But he was fortunate to have been working at M-G-M in the mid-twenties, where his material was carefully chosen by Irving Thalberg. Lon found an ally in Thalberg, who recognized his unique talent and showcased it with the proper material. It's doubtful that any other studio executive would have had the foresight to place Lon in *Tell It to the Marines*, proving to the skeptics that he truly could play any role. It's a shame that Chaney wasn't given the opportunity to play in more comedies or that the camera never caught him singing and dancing. The roles Lon could have played in talking pictures appear to be endless, and it frustrates the Chaney fan to realize that such a promising career in sound films was cut far too short.

After Lon's death there was speculation that Wallace Beery would play the roles that had been planned for him. Some writers have suggested that Beery's role in *The Big House* was actually written for Chaney, who was too sick to do the film at the time. There is no evidence to indicate that this role was planned for Chaney, although he certainly could have played the part. Others suggested that Boris Karloff would take up where Chaney had left off. While both Beery and Karloff were fine actors, they lacked Chaney's unique talent. Beery was generally typecast as the same character in most of his M-G-M films, with the notable exceptions of *Grand Hotel* and *Viva Villa*. Because of his height and weight, he could not assimilate himself into a role the way Chaney did. It's hard to imagine Beery playing *Mr. Wu* or the tragic clown in *Laugh, Clown, Laugh*, yet it is easy to picture Lon in Beery's role in *Grand Hotel, Dinner at Eight, Viva Villa*, or numerous other films.

Boris Karloff is another who has been labeled a horror actor. Although most of his roles were in the horror genre, it is unfortunate that his notable performances in *The Lost Patrol* or *The Unconquered* go unnoticed. When an interviewer in the 1960s made the observation that Chaney was a "monster man," Karloff quickly refuted the claim. "Well I wouldn't say 'Monster Man,' but he was a brilliant make-up artist, and a very, very, very fine actor," he replied. [4] Unlike Chaney, Karloff didn't have a Thalberg to properly select his material at Universal. Karloff was placed in horror film after horror film and was never given the opportunity to play other roles. Although he was a fine actor, he nevertheless lacked a certain warmth and appeal that Chaney brought to his roles. While Karloff could assimilate himself into more diverse roles, he was still limited because of his distinct accent and unique facial structure. No matter how much make-up or what the disguise, there was always that unmistakable Karloff visage underneath.

When Lon's son, Creighton, entered pictures in 1932, the young man was insistent that he make it on his own and not cash in on his father's famous name. Unfortunately, while Creighton's work was adequate, it did not stand out from that of other actors. At first, he flatly refused to change his name to Lon Chaney, Jr. Creighton claimed that he was almost starving before he gave in and reluctantly took his father's name. It was a move he would always regret, and he once bitterly remarked, "I'm proud of the name Lon Chaney, but not Lon Chaney, Jr." [5] Lon never wanted his son in the industry; he knew all of the industry's pitfalls and had hoped to keep Creighton away from them. He felt that being a bank manager or plumber was a better profession, and he made the picture business appear as

A Thousand Faces

difficult as possible to discourage his son. Another reason why Creighton would have had a hard time finding success in films was that, at 6-feet-2, he would have had difficulty integrating himself into a role. Instead, roles had to be built around him, but this, with very few exceptions, was rarely successful. [6]

Creighton also had to endure the inevitable comparisons with his father's talent, something that he sorely lacked. Comparisons are a curse most children of famous acting parents must endure and, unfortunately, most do not weather the correlation successfully. Creighton was a good supporting player, as evidenced in numerous roles such as those in *High Noon* or *Of Mice and Men*, yet he lacked the range his father displayed. While many horror fans claim he was as big a star as his father, in reality he is looked upon by Hollywood and film historians as a minor star of B pictures and a competent character actor. Creighton never reached, let alone equaled, the pinnacle of popularity his father had enjoyed — no doubt something that haunted him for the duration of his career. After his contract at Universal expired in the late 1940s, his career was reduced to appearances in B pictures, many of them low-budget horror films. Occasionally he was given a meaty role, such as in *High Noon* or *The Defiant Ones*, but they were the exceptions. He continued to appear in pictures and in guest spots on numerous television shows. By the late 1960s he was appearing in such trash as *Hillbillies in a Haunted House* or *Dracula vs. Frankenstein*, and displaying the ravages of alcohol, which had aged him beyond his 65 years. He once said he wanted to top his father, [7] but sadly he never equaled his father's success.

It's unfortunate that an actor is often remembered for only one or two outstanding roles, with the rest of his accumulative work overlooked or simply forgotten. I hope that this book and my previous biography will help the reader understand what a unique talent we had in Lon Chaney. Those who remember him as merely a "horror actor," focusing on a handful of pictures, not only are doing a disservice to Chaney's memory but are shortchanging themselves. Often people who express no interest in seeing a film such as *Tell It to the Marines* or *While the City Sleeps*, simply because Chaney plays a "straight" role, change their opinion after seeing the films. They even express surprise at the fine performances Chaney rendered.

There will never be a successful heir to Lon Chaney. Nor will there be one to Wallace Beery or Boris Karloff. Each actor was different and unique in his own right, and that it is what made them popular. Words like "immortal" or "legendary" are, like the term "charisma," badly abused when describing celebrities. But there are a few who are truly deserving of being knighted with these titles. Their work withstands the test of time, and their performances are as fresh and exciting to new generations of film lovers as they were to those who first saw their pictures 70 to 80 years ago. The continued viewing of their films at revival theatres and libraries and on cable television proves that they remain a vital influence on our American cinema culture.

Sixty-five years after the release of Lon Chaney's last picture, his performances still reach out and touch new admirers. The compendium of his work can influence a thirteen-year-old watching him perform for the first time, a writer like Ray Bradbury, or an actress like Whoopi Goldberg. This, combined with his unique talent, has earned Lon Chaney legendary status in motion picture history.

A rare picture of Lon (left) posing with an unknown performer from his musical comedy days. The baldcap with wig, putty on the tip of his nose, and goatee are proof that Lon was experimenting with make-up in his early days on the stage. (Courtesy of Loren Harbert)

A Theatrical Education

_____

(1883 -1913)

Colorado Springs' Antler's Hotel at the foot of Pike's Peak and Cascade Avenues in 1902. This picture was taken of the famous hotel shortly after its re-opening after the 1899 fire. This was the hotel where Lon helped lay carpets and hang wallpaper during his employment at Brown's Wall paper and Paint Company. (Courtesy of Pioneer's Museum)

Champion Benj F, tinner Lowell Meservey Hdw Co, bds 209 Moren ave, Colorado City.

Champion Consld M Co The, F G Black pres, J W D Stovell sec 21-22 P O bld.

Champion Maria S, dom 1431 N Tejon.

Champlin Belle, music tchr, bds 1417 N Weber.

Chandlee Allen, emp Whitaker Ptg Co, bds 415 N Oak.

Chandler Chas (Wilson & Chandler), res Ye Chelton Inn.

Chandler Earle, clk W P Bonbright & Co, bds 1023 N Corona.

Chandler Harry F, mining, bds 1023 N Corona.

Chandler Jacob G, contr & bldr, res 1023 N Corona (Mrs Anna B)

Chaney Frank H, barber, res 621 E Boulder (Mrs Emma A).

Chaney Jno O, stage carp, res 604 N Pine (Mrs Belle).

Chaney Leonard, emp Opera Hse, bds 621 E Boulder.

Chapin Raymond E, letter carrier, res 1307 Washington ave (Mr Emma M).

Chapman Bertha Miss, waitress 1123 N Cascade ave.

Chapman Charles, labr, bds 405 S Nevada ave.

Chapman Chas H, mason, res 1631 Grant ave (Mrs Emily).

Chapman Dora B, bds 1213 N Walnut.

CHAPMAN HARRY C, res 1730 Wood ave. Tel Main 689 B (Mr

Page from the Colorado Springs City Directory of 1902. Lon, listed as Leonard, had given up the wallpapering and carpet-laying trade to work full-time as an employee at the local Opera House. Lon' brother John is listed above him, as is his father.

No dramatist could have created a better background for a protagonist than Lon Chaney's own life and career, which contained the ingredients of every playwright's dream for a successful production: drama, comedy, irony, and triumph. Although he lived only forty-seven years, Lon Chaney was dealt a life full of the experiences that would serve him well in his chosen profession, for he would become known as the world's greatest character actor.

Born to deaf parents on April 1, 1883, Leonidas Frank Chaney seemed destined to excel in silent pictures. His birth name was anglicized to Leonard, and Lon became the nickname that would later burn brightly upon the marquees of movie theatres around the world. His maternal grandparents founded the Colorado School for the Deaf in Chaney's hometown of Colorado Springs in 1874. His mother Emma taught there during Lon's early years. His father, Frank, was one of the town's most popular barbers for over thirty years. But the Chaney household was far from being financially comfortable, especially after Emma was stricken with inflammatory rheumatism. Every penny had to be counted; there was no room in the family's tight budget for expenditures such as a nurse to see to her comfort. That duty fell on Lon's young shoulders, and because of it, his formal education came to a halt in the fourth grade. For three years, he took care of his mother and saw to the household chores. According to Lon's second wife, Hazel, he would often sit next to his mother and draw sketches for her amusement. [8] He was very fond of his parents and was their favorite, an issue the other siblings accepted without jealousy. [9] Hazel said that Lon's father once told her that when they were scolded, the other children would turn away from their parents in order to avoid their scathing gestures. Lon was the only one who would face them and watch their sign language movements.

As a deaf person, Emma Chaney was shut out from the hearing world, and now, because of her illness, she was also cut off from any social activities. The seed of Lon Chaney's pantomime talent was first sown during this time of family crisis. In order to communicate with his mother and to help take her mind off her illness, he would act out the events taking place in the city or around the world. He often would amuse his mother by mimicking his friends or their neighbors. As Lon grew, so did his talent, and soon he had broadened his repertoire to include performing skits with graceful movements and expressive body and facial gestures, all of which would later serve him well. It is a shame that Emma did not live long enough to see her son reach the heights of stardom, because she inadvertently had had a hand in its beginning.

When his younger sister, Carrie, and brother, George, were old enough to take over the household duties, Lon went to work to help with the family finances. During the summer months of 1897, he worked as a guide at Pike's Peak, taking tourists up the famous mountain by burro. In later years, Lon would find the mountains and his love of fly-fishing a welcome diversion from the cameras and bright lights of Hollywood. Asked by a writer if fishing were his favorite recreation, Lon replied,

> Absolutely. I've been fishing for trout ever since I
> was a kid when I got a job guiding tourists up Pike's
> Peak.There were some great streams up there and I
> learned to regard a mountain trout as the greatest
> adversary for a fisherman's skill in waters anywhere.

I've never cottoned to this deep sea fishing they
rave about out here. Give me a mountain stream,
and trout. [11]

It was also around this time that he was introduced to the
theatrical world by his older brother, John, who was working as a
stagehand at the local Opera House. John obtained a position for Lon
as a prop boy, which opened the door to Lon's lifelong career. One
can only imagine the impression that a theatre must have made on
the fourteen-year-old Lon Chaney: the hectic callings of the stage
manager, the prop men scurrying to place the props in the right
places, stagehands moving flats and furniture with quick, easy
movements. And then there were the actors. A young man assigned
the part of an elderly seventy-year-old on stage might be joking
around backstage or perhaps even chasing a chorus girl. There
would be people talking in normal voices one moment and then on
stage speaking with a dialect. For a boy of fourteen, all this hustle
and bustle must have made a vivid impression. Contrary to popular
belief, Chaney never witnessed the noted stage actor Richard
Mansfield perform in Colorado Springs. Mansfield's only known
performance at the Opera House was in 1880, three years before
Chaney's birth. [12]

It was the turn of the century and an era when being an actor
was hardly looked upon as a decent profession. Many boarding
houses would display signs that stated, "No Dogs or Actors," and
Frank Chaney was insistent that two sons in the theatrical business
were two too many. He wanted Lon to earn his living at an "honest"
trade. So Lon began to learn the craft of carpet laying and wallpaper
hanging, and in 1900, he helped install the carpets and wallpaper at
the Antler's Hotel when it was being rebuilt after the devastating fire
of 1899. This trade would later help Lon during the many dry spells
of his early acting career, and he once stated that a man should have
a trade to fall back on. [13] However, the theatre was in his blood, and

by 1902, he had turned in his tack hammer for a life in the theatre. Lon became a full-time employee of the Colorado Springs Opera House, and that April marked Lon Chaney's acting debut in *The Little Tycoon*. *The Colorado Springs Gazette* noted that Chaney's performance

> provoked laughter whenever he appeared on the stage and his dancing was received with loud acclamations of approval. As a comedian he is irresistible, and it would be hard to find his equal in dancing among many first class vaudeville performers. [14]

Buoyed by this review, Chaney appeared in two more productions in the following year, *Said Pasha* and *The Chimes of Normandy*. He left Colorado Springs in 1904 to tour the midwest with the Columbia Comic Opera Company as an actor, stage manager, stage hand, and wardrobe and transportation handler. In 1905, the Columbia Comic Opera Company performed a two-week engagement at the Delmar Gardens in Oklahoma City. It was there that Lon met a stage-struck sixteen-year-old girl named Cleva Creighton, who joined the troupe as one of the chorus. A romance bloomed and marriage quickly followed. When Chaney's only child, son Creighton Tull, was born in Oklahoma City on February 10, 1906, Lon abandoned the theatre for more honorable work in a furniture store, falling back on his old trade of carpet laying.

But the footlights were calling to him and before long, with his young family in tow, Chaney returned to the theatre, traveling with numerous musical comedy troupes. Once again he performed the jobs of several people, making him extremely useful to any producer trying to save a dollar here and there. Lon returned to performing (and co-directing) with a local troupe in Oklahoma City at the Delmar Gardens. *The Daily Oklahoman* stated in its review of *La Mascotte*:

A Theatrical Education

> Lon Chaney, as Prince Lorenzo, was easily the
> favorite character in the play. He and Charles Pryor,
> as Farmer Rocco, made an excellent team. They
> were the life and zest of the show. Cleverly
> changing the lines of their jokes to satire on
> prominent persons and familiar places, they earned
> the applause of the audience. [15]

By 1910, the Chaneys had arrived in Los Angeles, where John
Chaney was working at the Burbank Theatre as a flyman. [16] The
Chaneys found work at the Olympic Theatre, performing with the
Charles Alphin Amusement Company. Six months later, Lon and
Cleva joined the Ferris Hartman Company, playing opposite Roscoe
"Fatty" Arbuckle and Robert Z. Leonard. During the run of *The
Gingerbread Man*, Lon, playing the title role, and Roscoe Arbuckle,
playing the Good Fairy, performed what must have been an
extremely entertaining duet called "Do You Believe In Santa Claus?".

After finishing his engagement with Ferris Hartman's company,
Lon went on to perform with Max Dill, in San Francisco and Los
Angeles, in *The Rich Mr. Hoggenheimer*. Lon not only essayed two
small roles in the play, the First Custom House Inspector and the
Head Waiter, but also served as stage director for the production. It
was something of a family affair because Cleva played the Lady
Dedbroke and George, Lon's youngest brother, was master of
transportation for the company. [17] From February through August
1912, Lon served as actor, choreographer, and stage manager for
Fischer's Follies, performing in three weekly matinees and one
evening performance, seven days a week. Lon Chaney's work, which
had previously been overlooked in Los Angeles, caught the eye of the
Los Angeles Times theatre critic, Julian Johnson. Whether being
reviewed in a play or mentioned in Johnson's theatre column,
Chaney's talent was now becoming recognized.

The musical comedies of that period provided Chaney, as well as
many other actors, with a training ground upon which to build a

career. Good material was scarce, which meant that the different troupes would often perform the same plays. This required an actor to come up with fresh ways to make his character different to avoid the inevitable comparisons with the many others who essayed the same role. Most traveling troupes had a repertoire of five or six plays they would perform during an engagement. Some of the larger troupes, like Ferris Hartman or Fisher's Follies, who enjoyed extended engagements at one theatre, would have ten to fourteen plays on their rosters. Again, the weekly or bi-weekly program changes allowed little time for an actor to work up a detailed characterization. This was a point Julian Johnson noted in his review of *An American Idea*, stating, "Considering the enormous amount of toll Chaney has in getting out the choral numbers in these weekly pieces, the fact that he found time to get up such a bright, clean-studied characterization of his own speaks loudly for his superior talent." [18]

Performing with these musical comedy troupes was demanding work, both physically and mentally. While performing one play at night, actors spent their days rehearsing the following week's production. For Chaney, the work was doubly demanding because he not only played a role, but also choreographed the musical numbers and served as stage manager. The pay was low and the hours long, with some companies performing three matinees and two nightly performances every day, seven days a week. Adding to the pressure of these demands was the constant threat that a company's engagement could be canceled at any time if the box office receipts were lacking, and the performers might simply be left stranded. Chaney considered himself lucky when he latched onto a show that ran for six months. He and Cleva would then diligently save every penny they could, only to see their meager savings eaten up when they were unemployed. The fear of being without work and money was something that became so ingrained in Chaney's personality that it never left him, even after he achieved stardom.

Chaney rejoined Kolb and Dill's company in San Francisco in September 1912, to act in and also stage the musical numbers and serve as the company's stage manager. The *San Francisco Chronicle* noted the following about Kolb and Dill's production of *In Dutch*:

> In the second act she [Olga Steck] has a dance
> number with Lon Chaney which is actually acrobatic
> and whirl-windy and all but unbelievably agile. This
> number wits wild endorsement from the
> house...[with] Lon Chaney proving his worth to the
> company in goodly fashion. [19]

Despite the positive reviews, Lon Chaney was still a long way from obtaining stardom. It was at this time that Cleva found favor as a cabaret singer. While working with Lon at the Olympic Theatre in 1910, she originally had been billed as Cleva Chaney, eventually becoming the company's prima donna. In 1912, she reverted to using her maiden name, Creighton, while working in Fischer's Follies, and shortly after that she branched out into the cabaret scene. Here, Cleva's popularity soared while her marriage to Lon began to unravel. Cleva's inability to handle liquor, coupled with her quick success, led to many arguments between them. No doubt Lon was jealous of her rapid rise in popularity while he himself was still considered a second-rate performer in musical comedies. Cleva's problems with alcohol eventually led to an irrational suicide attempt in the wings of the Majestic Theatre in Los Angeles. Finishing her supper show at the Brink's Cafe, she walked over to the theatre, where Lon was working with the Kolb and Dill company. The two quarreled backstage and, while Lon was performing, Cleva swallowed a vial of bichloride of mercury, which robbed her of her beautiful singing voice. When her recovery was assured, Lon separated from Cleva and filed for divorce in December 1913.

A Thousand Faces

In 1931, Cleva was upset over the way she was portrayed in a detailed article about Lon by writer Adela Rogers St. Johns. Cleva threatened to sue, but lacked any legal grounds because Ms. St. Johns had based her story on a personal interview with Cleva, as well as newspaper and court documents. [20] In a feeble attempt to paint herself in a more positive light, Cleva penned her own version of how she and Lon met and claimed that when Lon learned of her pregnancy, he urged her to abort the child. She never mentioned any of her court-documented infidelities or her attempted suicide, and while her written version was officially notarized, it was never published. [21] Cleva's attempted suicide caused much unwanted attention, and Lon Chaney's theatrical career in Los Angeles was now at a dead end. No matter how talented Chaney was, he would always be associated with this scandal, giving theatrical producers second thoughts when it came to hiring him.

With a small son to support, Lon Chaney was forced to look for another way to provide an income and, more importantly, a stable future. The growing motion picture industry offered steady work and did not require much travel — an ideal circumstance for a single parent. And a theatrical background was considered an asset when it came to obtaining film work. So Lon Chaney gave up the footlights of the theatre to take his chances with the new medium of motion pictures, working for an independent studio at the corner of Sunset Boulevard and Gower Street called Universal Pictures.

A Fledgling Career at Universal

(1913 -1918)

Universal Studios during the teens. (Courtesy of Marc Wanamaker/Bison Archives)

This picture was taken from a Universal Weekly, when Lon was directing one of six films for studio's Victor Company.

In 1913, when Lon Chaney came to Hollywood, the motion picture business had yet to develop into the thriving industry it would soon become. There were no written rules for filmmakers or actors to follow; everything was experimental. What one developed, another tried to take a step further. The length of films grew from one reel (ten to twelve minutes long) to two or three reels, and later they expanded to five and eventually eight or ten reels. Theatres were built specifically for movies, and soon the art of promoting a picture became a specialized field unto itself. Suddenly actors were no longer just actors but *movie stars*, and the public eagerly awaited their favorite star's next film. As the stars' popularity grew at the box office, so did their salaries, until they reached unbelievable proportions, especially when compared with the average person's income at that time.

Movie studios were virtually unheard of in Hollywood before 1911. That was the year when members of the Nestor Film Company arrived in Los Angeles because David Horsley, the director of the company, had been advised to speak with a local photographer about filming conditions in the Hollywood area. Horsley rented the Blondeau Tavern at Sunset Boulevard and Gower Street for thirty dollars a month, and Hollywood had its first official movie studio. [22] Until the arrival of the Nestor Film Company, most studios operated out of downtown Los Angeles or nearby Edendale. Within two years, however, other filmmakers, including Cecil B. De Mille and D. W. Griffith, would follow the lead of Nestor and move their operations to the Hollywood area. This young industry was growing fast, and it didn't take long for the scene to change once again. The small clusters of disheveled buildings that made up most motion picture studios in Los Angeles and Hollywood had to give way to a new form of motion picture production. When Carl Laemmle dedicated Universal City Studios on March 15, 1915, it gave filmmakers vast amounts of acreage within which they could create their fantasies, and the studio itself began to take on an aura of organization much like that of a small city. Buildings were erected for a hospital, cafeteria, film lab, dressing rooms, a large warehouse to handle the numerous props, and a costume department that could clothe a performer as anyone from a Roman soldier to a socialite dressed in the current fashions. Universal City was the studio system in its infancy.

Universal Pictures was formed in 1912 by Carl Laemmle and was first known as The Universal Film Manufacturing Company. Its original purpose was to serve as banker and distributor for the several independent producers who would release their films through Laemmle's company. [23] By 1913, Universal was supporting fourteen production companies, most of which operated out of the hodgepodge of buildings at the corner of Gower Street and Sunset Boulevard. [24] But the public was clamoring for more moving pictures, and Laemmle realized that in order to keep up with the demand, he would need a bigger facility. Thus in May 1914, construction began on a former 250-acre chicken ranch on the other side of the hill from Hollywood, for which Laemmle had paid a price of $165,000. [25] Although Laemmle probably didn't realize it at the time, he was creating history by building the first all-inclusive motion picture studio. Even though the official opening of the studio wasn't until March 1915, just as quickly as the buildings and stages were completed, production companies moved in to finish their products.

A Fledgling Career at Universal

Damon and Pythias was shot entirely on the new studio grounds in 1914. [26] Before Laemmle's purchase of the property, D. W. Griffith had used the area to stage several of the battle sequences for his landmark film, *The Birth of a Nation.*

On the opening day of Universal City Studios, newspapers across the country reported that an entire city had been given over to the making of motion pictures. Just inside the front gates were two theatres, an administration building, a barber shop, technical shops, costume department, and cafeteria with a special area that posted the sign, "For directors and leads only." There was an enormous outdoor stage that measured 300 feet long and 65 feet wide, which could support sixteen film companies at one time. Farther back on the studio property was another stage 200 feet long by 50 feet wide, which had additional dressing rooms, carpentry and scene painting shops, and a prop building. The backlot was littered with a multitude of sets ranging from European villages to western towns. Because the studio produced numerous westerns, a large stable of horses was kept on the backlot, along with a bunkhouse for the wranglers. [27] A small creek running alongside the property was used extensively, even when it became a roaring river during the rainy season. Flooding was commonplace and, in typical fashion, stories were devised to take advantage of Mother Nature's torrents. An enclosed stage was built to allow filmmakers to proceed with filming on those not-so-sunny California days, which gave a director the luxury of not being forced to strike his set and props whenever the weather turned threatening. With arc lights, a company could continue filming even when it was pouring outside — that is, if the director could make himself heard over the tremendous noise caused by the pounding rain on the galvanized metal roof! [28]

The public was fascinated by the mystery of filmmaking, and visitors on opening day were shown how the studio could simulate a flood. Located on one of the hills was a large reservoir that held a half million gallons of water. [29] Studio workers would "create" a flood by releasing several thousand gallons of water, which unfortunately would also flood the nearby sets.

On that first day, the crowds of theatre exchange owners and the general public grew to nearly twenty thousand by midday. Seizing on the public's fascination, Laemmle once again became a pioneer. He came up with the idea of charging a twenty-five cent admission (which also included a box lunch) for the public to visit the studio to watch movies being made. [30] Hundreds of cars and buses jammed the road going through the Cahuenga Pass to Universal, as Laemmle opened the studio gate after being presented with a gold key (which cost $285) [31] by actress Laura Oakley. Newspapers also noted that Thomas A. Edison and Buffalo Bill Cody were among the many celebrities in attendance. [32]

Universal Studios was a training ground for names which would later become part of Hollywood history. Actors such as Harry Carey, Mary Pickford, Lewis Stone, and Jean Hersholt either got their start at the studio or worked there for some time before moving on to greater things. Several directors, including Clarence Brown, Jack Conway, Allan Dwan, Tod Browning, and John Ford, spent their early careers at Universal. Like many others at Universal, Lon Chaney was given the opportunity to sharpen his theatrical talents before the motion picture camera. Movies during those early years tended to be stereotyped into the categories of slapstick comedies, westerns, or broadly-acted melodramas. Yet many of these early movies dealt with adult themes, albeit discreetly compared with the current crop of adult fare. Illegitimacy, abortion, and alcoholism were some of the subjects producers tackled. These storylines and others made up some of the scenarios of Chaney's early films, which usually found him playing the role of the villain.

Although many of his roles were of a villainous nature, Chaney was allowed to play them as numerous character types, much as he had done in his musical comedy days. The villains ran the spectrum of several nationalities, from Spanish or Mexican (*The Tragedy of Whispering Creek, Her Grave Mistake, A Ranch Romance, Her Life's Story*), French Canadian (*The Honor of the Mounted*), and Italian (*The Gilded Spider, Star of the Sea, The Violin Maker, The Menace to Carlotta*), to a Southern plantation owner (*The Grip of Jealousy*). His proficiency at character work enabled him to play a broad range of roles, from a hunchback fisherman (*The Sea Urchin*), a half-wit (*Remember Mary Magdalen*), old men (*Red Margaret, Moonshiner, A Mother's Atonement, If My Country Should Call*), half-breeds (*The Unlawful Trade, Place Beyond the Winds*), and heroic mounties (*The Measure of a Man, Bloodhounds of the North*) to a blind man (*Her Escape*). Despite the heavy dramas, Lon did perform in several slapstick comedies (*Poor Jake's Demise, Almost an Actress, An Elephant on His Hands, Felix on the Job*) and even exhibited his dancing skill (*Father and the Boys*). Sadly, only three of the above-mentioned pictures still survive.

Even then, filmmaking was hazardous work for everyone involved. Veteran stuntman Harvey Perry summed up the risk by saying that if you got hurt, the studio paid your hospital bills and hired someone else to take your place. [33] The brisk pace of making these two or three-reelers could cause some mishaps. For example, while filming *Bloodhounds of the North* and *Honor of the Mounted* in the Mt. Lowe section of California, Lon and actor Arthur Rosson became lost in a deep canyon and were not located by rescue teams until late in the evening. [34] Also, the company became stranded at the Ye Alpine Tavern for five days when heavy rains made filming impossible. In order not to lose any time, director Allan Dwan rehearsed indoors with the cast for his upcoming production of *Richelieu* during the deluge. When the rain cleared, the filming of the two Northwest-themed pictures was completed in two days. [35]

Some film historians believe that Lon did not begin

A Thousand Faces

experimenting with make-up until late 1915 or early 1916. One writer claimed that Chaney's talent with greasepaint blossomed only after working in *Father and The Boys* (1915) with veteran stage actor Digby Bell, who taught him some secrets. This is simply not true. Before ever setting foot in front of a motion picture camera, Chaney was using make-up in musical comedies. Edwin S. Felch, who performed with Lon as early as 1906, taught him several techniques with greasepaint. [36] Make-up, whether on the stage or in the movies, was an essential part of an actor's stock-in-trade. In the early days of motion pictures, actors did not have the accessibility of a make-up artist on the set, and every actor was required to apply his own make-up. If someone such as Chaney were proficient at the craft, he would often help others apply their make-up. Sometimes this knowledge allowed an actor to earn a few extra dollars by creating what a director envisioned. Further support that Chaney used make-up early in his film career is found in the July 25, 1914, issue of *Universal Weekly*. In an article featuring actress Pauline Bush, who was heading a new production company at Universal, Lon, along with actor Joseph King and director Joseph De Grasse, was mentioned as being one of the new company. The story further stated,

> Lon Chaney has worked opposite Miss Bush
> continually since her engagement by Universal. He is
> almost as well known as Miss Bush and is considered
> to be the most versatile make-up artist and the most
> capable 'heavy' in his own line in the business.

The precise date of Lon Chaney's debut in motion pictures will probably remain a mystery forever. Chaney never mentioned when he actually entered films, presumably because he feared that some writer would discover Cleva's suicide attempt and once again dredge up all the adverse publicity it had generated. Working in motion pictures enabled Lon to bury the past and start his acting career anew. It is entirely possible that Lon may have dabbled in films as early as 1912, while he was unemployed. Most industry trade journals at the time rarely listed supporting or bit players, and sometimes even omitted the names of the leading actors. The ads in Universal trade journals from May to August 1913 show faces that *might* be Lon, possibly in make-up. In Chaney's personal photo album is a picture of him dressed as a Roman soldier. It is entirely possible that he may have played a small part in *Damon and Pythias* (1914) because no other picture in his filmography lists him as playing such a role, and he was at the studio during that period.

The cover of the July 5, 1913, issue of *Moving Picture World* features a photograph from *A Woman's Folly*; standing in the background is a man who strongly resembles Chaney. Another example of this guessing game is a March 1914 issue of *Universal Weekly*, which features an ad for *Who Won in the First?*. One of the actors, wearing long sideburns and top hat, looks similar to Lon. But again, since there is no credit for the cast, one is left to speculate. For years, it has been assumed that Chaney made an unbilled appearance in Lois Weber's *Suspense* (1913). He was supposedly seen in a brief glimpse as a vagrant walking along the road as the police race by. But recently having had the opportunity to look at this film frame-by-frame, I am confident that Lon Chaney does *not* appear in it.

All this speculation can drive any film historian crazy while attempting to document Chaney's early film career. Collections of industry trade journals are woefully lacking complete volumes, leaving numerous gaps in the history of early cinema. This problem is further compounded by the scant amount of surviving film prints. Sadly, of the 107 films Chaney made during this period, only eleven survive in either complete or partial form. It is therefore difficult to analyze fully the growth of Chaney's talent during this time. The smattering of his films that does survive allow one to see the potential he displayed to a greater extent later in his career.

As Lon Chaney's career in motion pictures began to grow, his personal life also began to regenerate when he became reacquainted with Hazel Hastings, a former chorus girl. The two had first met while working together for the Ferris Hartman troupe before Hazel left the company to return to her native San Francisco. [37] She later joined the Kolb and Dill company, where Lon replaced Frank Stammers as stage manager. Because Lon had three jobs — stage manager, choreographer, and actor — he had precious little time to care for Creighton. So, Hazel and some of the other chorus girls took turns caring for the young boy during the company's engagement in San Francisco. [38] She said Lon was separated from Cleva during this time. When the Kolb and Dill company went on tour, Creighton was taken care of by Lon's sister, Carrie, who lived in Berkeley. [39] Hazel said that at that time she and Lon were merely friends, yet she grew fond of Creighton. After Cleva's suicide attempt in Los Angeles, Hazel did not see Lon again until November 1913, while she was appearing at the Jahnke's Cafe on Spring Street in Los Angeles. Upon meeting after the show, Lon told Hazel that he and Cleva were divorcing and that he was working steadily in motion pictures as an extra and bit player. [40] She said that at that time, Lon's ambition was to become a film comedian, aspiring to the likes of Chaplin or Ford Sterling. Lon became a steady customer at the cafe, having his dinner there every evening and, after his divorce, Hazel noted, "He became more attentive to me." [41] She returned home for her sister's wedding and from there took a job performing in Portland, Oregon before returning to the Jahnke's Cafe. [42]

She and Lon renewed their relationship upon her return to Los Angeles, and for almost a year and a half, he met her every night after the show to take her home. He was anxious for her to secure a divorce from her husband, with whom she had lived only eighteen months during their seven-year marriage, so that they could settle down together. [43] Her divorce was granted in early November 1915, and Lon and Hazel were married in Santa Ana, California, on

A Fledgling Career at Universal

November 26, 1915. From that point on, Hazel gave up her career, explaining, "I had never been stagestruck, but as it was necessary for me to earn a living, I had followed the line for which I had the most talent." [44] At the time of their marriage, Lon was earning $45 a week even though he did not have a signed contract with Universal. Hazel said that when he was not appearing in a picture, he would work as a prop man or do anything until the next role came up. [45]

By the Sun's Rays (1914) is typical of the two-reel westerns Universal produced at that time and is one of the few complete films in Chaney's career still existing from this period. Lon plays Frank Lawler, an employee of a mining company and the lead villain. Because Chaney is allowed a good deal of screen time, *By the Sun's Rays* becomes a significant film by which to evaluate the beginnings of his film career. It illustrates Chaney's pantomimic ability because the movie uses only nine title cards to advance the story line. It was up to the actors to convey the emotions of the scenes to the audience. At the beginning of the film, Chaney, as Frank Lawler, communicates by furtive glances that he covets the gold sacks that are placed into a strong box. His whole demeanor projects that he is up to something underhanded, especially when he quickly places a mirror under his vest that he will later use to signal his gang that the gold shipment is on the way. As he leaves the office, he encounters the mine superintendent's daughter. Lon smiles and tips his hat. When she does not return his greeting he turns sullen and walks off. Another example of his efficient use of pantomime to convey a change of emotions takes place when he is introduced to the detective who has been sent to stop the robberies. The detective is speaking with the superintendent's daughter, and it's obvious that she is attracted to him. When Lon is introduced to the detective, his amiable expression quickly changes to one of jealousy when he sees the woman he loves show interest in another man.

This role is typical of the ones Lon would essay throughout this period, portraying the villain and meeting his demise by the end of the film. Despite playing the heavy, Lon made his characters realistic, not stereotypical. He used subtle gestures to give his parts depth and texture. Again, in *By the Sun's Rays*, when news arrives that the gold shipment has been stolen, he gleefully smiles, takes the pencil from behind his ear, and touches it on his lips, lost in thought. In another scene, when the superintendent's daughter has her back to him, Lon gently raises his hand and is about to touch her shoulder, but then hesitates and doesn't follow through. In that moment, he brings a sense of humanity to the character despite the villainy of the role. It is a gesture similar to the one he uses later, when he first encounters Mary Philbin in *Phantom of the Opera*.

The ability of an actor to use his face and body to convey the many emotions of a character is essential, especially in silent pictures. Many actors in the early days of cinema used broad gestures and facial expressions. Unfortunately some performers failed to change their technique as acting grew from theatrical melodramas to more realistic performances. Even Chaney was occasionally guilty of this early in his career.

Lon's next film, *The Oubliette* (1914), a dated and slow-moving costume drama, doesn't give him much screen time, which does not allow him to build his character. Yet when on camera, he displays a powerful presence. Lon appears midway through the film and once again plays the villain, who is rather quickly dispatched. His character, Chevalier Bertrand de la Payne, is a man of prominence and exudes an air of authority. Lon's body gestures are entirely within the confines of his part, especially compared with the overacting of the lead, Murdock MacQuarrie. The two men engage in a sword fight in which Lon's character meets his demise. It appears as if Chaney performed his own stunt when his character falls from a second-story balcony onto a table below. Unfortunately, this film does not showcase his talent as well as the next available picture.

A Fledgling Career at Universal

This film, *A Mother's Atonement* (1915), although missing the last of its three reels, presents Chaney in one of his best roles during his early tenure at Universal. Lon plays Ben Morrison, an old man of the mountains, who sports a scruffy grey beard and bushy eyebrows. An old rumpled hat and beat-up clothing complete his appearance, providing a sharp contrast to the character as he appears in flashback sequences, in which he is seen as a younger man. Unlike *The Oubliette*, this film is not badly dated, and the acting is fairly competent under the direction of Joseph De Grasse. This is an important film in judging this period of Chaney's career because it allows us to view Lon's work as directed by De Grasse. From 1914 to 1918, Lon appeared in 64 films for De Grasse and his screenwriter-director wife, Ida May Park. Working for this husband-and-wife team, Lon was given the chance to play various characters and to experiment with make-up. This is readily apparent in this film, in which Lon plays the same character over a thirty-year span.

Lon portrays old Ben Morrison with stooped shoulders and a stiff gait. He often plants his hands in the back pockets of his pants to suggest the hunched appearance of old age. Lon lets his character scratch his beard, giving the facial hair a realistic appearance rather than something that is simply stuck on. His portrayal of old Ben is one of a man who seems consumed by hatred for his daughter, who conjures up the memory of his wife who deserted them years earlier. Like her mother before her, Jen has fled to the city. It appears that Ben doesn't care for his daughter until the last shot in the surviving two reels. The camera fades in on old Ben, staring dejectedly into space, alone in the mountains; but as the fade out begins, he sighs, illustrating his loneliness at the loss of his only child.

As the younger Ben Morrison, Lon appears as a strong and virile man. His erect stature is in direct contrast to that of old Ben, (which further helps to signify the advancement of age). Young Ben is a man who sees his marriage crumbling — no doubt something with which

A Thousand Faces

Chaney could have easily identified. When young Ben enters the cabin after seeing his wife with another man, he stares at her, letting her know he is aware of the affair. Ben starts to turn away and then turns back as if to say something to his wife. He can't and instead sits dejectedly in a chair. This subtle gesture of Lon's character, wanting to say something but hesitating, brings a realistic touch to a scene that could easily have been overacted.

De Grasse's *The Scarlet Car* (1917) gave Lon the opportunity to portray another character with a certain twist. Lon plays Paul Revere Forbes, a bank cashier who discovers that his employer has embezzled a large amount of money. When he confronts his boss about the missing money, a fight erupts between them, and Chaney strikes his head against a file cabinet. Believing him dead, his boss has his body dumped in the country. We are led to believe that Forbes has indeed died, until a flashback sequence shows that he was merely unconscious. The blow to the head causes Chaney's character to have delusions that he is a general during the Revolutionary War, holding a secret document (which is actually a page from the bank ledger implicating his boss). As the bank cashier and father, Chaney presents himself as a dedicated man. Wearing a grey wig and a goatee gives him a dignified appearance, emphasizing the contrast with his character later in the picture. By rubbing his hands and appearing to be lost in thought, he establishes his character's preoccupation with the trouble at the bank. After the fight, however, the mental status of Chaney's character degenerates. His hair becomes disheveled, and the carefully groomed goatee grows into a wild beard, emphasizing his frantic state of mind. Unlike many actors who might have worn a fake beard, Chaney appears comfortable with his, pulling, tugging, and scratching at it, giving it a life-like appearance and making his character all the more believable. In this sequence of the film, Chaney's role permits him to convey the instability of a man who has suffered a blow to the head. When

Forbes displays moments of lucidity, Lon makes his gestures and expressions more subtle, but then just as quickly reverts to his dreamlike state of mind. When he comes face-to-face with his boss, Chaney does not simply stare wildly at the man but conveys a cloudy sense of recognition that helps to expose the true criminal by the end of the picture.

Despite his successful character roles and positive reviews, Lon was still working without a contract at a paltry $75 a week, while other, less talented actors enjoyed the benefits of both better salaries and contracts. When he requested a raise from Universal, they responded by offering him $90 a week. [46] Hazel Chaney recalled, "I could not bear to see him working so hard for so small a salary, after doing such good work with such consistent improvement." [47] She said they both felt he was deserving of a better raise, but Lon was afraid that if he left Universal, he wouldn't find work elsewhere. He countered Universal's offer with one for a weekly salary of $125 and a five-year contract. William Sistrom, the studio manager, rejected his counter-proposal and reportedly remarked that Lon would never be worth $100 a week. Lon left his "home" lot after five years of steady employment and engaged the services of Willis and Inglis as his agents. [48] This was an extremely courageous move on his part, considering the infrequency with which freelance actors had been employed over the years. But Lon felt certain that with the help of his new agents, he was sure to find work elsewhere in Hollywood. Alas, even though he had created many characters and had received encouraging reviews, Lon Chaney was still basically an unknown commodity outside Universal Studios. Weeks of unemployment grew into months, and the actor's old fear of never working again began to set in. Lon later admitted that he considered returning to Universal to take whatever he could get and count his blessings. [49]

But all that changed when he landed the role of Hame Bozzam in *Riddle Gawne* (1918). Contrary to the accepted story that William S.

A Thousand Faces

Hart insisted that Chaney play the villain, it was director Lambert Hillyer who had to sell the idea of using Chaney to Hart. [50] Hazel said that Lon spent several days at home building up his shoes to give him the proper height to play opposite Hart. She also said that when Lon received his salary of $125 a week, they felt as though they were rich. [51] Despite the early doubts of William S. Hart, Lon turned in an effective performance.

Evidently Universal didn't hold a grudge against Lon because after completing *Riddle Gawne* at Paramount, he went on to make three more pictures at his former studio. One thing that did change, however, was his salary; the studio was obliged to meet his original demand of $125 a week. The following year, 1919, proved to be a milestone one for Lon Chaney as he established himself as a prominent character actor with a flair for make-up. Helping him would be director Tod Browning and the ground-breaking role in *The Miracle Man.*

Father and the Boys (1915) is one of Chaney's lost Universal pictures. It is also one of the few films that captured his dancing talents, as this picture illustrates.

Edith Johnson, Lon, and Franklyn Farnum in *The Scarlet Car*. (1917)

Lon and William S. Hart struggle over a six-shooter in *Riddle Gawne* (1918). Leon Kent lies on the ground.

Chaney's first picture with director Tod Browning, *The Wicked Darling* (1919). Left to right: Lon, Kalla Pasha, Spottiswoode Aitken, and Priscilla Dean.

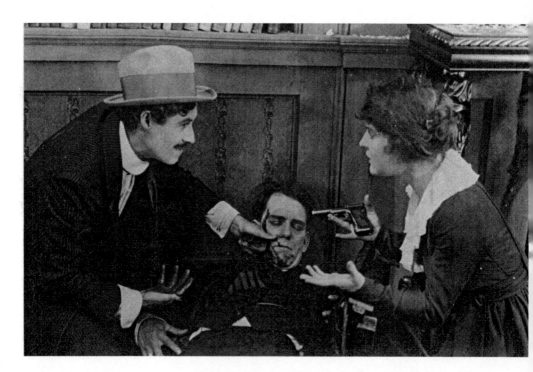

Henry B. Walthall prepares Chaney for his dramatic death scene in *False Faces* (1919), as Mary Anderson watches.

From Freelancing to Stardom

_____

(1919 -1923)

The two faces of "The Frog" — before and after his spiritual transformation in *The Miracle Man*.

By 1919, the motion picture industry had experienced enormous growth. Unfortunately, World War I was destined to hinder the spread of this budding industry to other countries. Britain, France, and Germany were much too involved in the war to produce motion pictures in any substantial number, and even after the war, the European film market was affected by the subsequent rebuilding process. America was fortunate to find herself in the enviable position of being the predominant supplier of motion pictures to the rest of the world. New theatres were being constructed all over America to replace the small nickelodeons that had given birth to the industry, and it has been said that many of these theatres were so grand that they rivaled the great palaces of Europe. Budgets for motion pictures grew from the 1916 average of $25,000 to upward of $80,000 by 1920, with some even soaring to $125,000 when a big-name star was featured. Mary Pickford, Charlie Chaplin, and William S. Hart had developed large followings among moviegoers, which gave them an advantage when negotiating for higher salaries or fringe benefits — much to the dismay of the producers and theatre exhibitors.

Leaving Universal was probably the smartest move Lon Chaney could have made during this period of his career. Had he remained at Universal, he most likely would have been relegated to supporting or secondary lead roles and might never have moved on to become one of Hollywood's predominant character actors. Universal was considered by the industry to be a factory. The studio regularly turned out melodramas, westerns, and comedies to be seen in independent theatre chains across the country. Although Chaney's work was impressive and some of Universal's pictures were well received by critics, Hollywood regarded the studio as capable of producing only program material, certainly nothing of any consequence. *Riddle Gawne* gave Chaney the prestige and boost his career needed, and after working with Hart, Chaney's career took a new course. By freelancing, Chaney was allowed to work with a larger roster of stars and make more money than if he had simply remained under contract to one studio. Each film guaranteed him a certain number of weeks' work, and his salary was raised accordingly. If he had been under contract to only one studio, he would have been forced to play whatever roles were assigned to him. Freelancing gave Lon the opportunity to be selective when choosing his parts. [52]

Producers began to look at him in a different light, recognizing his talent and growing appeal. One such person, who not only recognized but also astutely took advantage of Chaney's talent, was Tod Browning, a rising young director with a flair for underworld films. *The Wicked Darling* (1919) was the first of a ten-picture collaboration between Chaney and Browning, making theirs one of the most successful pairings in motion picture history. This film was one of the first starring vehicles for Priscilla Dean, Universal's leading female star in the early twenties. Although Chaney's role was a supporting one, his performance was praised by critics, and this picture sent him on his way to becoming a leading player of characters and villains. Unfortunately, no print of the film exists, but reviews indicate it was a money-maker for Universal.

False Faces, made during the final months of World War I, was a typical movie of the period, portraying the Germans as beasts determined to unleash their wrath upon the world. By the time it was released in February 1919, the war was over, and the public had tired of "kill the Hun" pictures. Although *False Faces* uses World War I as its background, most of the story takes place aboard an ocean liner, a U-boat, and in New York City. One of the interesting aspects of this film is the artwork of the title cards. During this period, many producers began to experiment with artwork on their title cards to emphasize events taking place in a scene. For instance, the title card referring to Eckstrom, the villain in *False Faces*, displays an artistic rendition of a coiled snake baring its fangs, over which the title caption is superimposed.

The movie conjures up memories of Saturday matinee action films or the recent *Indiana Jones* pictures because of its non-stop action and the hero's narrow escapes from nail-biting situations. Lon is the despised Karl Eckstrom, a role he appears to have thoroughly enjoyed, portraying the man as cunning and vicious. Eckstrom, like many of the German villains during this period and later in World War II-period films, takes delight in his own cruelty. He is a man totally without conscience, a quality which Lon later would endeavor to instill subtly in many of his villains. Even though his role as the wretched antagonist is typical, Lon employs such a menacing glee in his character that when he is killed, the audience can't help but applaud. In that respect, Chaney succeeds in his performance. Especially noteworthy in *False Faces* is a scene that takes place aboard the ocean liner, in which Eckstrom is seen putting on a fake beard as part of his disguise as the boat captain. This is the only time Lon was ever filmed applying his own make-up.

The role that firmly established Chaney as one of the industry's leading character actors was that of the Frog, a fake cripple, in the film that was one of the biggest hits of 1919, *The Miracle Man*. Based on the novel by Frank L. Packard, *The Miracle Man* was originally produced on Broadway in 1917 by George M. Cohan, who had played the lead role of Tom Burke. The film version was written

A Thousand Faces

and directed by George Loane Tucker, who had made a name for himself in the early years of motion pictures by producing the popular *Traffic in Souls* (1913) for Universal. Because of Tucker's success, he was made director-general of the London Film Company, for which he produced several films in England before returning to America. Tucker then went to Goldwyn Pictures, accepting the position of production supervisor. But he soon tired of supervising and returned to directing, turning his attention to *The Miracle Man*. Tucker caused a sensation with this movie, which critics unabashedly called "the greatest picture ever made." At the première on August 26, 1919, at the George M. Cohan Theatre, *Exhibitors Trade Review* noted:

> There was no doubt about the reception this feature received at the hands of the patrons, and many of them are judges of what is, and what is not, good. They were held in a spell until the final scene, when a thunder of applause was heard through[out] the entire house.

Perhaps the most interesting response to *The Miracle Man* was received after a screening for the inmates at Sing Sing Penitentiary. Following the presentation, a representative of Paramount Pictures stated:

> The picture went over beyond all my expectations. I never before saw such a crowd of enthusiasts....Louis Jacobs [chairman of the entertainment committee] said: "The picture carries a message that gets to the men without their knowing why. It isn't crammed down their throats like a preachment. That's why it made a hit with them." [53]

One inmate reportedly paid the highest compliment to director George Loane Tucker when he said, "The guy that directed that

44

picture was a fourth timer, I'll betcher." [54]   The picture was an enormous money-maker and was one of the top ten picks of the year by film critics.

The role of the fake cripple who preys upon the sympathy of the unsuspecting public gave Chaney the chance to exhibit his talents in a unique way. The Frog is introduced as a disheveled man with a twisted body and useless legs, dressed in soiled clothes, who causes a traffic jam in a section of Chinatown as he attempts to cross a street.   However distasteful he may appear, he manages to arouse sympathy from the tourists, allowing him to earn a few dollars. Later, at the apartment of one of the crooks, we see the Frog unwind his legs and learn that he is a fraud. By using the Frog's talents, Tom Burke (Thomas Meighan), the leader of the crooks, lays out his plan to swindle money from the unsuspecting believers of a blind faith healer. Chaney's character is seen as a scheming knave, out to take advantage of "the suckers" who believe his act. When he appears before the faith healer, the Frog is clean shaven and dressed in nicer clothes, which helps to lay the foundation for his character's redemption. As the Frog is being "healed," Chaney employs body movements and facial expressions that propel the dramatic climax of the scene when a little boy who is truly crippled throws down his crutches and runs up to the faith healer. The criminal's self-assurance in the certainty that his "act" is being believed quickly crumbles when he witnesses this true miracle. Chaney was able to register these divergent emotions by expressive facial and body gestures alone.

Existing scene stills from the film illustrate this change in Chaney's character, as the righteousness of the faith healer begins to inspire him. The grimacing criminal is replaced by a gentle and caring man who lovingly wipes the mouth of the blind faith healer after he has a drink of coffee. Taken in by a childless widow in the small town, he becomes a devoted son. Chaney's ability to transport his character from one dimension to another caught the eye of critics, the public and, most importantly, Hollywood producers. Hazel Chaney said that before this picture went into production, there was much speculation and skepticism about its chances for success. She said that Lon realized the tremendous potential of the picture after he read the novel and through the efforts of his agents, Willis and Inglis, he was able to secure an interview with Tucker. Once Tucker approved him for the role, Lon's salary increased to $150 a week. [55] Hazel said that Lon spent hours crawling on the floor, twisting and untwisting his arms and legs to arrive at the proper effect. [56] During production of the picture, Lon was not just enthusiastic about his role, but about the whole story. He would do anything to help on the set, from moving the camera to assisting the prop man. [57]

Existing footage from *The Miracle Man* is minimal at best. Only two brief scenes survive: that of the crooks hatching their plan and the healing sequence. The rest of the picture remains lost. However, film historians have another avenue available to them to recount a movie scene-by-scene. This is the cutting continuity. A cutting continuity is a manuscript compiled by either the editor or his assistant that lists (in order of appearance) every shot and every title in the final print. Through these accounts, a film historian can get a pretty good idea of how the film was assembled and might even be able to discern the deletion of a filmed sequence. The following transcript of the healing sequence from *The Miracle Man* illustrates how a cutting continuity works. [58]

("Ext." is an exterior or outdoor location. "Reverse" means in the direction opposite that of the previous shot — for example, someone shown walking away from camera in one shot is seen walking toward the camera in the following shot. A "panel shot" is another term for a two-shot, featuring a fairly close shot of two players.)

Scene 349 — Fade In — VLS [Very Long Shot]—Ext. Patriarch's House. Over the crowd's heads — Cripple boy and Frog on the path leading to the house.

Scene 350 — MDS [Middle Distance Shot] (reverse) — Frog and the boy — with the crowd in the background. Boy pointing to the house.

Scene 351 — CU [Close-up] — Boy pointing to house.

Scene 352 — CU — Frog looking up toward the house.

Scene 353 — MDS — Patriarch's Living Room. Patriarch suddenly awakens — Rose is surprised — he rises and walks off — Rose looks after him.

Scene 354 — LS [Long Shot] — Through door. Patriarch goes out.

Scene 355 — VLS — Over crowd's heads. All look at the Patriarch.

Scene 356 — MDS (reverse) —Frog and the boy with the crowd in the background — looking toward Patriarch.

Scene 357 — CU — Frog looking toward Patriarch.

Scene 358 — CU — Patriarch at door.

Scene 359 — BCU [Big Close-up] — Tom looking cynically toward Patriarch.

Scene 360 — CU — One of the salesman looking toward the Patriarch.

Scene 361 — CU — Claire looking hopefully toward Patriarch.

Scene 362 — MDS — Frog and the boy — with the crowd in background. Boy tells Frog "There he is!"

Scene 363 — VLS — Over crowd's heads. Frog starts to drag himself up the path.

Scene 364 — CU — Boy telling him to go on.

Scene 365 — VLS — Frog continues dragging himself toward the Patriarch.

Scene 366 — CU — Rose at window smiling cynically.

Scene 367 — LS — Through door. Frog dragging himself toward the Patriarch.

Scene 368 — CU — Patriarch with his head raised heavenward.

Scene 369 — VLS — Frog reaches the Patriarch.

A Thousand Faces

Scene 370 — CU — Claire looking on.

Scene 371 — PS [Panel Shot] — Patriarch and Frog. Frog straightens out his arm.

Scene 372 — CU — Jewish salesman — opened mouth.

Scene 373 — PS — Patriarch and Frog. Frog straightens out his leg.

Scene 374 — CU — Newspaper man's eyes wide open with cigarette hanging in his mouth.

Scene 375 — PS — Frog and Patriarch. Frog raises up on his feet.

Scene 376 — CU — Fat farmer boy with tears in his eyes.

Scene 377 — PS — Frog and Patriarch. Frog straightens up.

Scene 378 — CU — Woman fainting in man's arms.

Scene 379 — PS — Frog and Patriarch. Frog straightens up completely.

Scene 380 — CU — Patriarch with his head raised — his lips moving as if saying "Forgive them for they know not what they do," etc.

Scene 381 — VLS — Frog sinks at the Patriarch's feet.

Scene 382 — CU — Patriarch still in same position.

Scene 383 — CU — Cripple boy smiling.

Scene 384 — VLS — Cripple [boy] gets in center of path.

Scene 385 — CU — Patriarch in the same position.

Scene 386 — VLS — The Cripple [boy] drops one crutch.

Scene 387 — CU — Cripple boy smiling.

Scene 388 — VLS — Everyone surprised and moving forward.

Scene 389 — MDS — Cripple [boy] drops other crutch

Scene 390 — VLS — The boy balances himself — everyone astonished.

Scene 391 — CU — Frog looking toward the boy in surprise.

Scene 392 — VLS — The boy runs up to the Patriarch who pets his head.

Scene 393 — CU — Tom wide-eyed.

Scene 394 — CU — Rose at window excitedly tearing her handkerchief.

Scene 395 — CU — Claire looking on hopefully.

Scene 396 — CU — King looking on in surprise — passes his hand over his eyes.

Scene 397 — MDS — of the crowd. The postmaster sinks on his knees and starts to pray.

Scene 398 — MDS — Patriarch petting the boy's head — Frog looking on in surprise.

Lon's next film, *Victory*, based on Joseph Conrad's novel, marked the first time he worked for director Maurice Tourneur. [59] Chaney won praise from the critics for a portrayal that totally overshadowed those of the other members of the cast, including Wallace Beery. Lon is deliciously villainous as Ricardo and goes all-out in his performance. At this point in his career, Lon was determined to make an indelible impression, and from his first scene in the picture until his character's violent death, he succeeds. We are introduced to Ricardo and his two traveling companions, Mr. Jones (Ben Deely) and Pedro (Bull Montana), when Schomberg (Beery) (who has hired the three to track down Heyst [Jack Holt] and Alma [Seena Owen]) takes a launch to a boat in the harbor off his island. Boarding the boat by means of a ladder, Schomberg pauses when he sees the three men looking down at him. The shot of the three impassive faces leaves him with an eerie feeling, which is only accentuated by Ricardo's slow smile — Chaney's first hint of his character's capacity for villainy.

The scene that truly showcases Chaney's bravura performance takes place after the trio has taken up residence in Schomberg's hotel. Ricardo, playing with a deck of cards, calls Schomberg over to the table. He displays great dexterity with the cards (a credit to the performer who makes this difficult piece of business look effortless). Schomberg picks a card from the deck, and Ricardo is able to identify it. Unimpressed, Schomberg remarks that this isn't the first trick he's seen performed by a card shark. This comment infuriates Ricardo, who deliberately drops the deck of cards onto the table and slowly rises from his chair. He pulls up one of his pant legs to reveal a sheathed knife strapped to his leg. The character's propensity for violence comes to the fore in the delight he takes in instilling fear into Schomberg. As Schomberg tries to get away from Ricardo, the villain throws his knife, pinning Schomberg's coat sleeve to the door. When Ricardo frees him, he orders Schomberg to sit down, while calmly scratching his head with the tip of the knife blade. Relating to Schomberg how he almost used this knife once to kill Pedro, Ricardo bursts out laughing with malicious glee and slowly moves his thumb up and down the sharp edge of the blade. This gesture and the maniacal outburst help magnify Ricardo's inclination toward violence. As he recalls the tale, the story flashes back to an incident in which Ricardo suspected that he and Mr. Jones were going to be murdered by Pedro and a mysterious companion of Pedro's. When tensions erupt in violence, Mr. Jones kills Pedro's unnamed companion but he later prevents Pedro from being murdered by Ricardo. As a result, Pedro becomes devoted to Mr. Jones—or so he wants Jones to believe. Ricardo tells Schomberg how Pedro can break a man's back as easily as one could snap a dried stick. As he makes this comment, Chaney is featured in a medium close-up, holding a matchstick. He stares at it intensely, mesmerized. Then he snaps the stick, breaking it in two. Holding the two pieces in his hands for a moment before letting them fall, Ricardo slowly lifts his eyes from the discarded sticks to Pedro. This glance, without any movement of his head, brings a chilling touch to the scene.

Victory is a well-made picture and moves at a brisk pace. For a 1919 film, it contains two ruthless scenes of torture that probably had the censors reaching for their scissors. When Mr. Jones kills Pedro's companion at the campfire in the flashback mentioned above, we see the mysterious companion (obviously a dummy, but a good match) fall face first into the campfire in a close-up! The shot is only on screen for a few seconds, but it gives the film a gritty edge. The other sadistic scene comes completely by surprise. As Ricardo meets his end, shot to death by Heyst, Pedro straps Mr. Jones into a chair in their bungalow on Heyst's island. As Pedro builds a blaze in the fireplace, Jones pleads for his life, and we learn that Pedro's mysterious companion was actually his brother. To avenge his brother's brutal death, Pedro throws Mr. Jones face first into the raging fire!

Despite such gripping scenes, however, *Victory* displays some weaknesses. The romance between Heyst and Alma blooms rather quickly, which does not allow the characters to build up to a believable embrace. Another problem is that the development of Wallace Beery's Schomberg is rather unsatisfactory. We are told, through actions and title cards, that he is interested in Alma and sends the trio of criminals after her and Heyst by leading the three to believe that Heyst has a cache of money on his island. But Schomberg never reappears in the picture after the trio's arrival on the island, leaving a lead character in the film poorly defined. Shots of a smoking volcano on Heyst's island suggest to the audience that it will play a part in the storyline, especially after the criminals arrive on the island, yet it never does. But overall, despite these points, *Victory* is a satisfying film and allows Chaney to bring a vivid character to life.

Chaney again worked under Maurice Tourneur's direction in the second film version of Robert Louis Stevenson's *Treasure Island* (1920), playing both the blind pirate, Pew, and another pirate, Merry. Taking on dual roles became something of a trademark for Chaney during his career. [60]

His next appearance earned him good notices but was really nothing more than an average programmer titled *The Gift Supreme.* Unfortunately, the surviving footage gives the viewer little to go on to form an opinion of Lon's character. He is seen only briefly (for approximately five minutes) as he walks into a saloon with another man and sits at a table. However, this small segment does allow us to see Chaney playing a "straight" role without the use of any character make-up.

Nomads of the North allowed Lon the rare opportunity of playing a leading man, a departure from his usual roles. Based on a popular novel of the Northwoods by James Oliver Curwood, Lon plays Raoul Challoner, a French-Canadian trapper. The plot was a typical melodrama of the time, with a bear and a dog providing some would-be comical moments. The film, which James Oliver Curwood produced, is reminiscent of the live-action family pictures Walt Disney later made. [61] Lon's performance is overdone in many scenes and the emphasis of the character's good nature and expressive gestures can at times wear on today's viewer. This is quite obvious in the opening scenes of the picture. Yet Lon also displays tender, underplayed emotion in the scene in which he watches the bear cub smelling the lifeless fur that was once its mother. Remorseful that he was forced to kill the bear, Raoul adopts the cub, a gesture that gives his character some substance. When Raoul returns from the Northwoods, he finds his sweetheart (Betty Blythe) is about to marry his rival, Bucky McDougall (Francis McDonald). Naturally this triggers a confrontation between the protagonist and the antagonist, who frames Raoul for a murder.

The role of Corporal O'Connor (Lewis Stone), the mountie who arrests Raoul and ultimately frees him after he saves O'Connor's life, seems more akin to the roles Chaney later played at M-G-M. O'Connor is in love with Nanette but realizes her heart belongs to Raoul, and in the end he becomes the tragic hero of the piece when he frees the two lovers, letting them escape into the wilderness. A forest fire becomes the *deus ex machina* that allows Raoul to save O'Connor, thus ultimately winning his own release, and serving also to cause the demise of the villain, McDougall. Unfortunately, the entire cast, including the venerable Lewis Stone, is guilty of overacting, and the direction is lagging and labored. The animal antics are amusing, but when the film resorts to the inclusion of a title card of two animals supposedly speaking to each other, it becomes obtrusive. The scenery and the animals are the strongest features going for this film, leaving the viewer feeling indifferent.

On the other hand, his next film, *The Penalty,* remains one of Chaney's most impressive character performances. Written in 1913 by Gouverneur Morris, a popular writer of the period, the novel doesn't immediately strike one as being great material for a movie, yet someone at Goldwyn Pictures realized its potential. Fashioned into an effective scenario by Charles Kenyon and Philip Lonergan and ably directed by Wallace Worsley, the film still carries a powerful punch. Borrowing the essence of the plot from the gangster and melodrama themes of the time, the film also incorporates references to the Red Scare of 1919. With the end of the war and the rise of Lenin, the threat of a Communist takeover in Europe fueled the flame of fear in the United States. Hundreds of people were rounded up and deported to Russia, and this picture develops the premise of disgruntled immigrant workers who are encouraged by a legless crime boss, Blizzard (Chaney), to become part of his plan to take over the city of San Francisco.

In playing Blizzard, the double-amputee who rules San Francisco's underworld, Chaney had to be careful that the physical aspect of the role did not overshadow his acting. Refusing to use trick camera angles, Lon designed a leather harness to strap his legs behind him, which actually allowed him to walk on his knees with the aid of crutches. There are occasional medium close-ups in which it is apparent that Chaney is standing on his knees without his legs strapped behind him. Hazel Chaney said that to dispel the rumors that he was doubled by a true amputee, Goldwyn Pictures added a sequence at the end of the film showing Lon walking down a flight of stairs as himself. [62] She also said that her husband spent many hours at home practicing the things he had to do in the film while wearing the stumps. [63] As the star of this production, Lon saw his salary rise to $500 a week, only to learn later that the studio had been willing to pay him $1,500 a week. It was a costly lesson for Lon, but it did manage to impress upon him his true monetary value to a production.

Chaney's Blizzard is a force to be reckoned with. He rules his underlings with a strong hand, allowing no one to question his motives. One particular scene that exemplifies Blizzard's iron rule takes place when he enters a room where several women are making straw hats. He climbs onto the table to examine their work and finds a defect in one. Rebuking the worker, he slaps her face with the hat and grabs her by the hair, pulling her close to him. The anger expressed by Chaney and the reaction shots of the other women heighten the intensity of this scene. After issuing orders, Blizzard starts to leave, and as an afterthought, tells them about one of the girls who left his enclave. Sneering, he states that she now sleeps upon a marble slab in the morgue, and exits laughing. In another scene, he taunts Wilmont (Kenneth Harlan), Barbara's (Claire Adams) fiancé, by remarking that he has an admirable pair of legs. Blizzard then looks down at his stumps and replies, "I gave mine to science," and laughs. This line provides the audience enough of a chill without overstating the diabolical undertone of the character.

Instead of portraying Blizzard as a complete villain, Chaney reveals a human side to the character. He cannot bring himself to kill Rose (Ethel Grey Terry), even though he knows she is a government agent, because of her help in manipulating the pedals of the piano he plays. The music seems to soothe Blizzard's "beast" and allows him to display a moment of compassion, which is in direct contrast with his evil deeds. It also prepares the audience for his eventual transformation when a doctor removes the pressure on his brain that governed Blizzard's evil motives. After the operation, Chaney is careful to temper and soften his expressions, showing remorse for his past deeds, which makes his previous villainy even more vivid in retrospect.

Director Worsley makes good use of Chaney's agility, rather than resorting to trick photography. By the use of wide shots, he shows Blizzard walking up a flight of stairs on his stumps and descending a pole using only the strength of his arms. Because of these unusual physical demonstrations of strength, Chaney's performance is all the more effective and leaves the audience wondering, "How did he do that?" While Chaney's facial contortions are effective, there are a few instances when it becomes a little overdone; yet his overall performance makes amends for such transgressions. The intensity he displays while revealing his plot to his lieutenant, O'Hagan, is mesmerizing and attests that it was Chaney's acting, not the physical grotesqueness of the role, that dominated the picture.

Lon is ably supported by a strong cast, with James Mason providing an effective performance as Pete, the dope addict and one of Blizzard's henchmen. The entire production displays a craftsmanlike quality, and for many first-time viewers, it is a surprise to learn that it is not an M-G-M picture. [64] Adding to the potency of the film is a scene in which Blizzard tantalizes Pete, who is going through withdrawal, with a portable dope kit. Had this film been made a few years later, it is very doubtful that this scene or some others would have been included. A dope fiend getting away with murder, a prostitute picking up a customer, a murder on screen, and a nude model would have had the censors in the Hays Office jumping.

The only serious detriment of the picture by today's standards is that some of the title cards induce chuckles because of their naiveté. For example, in one scene, Blizzard warns a girl who is helping him play the piano that she may not live long enough to see his plan come to fruition if she doesn't pedal the piano better! When the head of the Secret Service (Milton Ross) warns Rose that infiltrating

A Thousand Faces

Blizzard's domicile could mean her death, she casually replies, "That's all in a day's work." Others will shake their heads at the sequence in which the doctor who originally maimed Blizzard as a child pleads with the head of the Secret Service to free the criminal. The doctor claims that after performing brain surgery on Blizzard, the mastermind could do as much good in the future as he has evil in the past. (The censors would have been in an uproar over the Secret Service agent agreeing to allow Blizzard to escape any criminal prosecution.)

The original draft of the screenplay had a very weak ending in which Blizzard, after recovering from his surgery, returns to the studio of the doctor's daughter to finish posing for her sculpture of Satan. Rose, having married Blizzard after his surgery, and Wilmont, Barbara's fiancé, are also present. They watch Barbara as she struggles with the sculpture and then, in frustration, throws it to the floor, smashing it to pieces. She explains that the sculpture simply can't be done because the evil expression is now gone from Blizzard's face, but that she is glad for him nevertheless. The two young lovers embrace as Blizzard and Rose smile. Needless to say, this insipid ending would have left the picture without the dramatic punch of having Blizzard pay the ultimate price for his actions. [65]

In November 1920, Lon retained Alfred Grasso to act as his business manager. He continued in this capacity for four years while taking care of other clients, including actress Betty Compson, character actor William V. Mong, and later, director Wallace Worsley. Grasso began his career on the executive staff of New York theatre producer Henry W. Savage. He entered motion pictures about 1917, working in the scenario department of Goldwyn Pictures, where he became acquainted with director George Loane Tucker. When Tucker left the company, Grasso followed him to Hollywood, working as an assistant director on *The Miracle Man*. It was on this picture that he and Chaney became acquainted. Grasso stayed with

Tucker until the director's death three years later, then went on to serve as general manager of Betty Compson Productions. Unfortunately, her company quickly folded, but Grasso moved on to become an assistant director on John Stahl's picture *One Clear Call* (1922). From there he went to Universal, working as an assistant to Irving Thalberg. All during this time, he served as business manager to Chaney and others. According to his daughters, Lillian Broadbent and Mary Clark, Thalberg had approved a large contingent of horses for a certain production, but something went wrong. Rather than owning up to the mistake, Thalberg fixed the blame on Grasso, who accepted the accusation rather than confront his boss. But his noble act did not earn him any reward for loyalty because he found himself the victim of Thalberg's blacklist, and he was never able to find work at any of the major studios again. Despite Thalberg's actions, Grasso continued to work in the industry, supervising such independent productions as *Hawaiian Love*, *Savages*, *Assorted Nuts*, *The Doctor*, *Never Say Can't*, *The Blonde Captive*, and *A Western Welcome*. With the advent of World War II, Grasso decided to leave the film industry and found work at the growing Lockheed Company, where he had a long career. He died in 1956. (In 1932, Hazel Chaney contacted Grasso to serve as her agent for a planned biography of Lon but, because the Depression had wrought an overall poor financial climate, publishers turned down the proposal. After Hazel's death in 1933, nothing further was done with this material until it was brought to this author's attention.)

Lon's next project, *Outside the Law* (1921) remains one of the better crime melodramas of the period and clearly illustrates Tod Browning's talent at storytelling, directing, and creating suspense. Other than incorporating a few slang terms of the day, the film is not dated, and it maintains a strong pace. Browning adds a sense of realism to the film with his careful casting of bit players and extras. His special attention to the proper casting of an actor or an extra, as well as to the details of a set's appearance, added to the subtle quality of Browning's pictures. This became especially obvious when the director set up shop at M-G-M and took full advantage of the studio's support staff.

Chaney literally steals the picture from the lead, Priscilla Dean, with his performance as the crafty and vicious "Black Mike" Sylva, playing him as a shrewd, cold-blooded criminal and employing tremendous energy in the role. While questioning his partner, Bill (Wheeler Oakman), about his disappearance after a jewel heist, Lon acts cool and untroubled, and appears to accept Bill's explanation. Yet the audience knows that this trusting demeanor is merely an act and the fact that he doesn't really believe his partner makes Chaney's character all the more terrifying. (Lon's convincing portrayal of a villain apparently extended beyond the movie screen because, while on location in San Francisco, he was actually arrested by a police officer who thought he was criminal.) [66] Chaney plays dual roles in this picture, the second being that of a Chinese man named Ah Wing. This character has no real importance to the development of the story, yet it allows Chaney to present a realistic portrayal of an Oriental, his first interpretation of this ethnic group. Chaney's superior concept is particularly apparent when one compares his Ah Wing to E. A. Warren's Chang Low. Lon's character looks, acts, and walks like a true Oriental, while it is obvious that Warren's character is being portrayed by a Caucasian. In the May 1923 issue of *Picture Play*, Lon explained that playing an Oriental character "is infinite art. He is passive, repressed; by thought alone I have put over my three Chinese roles."

Chaney's rise in popularity is illustrated by an incident that occurred about this time at the Rivoli Theatre in Portland, Oregon. The Rivoli was screening *Outside the Law* and decided to add a two-reeler featuring Chaney, called *The Empty Gun* (1917), to the program. By the second day, it was clearly obvious that the Chaney two-reeler was attracting the crowds, and the theatre management changed its advertising, playing up *The Empty Gun* for the rest of the week. In South Carolina, a movie theatre employed a unique approach to advertise *Outside the Law*. They hired two men, one dressed as a cop and the other in prison stripes, to walk around the city with signs on their backs calling attention to the movie. Universal reissued *Outside the Law* in 1926 to capitalize on Chaney's popularity, giving him top billing over Priscilla Dean instead of the original "supported by" credit.

Playing the Chinese character furthered Lon's reputation as Hollywood's leading character actor and brought him to the attention of director Marshall Neilan. Lon played his second Chinese role in Neilan's *Bits of Life*, a film comprising four short stories featuring events in the lives of various people. Lon made his Chin Gow character both vile and realistic, earning praise for his performance. The picture garnered positive reviews for its unusual anthology approach of combining four different stories into one picture. Although the world première for *Bits of Life*, held at the Raymond Theatre in Pasadena, California, on August 9, 1921, had several stars in attendance whose pictures were being released by Associated First National, including Charles Chaplin, Buster Keaton, and Charles Ray, there was no mention of Lon's attending the event. [67]

Lon next appeared as the sympathetic gambler opposite Betty Compson in *For Those We Love*. His former costar from *The Miracle Man* had recently signed a deal with Goldwyn Pictures to form her own company, but the undertaking was short-lived. Many performers during this period attempted to establish their own companies in hopes of producing their own pictures; unfortunately, most of these endeavors were less than successful, and many of these actors found themselves bankrupt.

Chaney was quickly becoming one of the preeminent character actors of the day, sought out by numerous producers and directors, including Herbert Brenon. According to telegrams in the Alfred Grasso family collection, Brenon wanted Chaney for three weeks' work starting on September 19, 1921. The title of the project itself remains unknown, but the director offered Lon a salary of $1,000 a week. However, remembering how he had been short-changed on *The Penalty*, Lon rejected Brenon's offer and countered with $1,500. An interesting perception is found in these telegrams when Lon requests of Brenon,

> Please wire me type of story and character you wish
> me for so as not to conflict with my next
> characterization. [68]

This statement shows that Chaney was keenly aware of his work and was being careful to avoid playing the same type of role. In another telegram from the director to Lon, Brenon pointedly asks, "Have heard you signed with Universal. Is it true?" Lon replied,

> Only agreement I have made is for one picture only
> with Universal in which I have a very good part.
> Finishing in time to start with you on or about Sept.
> 19. Please wire type of story and character you wish
> me for and tell me frankly what rumors you heard to
> cause you to inquire about Universal contract. [69]

The deal with Brenon ultimately fell through after Lon received no further replies to his telegrams. The rumors of his signing a contract with Universal surfaced after the announcement "Lon Chaney Is Signed as New Universal Star" in the September 17, 1921, issue of *Exhibitors Trade Review*. The one-picture deal was for *Wolf Breed*, released as *The Trap*. To put the rumors to rest, Lon issued a press release on August 31, stating,

> Lon Chaney, whose portrayals in *The Miracle Man*,
> *The Penalty*, *Outside the Law*, etc., have made him
> famous as a character actor, makes an emphatic

denial to reports that he is to star in a series of
pictures for Universal Company. Mr. Chaney
declares that he has been engaged by the Universal
Company for one picture only and not for a series,
owing to the fact that he has practically arranged to
appear in other large productions, and is also
seriously considering proposals to head his own
company. [70]

Although it was originally thought to have been a publicity ploy,
letters from the Alfred Grasso family collection indicate that both
Chaney and Grasso were actively discussing financing for a film and a
production company. In June 1921, an agreement was drafted
between Lon, Abe Stern, Julius Stern, and Louis S. Jacobs to fund a
picture based on an original story by Chaney. The story, tentatively
titled *The Sacrifice*, was described in the agreement as "an Italian
love story written by Perley Poore Sheehan and the producer
[Lon]." [71] The agreement, which for reasons that remain unknown
never was consummated, would have allowed Lon to produce and
supervise the entire production, anticipated to run between 5,000
and 7,000 feet (or five to seven reels) and budgeted at no more than
$60,000. Despite the failure of the agreement, Chaney and Grasso
continued to discuss funding with several independent financiers,
including one H. A. Berg of New York. [72] In a July 28, 1921 letter to
Chaney, Berg offered the following conditions, after meeting with
Grasso and Hal Layton, a publicist and friend of Grasso's who had set
up the meeting:

> After the payment of the following weekly salaries
> during the period of production of each picture, Lon
> Chaney, $1,000, Grasso, $300, Berg, $200, Layton,
> $100, with an additional $400 per weeks for ten
> weeks advertising expense; the net profits from the
> picture [to] be divided equally on a fifty-fifty basis
> between yourself and the writer.

A Thousand Faces

> I agree on my part to advance $2,000 for advertising
> of State Rights production to be made with yourself
> in the chief male role, starred as such on all paper,
> printing, advertising, etc.; such production to be a
> minimum of eight reels (8,000 feet) in length. In the
> event the initial $2,000 is not sufficient, I am to
> advance an additional $1,000, making a total of
> $3,000; the State Right proposition then failing, this
> tentative contract may be dissolved within thirty
> days thereafter.

The term "state rights" referred to independent distributors who booked films with the various independent and small-chain theaters in a particular state. Sometimes, neighboring states would also be included by a certain distributor in what would then be defined as "territories." It was not uncommon for a producer or financier to raise capital by pre-selling a picture, similar to the way *Terminator 2* was pre-sold to foreign markets before even a single frame of film was exposed. This method sometimes proved to be a risky proposition for the independent distributors of the 1920s because many producers or financiers, after raising the capital, might never deliver the promised product. Someone like Berg would have used Chaney's popularity and growing box office draw to entice the state rights distributor into either financing or releasing the proposed film.

Replying to Berg's offer, Grasso outlined provisions for the deal. The film would be budgeted at between $75,000 and $100,000, with Chaney organizing his own company and having exclusive control over all details pertaining to the production and expenditures. Lon's salary, which would be included as part of the film's budget, would be $15,000, in addition to twenty-five percent of the picture's earnings. Grasso outlined four stories to be considered for the financed project: *The Sacrifice*, the original story by Lon and Perley Poore Sheehan (who would later write the screenplay for *The Hunchback of Notre Dame*); another scenario by Sheehan, *God's Lightning*, which originally was a project planned by George Loane

Tucker before his untimely death in 1921; a novelized story by *The Penalty* author Gouverneur Morris; and "an original idea of Lon Chaney's, being developed by Perley Poore Sheehan in collaboration with Mr. Chaney." According to Grasso's figures, if the first film cost $75,000 to produce and could be sold for $250,000, Chaney's twenty-five percent would be $43,750, which when added to his $15,000 salary would garner him a total of $58,750. While that amount appears relatively small compared with the multimillion-dollar deals being signed by stars today, one must remember that an average worker's salary at this time was roughly $25 to $30 a week.

As negotiations continued with H. A. Berg (they would eventually collapse), Lon continued to seek material for future projects. One interesting contact in this regard occurred in the form of a letter, a copy of which is held in the Alfred Grasso family collection, from Darryl F. Zanuck, who would later run 20th Century-Fox Studios. At the time, Zanuck was a struggling writer. In one letter to Lon, he discusses a current project:

> At last I have finished my new one, "*The Man Who Lived Twice*," and am submitting it to you before allowing any of the studios to see it. You suggested several times that I get a good ending for you, and in this I think I have.
>
> I will appreciate any changes or suggestions you care to make. I mentioned to Thalberg and Bender that I was working on one for you, and they asked to see it immediately, but I'll leave it to your judgment first. Undoubtedly this will appear as a serial in one of the cheaper magazines — *Argosy-All Story Weekly*, *Adventure*, *Wide World*, or possibly *Everybody's*. Will appreciate as quick action as is convenient to you. [73]

Lon returned to Goldwyn Pictures to star in *Ace of Hearts*, which marked his second appearance for Goldwyn and a reteaming with director Wallace Worsley. Although the film is not as strong as *The Penalty*, it is an example of the craftsman-like product the company was producing. The story concerns a group of extremists who meet to decide the fates of those they deem unsuitable to society. Whoever draws the Ace of Hearts must execute their latest chosen target. The method for disposing of their victims was a bomb, which would be on a timer set to explode shortly after being dropped off by the group member. Unfortunately, neither the reason for the formation of this group nor its background is ever explained (although it's suggested they are associated with Communists). Further, it is never established what crime(s) their victims have committed to warrant the punishment of death. In that respect, it is hard either to approve or condemn their actions. Nonetheless, Chaney's character and those of Leatrice Joy (Lilith) and John Bowers (Forrest) are able to redeem themselves by the end of the picture, gaining some sympathy from the audience. Lon's character, Farralone, is a man of quiet strength. He is a reserved, thinking man who has been painting a portrait of "the man who has lived too long" (the group's intended victim), and is described in the script as "stern, vengeful — rather splendid looking." [74] Forrest and Farralone are both in love with Lilith, and they naturally compete for her affections; but she refuses to become involved with either of them, thinking only of the "cause," until Forrest draws the fatal Ace of Hearts .

While the cards are being dealt, director Worsley builds suspense by intercutting close-ups of each recipient's reaction to the card drawn. He also places the camera above the card table, which gives the audience a voyeuristic sensation during this scene. Chaney is tightly controlled as he watches the events unfold, the anticipation of his character shown by his nervous fidgeting, following the cards as they are dealt. When his turn comes, he looks imploringly at Lilith, as if begging to be dealt the fatal ace. When he turns his card over, Lon hesitates a second before registering his disappointment. This subtle yet expressive gesture escalates the suspense. Chaney also incorporates small but suggestive gestures into his character to connote a man of education: while writing, he holds his pen between forefinger and middle finger and, when lost in thought, he grips the lapel of his jacket. These apparently insignificant gestures combine into a totality of character, making Lon's role individual and unique.

Ace of Hearts also promotes a continuous theme found in many of Chaney's pictures, that of a man who loves a girl so desperately that he is willing to sacrifice himself for her happiness or safety. When Lilith seeks Farralone's aid in stopping Forrest from carrying out his mission, Chaney's emotions range from the taciturn to sympathetic. Forrest returns to the group's meeting place relating that he failed to carry out his assassination, and places the bomb on the table before the group. Chaney's character remains stoic, knowing what he must do to protect the lovers. As Lilith looks imploringly at him, Chaney quickly brings his finger to his mouth, urging her to remain silent. After Lilith and Forrest leave, the remaining group sits at the table to determine who will kill the traitorous couple. Chaney brings forth the quiet strength of his character by calmly and surreptitiously triggering the bomb's timing device in front of him, remaining unemotional while watching the dealing of the cards until the bomb explodes. The calmness he exudes further emphasizes the determination of his character to save the life of the one he loves.

The original ending of the script found Forrest and Lilith living in a cabin with their child, happy yet concerned that the other members will find them. (A title suggested that they were unaware of Farralone's setting off the bomb.) An old man wearing an eye patch and missing an arm approaches their cabin. It is Morgridge, the leader of the group. He assures the couple that they have nothing to fear and relates, via flashbacks, how the bomb went off. The police held him for a time but because they could not prove anything, he was released. He has been searching for Forrest and Lilith to tell them that they have nothing to fear, and when he learns that their child has not yet been named, suggests they name him after Farralone. [75] This ending was filmed but eventually discarded in favor of one in which Forrest and Lilith exit a train in the country and later read about the bomb blast that killed the entire group. They realize that Farralone has set them free, and as the couple walk down a country road, the picture fades out. [76]

An interesting interoffice communication reveals Samuel Goldwyn's feelings about the bomb scenes and the first ending; he noted:

> Consider changes in *Ace of Hearts* very important.
> Don't agree that rehearsal scene lightens picture and
> feel it should come out as explained in previous
> wire. The less you show bomb scenes the better
> chance we have of picture remaining intact without
> censors hurting drama of picture. Ending of picture
> must be changed as it weakens story. You can still
> retain scenic investiture by showing how happily
> they live together and then Forrest picks up
> newspaper and reads of conspirator's death. We
> consider ending [of] *Ace of Hearts* ridiculous and
> picture cannot be released in present form. [77]

The Trap (1922) was a major career step for Lon because the scenario was tailored expressly for his talents. It also marked the first time that the appellation "Man of a Thousand Faces" was used in connection with publicizing Chaney's ability at altering his features; yet his only make-up in this film was a shoulder-length wig. The story was written by Chaney, Irving Thalberg, Luicen Hubbard, and the director, Robert Thornby, utilizing typical melodramatic plots. For the most part, the picture holds up well, and Chaney's work is admirable. In some sequences, Lon's facial and body movements are extremely fluid, illustrating his ability at pantomime, yet there are moments when he commits the sin of overacting. As Gaspard, Chaney plays the type of character he would come to portray frequently, particularly in his Tod Browning pictures — that of a wronged man consumed by the desire for vengeance against his betrayer. Gaspard is driven to revenge because Benson (Alan Hale) has cheated him out of his mine and stolen his sweetheart, Thalie (Dagmar Godowsky). When she marries Benson and gives birth to a child, Gaspard frames his betrayer for murder. After Thalie's untimely death, Gaspard takes care of the boy, hoping to use him as a pawn for further revenge against Benson. However, the innocence of the child slowly redeems Gaspard and he comes to love the boy as his own. When he learns Benson is to be released from prison, fear of losing the boy overcomes him. He fashions a trap (a half-starved wolf left in his cabin) to kill his betrayer when he opens the door. But when the boy almost becomes the unintended victim, Chaney's character intervenes, and fights off the wolf to save the boy's life. Gaspard comes to the realization that the boy belongs with his father and he reunites them, with a promise that the boy can visit his "Uncle Gaspard" anytime.

Now that movie theaters were plentiful, picture promotion was becoming as much an art as filmmaking was. The average picture played two or three days at a local theatre, with the exception of prestige pictures. These could run for up to a month at most large-city theaters, so an exhibitor had to devise unique ways to ensure the patronage of his theatre. In towns with one or two theaters, the competition wasn't intense; but it was a different situation when a city had four or more theaters. Theatre owners were obliged to come up with distinctive promotions, which could range from the simple placement of various posters and lobby cards [78] to more elaborate gimmicks such as giveaways or a staged prologue to the main feature.

A Thousand Faces

According to the May 20, 1922 *Exhibitors Trade Review*, during the engagement of *The Trap* at the Central Theatre in New York City,

> in the prologue the singer, a tenor, copied Gaspard's (Lon Chaney's) movements in every particular and sang the song Gaspard was supposed to be singing when he entered the village. He also had a bundle of furs, laying them on the stage as he stepped out of the canoe. The prologue closed with a duet, a contralto joining the tenor. This prologue created an atmosphere for *The Trap* that helped immeasurably to put over to the big business the picture enjoyed during its run at the Central.

Although Lon Chaney attempted not to become stereotyped as a portrayer of criminals, his next feature for Goldwyn Pictures cast him in exactly that type of role. *Voices of the City* was originally filmed under the title of *The Night Rose*, but this title was met with opposition from several state censor boards, who determined that it was too suggestive. While state censor boards may have felt the film didn't meet their standards, their actions increased audience interest in the picture. Directed by Wallace Worsley, the film was a profitable one for the studio, with Lon playing a fashionably-dressed criminal who uses his wits to achieve his illicit gains. In an undated script, his character is described as having a "dominating, dictatorial manner, always exacting but suave in manner — a man who never touches little things and [is] unquestionably intelligent." [79] It's regrettable that this picture does not survive because there appears to have been a scene, just before Chaney's character is killed, in which he and the character of Georgia engage in ballroom dancing. [80] This would have given us a rare opportunity to catch a glimpse of Chaney's little-publicized dancing talent.

Chaney's next film, *Flesh and Blood* was an independently produced picture featuring Lon as a man who is falsely imprisoned

68

but escapes, disguised as a cripple, to see his wife and child. The film boasted a cast of well-known players who were not major stars of the time but were recognizable enough to help sell the picture to independent theaters. Lon delivers a remarkably restrained performance as David Webster, carefully avoiding the temptation to overplay the sentiment of the moment. The relationship between Chaney's daughter, known as the Angel Lady (Edith Roberts), and Ted Burton (Jack Mulhall), son of Fletcher Burton (Ralph Lewis), the man who framed him, is the plot strategy that triggers the dramatic confrontation between the two fathers. Most of Chaney's characters sought to preserve the sanctity, decency, and virtue of a woman, whether she was his daughter or a love interest. In this picture, the David Webster character must keep his identity a secret while helping his daughter, ultimately sacrificing his freedom for her happiness. This desire consumes Webster, especially after learning that Fletcher Burton has told her she is not good enough to marry his son, and develops into the confrontation between the two men in which Webster forces Burton to sign a confession.

However, this confrontation scene is stodgily executed by the director, Chaney, and Ralph Lewis, and the intercutting of Li Fang's (Noah Beery) interrogation scene kills any tension or suspense the encounter between Webster and Burton might have created. Similarly, the scene in which both Chaney's daughter and Burton's son confront the elder Burton about his decision that they cannot marry is flawed, and both actors, Edith Roberts and Jack Mulhall, unfortunately deliver inferior performances. The ending, with Chaney returning to the prison gates as the cripple and standing up as the guards approach him, tends to exploit the gimmick of the actor's disguise. [81] The entire supporting cast is competent, with the exception of Noah Beery's performance as Li Fang, which lacks the realistic touch Chaney brought to his Oriental roles. (A notable sidelight to *Flesh and Blood* is a scene not found in any existing print, which showed Noah Beery relating a Chinese tale to the impatient Chaney. This missing scene was filmed in color and featured Chinese performers.)

Although the negotiations with H. A. Berg dissolved, Alfred Grasso continued to discuss funding a production unit with other financiers. In a July 8, 1922, letter from the Los Angeles finance firm of Bentley and Jenicek, C. E. Bentley laid out the following proposition:

> I propose to organize a producing unit for the purpose of starring Mr. Chaney in a series of productions which will reflect creditably upon his past successes and that will insure his future.
>
> I will offer Mr. Chaney a contract with this proposed organization for a term of four years at a salary of $15,000 per week each and every week during the life of the contract and will give him in addition to the above mentioned salary a 30% interest in the organization in its entirety.
>
> I will also agree that Mr. Chaney have complete control and supervision of all productions in which he appears and the privilege of selecting his own books and scenarios. [82]

But like all the previously anticipated deals, this one would fall through too. In spite of these setbacks, Lon remained one of the busiest actors in Hollywood during 1922, working from late April through the end of the year on six pictures, which allowied him very little time off. Examples of this hectic schedule are found in the numerous telegrams between Lon and Grasso. After completing *Flesh and Blood* in late May, Lon went directly to work on *Oliver Twist* for three weeks. By the end of June, he was at Universal working on *The Shock*, and only after completing that assignment was Lon able to take a much-needed vacation, visiting relatives and relaxing in San Francisco. But he wasn't to be given much time to rest, as is clearly illustrated in this July 20, 1922 telegram to Grasso. Lon asks,

> Wish you would find out if I have to be there on Monday. Find out if they have arrived from location yet. Get full particulars as to latest possible date I can stay up here. Am resting fine.

The movie to which Lon referred was the Metro Pictures production of *Quincy Adams Sawyer*. Lon stated he wanted to begin work on Wednesday, July 26, instead of the preceding Monday. On July 21, Grasso wired the following to Lon, who was staying at the famous St. Francis Hotel:

> Metro informed me their latest schedule calls for you to start Thursday July 27. However they said if you insist they will change schedule so you start Tuesday July 25. My advice you better start Tuesday otherwise you might have to rush in order to finish in time to start with Schulberg on or about August 15. Wire me whether you would rather start Tuesday or Thursday so I can take up with Metro tomorrow to arrange schedule accordingly. [83]

While Lon was quickly changing his vacation plans, several of his movies were being released across the country. *Light In the Dark* featured him as a crook who was more an offbeat hero than a true villain. Chaney's performance as Tony Pantelli gave him the opportunity to play a thief with a gentler side than he usually displayed. The compassion his character exhibits is evident when Tony brings Bessie (Hope Hampton) a newspaper and some flowers, which he hides behind his back. As he presents the flowers, Chaney's expression is reminiscent of a young boy giving a gift to his first love. Without overstating the gesture, he brings a tremendous amount of warmth to this moment, soliciting sympathy for his character. In the typical fashion of a Chaney character, however, Tony Pantelli gives up the girl he adores so that she may find happiness with her true love. A condensed version of the film, retitled *The Light of Faith*, was edited into a three-reeler that emphasized the subplot involving the Holy Grail. This version was shown around the country in schools and churches in the 1920s and, because it had to be transferred to safety stock before its distribution, this abridged version has survived. [84] Unfortunately, the performances of the other lead players and the direction by Clarence Brown fail to generate much interest, rendering the film a typical programmer of the period.

While making *Light In The Dark*, Lon struck up a friendship with author William Dudley Pelley. The film was based on Pelley's story, *White Faith*, which he had sold to producer Jules Brulatour, who envisioned the story as a showcase for his lover, actress Hope Hampton. The friendship between Pelley and Chaney certainly is an interesting one. While Pelley maintains that he and Chaney remained friends until the actor's death, it is obvious that the friendship between the two had cooled by 1928, when Pelley fell into disfavor with publishing and Hollywood circles because of his growing anti-Semitic sentiments. In 1933, he founded the Silvershirts, a group that espoused fascist rhetoric similar to that of Adolph Hitler. There were even reports that Hitler had promised to make Pelley the American Fuhrer had the German leader been victorious in World War II. Instead, Pelley served eight years in prison, was released in 1950, and resumed writing for a limited audience. [85]

But back in 1921, he was a fairly popular writer who had sold his first story to Hollywood and was about to embark on a seven-year career of writing screenplays. In his autobiography, Pelley recounts his first meeting with Lon Chaney at the studios in Fort Lee, New Jersey:

I was introduced to a soft-spoken, jovial-mannered
man of about my own years, with the most poignant
brown eyes into which I ever looked....We
discussed trade events in Hollywood at first, the
gossip of the West Coast from which Chaney had
just come. Then we got down to the story and the
role he was to play. "Somebody's got to go over-
town with me and show me where to find the right
clothes," he said an hour later.

"Pelley'll go with you," [director Clarence] Brown
responded. "He knows what's called by the plot."

I walked out to the Fort Lee, N.J., trolley-line with
Chaney. "So you wrote the story," he opened our
friendship. "Tell me the action on the way across
the ferry."

But I did not tell him the action on the way across
the ferry. He was far more interested in the fact that
across the river on Claremont Avenue I had a wife
and two babies. "Swell!" was his comment. "My wife
Hazel is down to the Commodore [Hotel]. Maybe
your wife can keep her from being lonesome while
we're here in New York."

Came the night when I phoned Marion, "Lon and
Hazel Chaney are coming up for dinner." It was the
commencement of an intimacy with the star of *The
Hunchback of Notre Dame* that practically endured
to the month of his death. [86]

Pelley said that the Chaneys were frequent visitors to their home
in Columbia Heights during the making of *Light in the Dark*.
Recounting these visits, Pelley recalled a different Lon Chaney from
the performer who appeared on the screen:

Night after night would find Chaney in our
kitchenette with one of Marion's aprons tied about
his waist, dexterously concocting savory messes

> while our wives laid the table. After the meal, Lon
> and I planned roles for his future screen career
> across the cleared cloth.[sic] His make-up for *The
> Hunchback of Notre Dame* was thus evolved, with
> many sketches and references to Hugo's works, in
> my New York apartment. One evening I came home
> from an afternoon's shooting at which his presence
> had not been required, to find this idol of photoplay
> millions squatted cross-legged on the rug with his
> tongue in his cheek, engrossed in showing Adelaide
> [Pelley's daughter] how to dress a doll. Of the pair
> of them, the screen's most famous bad man was
> enjoying that costuming more. [87]

While making the picture, Chaney had a close brush with death the day before Christmas, according to Pelley. A scene involved Lon's escaping from the police by swinging from the top of a moving bus to the Ninth Avenue elevated train tracks. He was to climb the ironwork and move onto the platform, where he would board an incoming train. Everything went well until Lon got onto the platform. One of the boards broke under his feet, leaving him dangling thirty feet above the ground. He was able to pull himself to safety by clutching a truss. [88]

When he and Hazel left New York, Lon urged Pelley to come to Hollywood to be his scenario man, adding, "We'll both clean up!" Pelley had given Lon a script based on his magazine story, *The Pit of the Golden Dragon*, which eventually was adapted as *The Shock*. Unfortunately, *Light in the Dark* did not become the success Pelley had hoped for. When the picture was assembled, it was obvious that Lon had walked away with the show. According to Pelley, both Hope Hampton and Jules Brulatour recut the picture, eliminating numerous scenes featuring Chaney, leaving the picture, in Pelley's words, "about as clear and progressive as a Chinese laundry check." [89]

One of Chaney's finest performances came in his next movie, *Shadows*. He gives a remarkably realistic portrayal of a Chinese man, far outshining his previous work in *Outside the Law*. What is most impressive is his complete absorption in the character. He literally appears to be a small, frail Chinese man, and it is hard to believe that this is the same actor who appeared in *The Penalty* and *Ace of Hearts*. His Yen Sin is a flawless interpretation, the performance far outdistancing that of any other Caucasian actor who played a similar ethnic role. In addition to the character's posture, which Lon often called "an attitude of body," the wardrobe played an effective part in shaping Yen Sin. His clothes are loose fitting, giving the appearance of a frail body. This, combined with a stooped posture and small footsteps aided the actor in presenting a realistic character. Priscilla Bonner, who appeared in the film, said that Chaney spoke with a Chinese accent during the scenes and virtually became Chinese in front of the camera. [90] As Yen Sin's health fails toward the end of the picture, his gestures and movements slow, signifying his advancing physical deterioration. But body posture or gestures were only a portion of what encompassed the overall character. For Chaney, any one aspect of a character, be it his gestures, wardrobe, or make-up, did not take precedence over another. All the characteristics were combined to create a total and meticulous portrayal. Lon used an old Chinaman who lived and worked in Colorado Springs as his model for the role, and he endeavored with his wig and make-up to look exactly like the old man when he had last seen him. [91] Viewed today, *Shadows* does not hold up well, mainly because of the overexaggerated performances of the supporting cast, which, unfortunately, date the picture rather badly. Therefore, what makes this picture worth viewing is Chaney's touching performance.

It was considered a courageous move on the part of producer B. P. Schulberg to have an Oriental as the film's protagonist since pictures of this period generally portrayed Asians as either villains or comic relief. Theatre distributors were hesitant to feature a film that had an Oriental as its hero and, in an attempt to appease theatre owners and distributors, the film's original title of *Ching, Ching,*

Chinaman was softened to *Shadows* (which had little to do with the plot of the story). [92] Curiously enough, a song based on the original title was released in conjunction with the film, featuring Lon (as Yen Sin) on the cover. Chaney's growing box office appeal, and praise from film critic Robert E. Sherwood, helped carry the independent production to moderate success at the box office. In *Best Pictures of 1922-1923*, Sherwood claimed that "Mr. Chaney's performance of the benevolent laundryman, Yen Sin, was the finest impersonation of an Oriental character by an Occidental player that I have ever seen." Industry trade journals reported that the film performed exceptionally well across the country, even breaking records at independent theaters in Newark, Washington, D.C., Los Angeles, Philadelphia, and Dallas. [93] While working on the picture's location in Del Monte, California, Lon noted in a letter to Grasso, "We have been working very hard since we've been here and I sure will be glad to get back home."

The year 1922 was indeed proving to be a prolific and profitable one for Lon as he literally went from project to project. While working on *Shadows*, he was offered a role in Warner Bros.' *Little Church Around the Corner*. Jack Warner was so eager for Lon's participation in the picture that he offered to have scenarist Olga Printzlau "re-write the part of Jude to conform with any suggestion you might make." Ultimately, Lon would pass on the project because of his involvement in *The Hunchback of Notre Dame*. [94]

A film based on a popular or classic novel has always provided an actor with substantial material upon which to establish a character. Not only is an actor able to obtain insight into his character (there is often less to go on in an original screenplay) but a novel also allows for a more accurate feeling for the overall theme and period. No doubt this helped Lon, who was the only choice of director Frank Lloyd and producer Sol Lesser to play the role of Fagin in *Oliver Twist*. [95] Chaney had his own ideas and interpretation of the character, stating that he "intended to play the part not essentially as a Jew but as a character with more universal appeal." [96] Young Jackie Coogan recalled his first impression of Chaney in make-up when he said, "He scared the bejesus out of me!" [97] Frank Lloyd, who proposed the idea of making the film to Coogan's father and producer Lesser, [98] captured the flavor of the period by displaying great attention to detail. The budget for the film was the then-unheard-of amount of $400,000, double the cost of most pictures being made at that time. [99]

Chaney's Fagin is a crafty petty thief who knows how to use people to his own advantage. He is initially charming, and almost fatherly toward young Oliver Twist. Although he seems to fear for the boy's safety when he is to accompany Bill Sikes on a robbery, Fagin does not interfere with the villainous plans formulated for his own personal benefit. Dealing with Sikes, he is careful not to provoke the man's temper, preferring to placate him and avoid any kind of trouble. Fagin ridicules the other boys when they fail to properly demonstrate the art of pickpocketing for young Oliver. When Oliver makes an attempt at the illegal trade, Fagin praises him like a proud father, winning the boy's trust, which of course is his sinister intention. Fagin is old, and while Chaney plays him with a stooped posture and slow gait, at times he appears to be a little *too* stooped, almost hunchbacked. Also, when Fagin learns that Oliver has told the authorities everything he knows about his group, Chaney tends to exaggerate his fear of being caught. Yet even with these occasional transgressions, his portrayal is believable, and the expressive and fluid hand gestures incorporated into the character are impressive.

Quincy Adams Sawyer, a popular novel when it was published in 1902, uses a small New England town at the turn of the century as its backdrop. The story went on to become a well-received stage play before being brought to the motion picture screen in 1912 and 1922.

A Thousand Faces

The 1922 version, which proved to be a big success with the critics and the box office, boasted several well-known performers including John Bowers, Blanche Sweet, Barbara LaMarr, Elmo Lincoln, Hank Mann, Louise Fazenda, and Lon as Obadiah Strout, the crooked lawyer. An interesting insight into Chaney's popularity at this time is revealed in a letter addressed to Lon and Alfred Grasso,dated March 6, 1923, from producer Arthur H. Sawyer:

> I have learned some very interesting things in the field through talking to exhibitors and exchange men; also a great many of the general public. I find that Lon Chaney's name in front of a theatre really means something, but the only reaction is from the big "first-run" theatre due to the fact that every time he advertises a picture with Lon Chaney, all of the "dumps" [100] take out the old ones and their advertising of "Lon Chaney" does not help the big house.

> I think you are remedying this to a great extent now owing to the fact that, during the time you are making *The Hunchback*, you ordinarily, under former conditions, would have been turning out three or four of the other type of picture. This means that during the next six months, there will not be anywhere near as many pictures in which you are featured, put on the market, and this fact will enhance your value to the "big" theaters.

> And I want to tell you that unless we can count on the big, first-runs throughout the country, we do not stand much of a chance to do a big gross. *Quincy Adams*, by getting the big rentals and playing the big theaters, cleared itself in the first two months, whereas some of the other pictures we made previously to that, have been playing for eight months and over, and some of them have not cleared themselves yet... [101]

I have also found a lot of criticism on my using you as "Strout" in "Quincy Adams." In other words, the masses (and also a good many Exchange men) and the supposedly more intelligent producers and managers feel that because you did a legless cripple or an East-Side Gunman, that you must always do that. However, am very glad to say that I found a number of intelligence to realize that you gave a very consistent and wonderful characterization of "Strout," even though some of them resented the fact that we would even dream of asking you to "put over comedy."

My observations have led me to believe that we have over-estimated the intelligence of the American Movie Picture audiences. However, I feel that as long as we consider carefully the character and minute consistency, we will please the "thinking" public, and if the part is well done, the others will follow in line. [102]

Without the help of a studio to carefully monitor the release of a performer's pictures, an actor was likely to become overexposed, and smaller theaters could then easily capitalize on a current production by running a previously distributed picture. (Later, when a performer's older pictures were sold to television, this would prove to be an even bigger problem because the old films would compete against current releases. This practice also hurt several television shows when their early episodes where sold to syndication while current episodes were still in production.) [103] Of course, this problem was remedied for Chaney when he signed with M-G-M; they not only carefully chose his material but also prudently monitored the distribution of his pictures so that the public would not lose interest. But Chaney, like other actors, was in danger of becoming stereotyped as a "crippled gangster" because of the tunnel vision of some producers who wanted to capitalize on this known commodity. Fortunately, he was able to convert most producers from this kind of thinking by his unrivaled performances in such films as *The Hunchback of Notre Dame, He Who Gets Slapped, The Unholy Three,* and *Tell It to the Marines.*

Despite the mindset of some producers, Lon continued to reinforce his reputation as a leading character actor by performing in several different kinds of roles. One was in Goldwyn Pictures' *A Blind Bargain,* which is also one of Chaney's most sought-after "lost" films. This picture is but one of a handful in Chaney's career that can truly be classified as a horror film. Lon plays the brilliant surgeon Dr. Lamb, who is consumed by the theory of using animals to prolong human life. One of his botched experiments is a half-ape/half-man character whom Chaney also portrays. Director Wallace Worsley used double-exposure photography to incorporate both characters in several scenes, and the studio played up Chaney's dual performance with a separate title card in the opening credits: *Presenting Lon Chaney in the dual role of Doctor Anthony Lamb and the Hunchback.* [104]

His performance as the ape-man, praised by the critics, tended to eclipse his characterization of Dr. Lamb. Unfortunately, the picture was met with mixed response from both critics and audiences. The premise of a doctor who considers himself God-like in his experiments to prolong life no doubt would have had censors and church groups calling for its banishment. [105] Therefore, the picture was severely edited, and four different versions of title cards were drafted before the film received its final approval on February 15, 1922. [106] Goldwyn Pictures proposed several ideas for the promotion of the picture. One idea was that theatre owners hold an amateur make-up contest offering two prizes, one for the most original characterization and one for the best disguise which could be done in the shortest amount of time. [107] Over the years, similar contests would be repeated by numerous theaters in an effort to capitalize on Chaney's talent with greasepaint.

From Freelancing to Stardom

While his films were busy ringing up profits at the box office, Lon tried once again to catch up on some much-needed rest from his rigorous schedule. After completing *Shadows*, he and Hazel returned to San Francisco in September, 1922. But Hollywood once again called for Lon's services in the Metro picture *All the Brothers Were Valiant*. Alfred Grasso wired Lon at the St. Francis Hotel on September 15:

> Metro wants you for Irvin Willat production offering $1,800 weekly starting September 20th in Frisco. Finishing about October 30th. Thalberg willing to extend your starting date to November 1st. Wire me your decision and when you expect to return. [108]

Lon replied that he wanted a salary of $2,000 a week and left all other arrangements up to Grasso, asking him to let him know at once whether or not Metro would accept the offer. The following day Grasso wired,

> I have Metro signed contract. You play part in Willat production at $2,000 weekly starting on or about September 20th finishing on or about October 30th. I have letter from Thalberg postponing your *Hunchback* starting date to on or about November 1st. Metro informs me Willat may need you before September 20th, therefore if you decide to remain in San Francisco, wire me. Also if you wish me to send you or take your make-up material and anything else you need.

Even the *San Francisco Examiner* carried the news of how Chaney's vacation was interrupted by the demands of Hollywood. The "Around the Lobbies" column noted:

A Thousand Faces

> It was recreation and rest that Lon Chaney, film
> actor, who is at the St. Francis, sought when he left
> Hollywood several days ago with Mrs. Chaney and
> came to San Francisco.
>
> For a few days there was motoring, horseback
> riding, etc., and then Irving Willat of the Metro Film
> Company came rushing up with the announcement
> that his leading man was ill, that he had expended a
> large sum of money in bringing his company to San
> Francisco and that Chaney could save the day. Well
> Chaney saved the day, and each morning now he is
> going out on locations for a picture and under
> conditions that were unknown to him when he
> went vacation hunting. And as soon as he has
> finished this picture, Chaney must go back to Los
> Angeles for a picture. So there is no vacation for
> Chaney. [109]

Based on the novel by Ben Ames Williams, *All the Brothers Were Valiant* (1923) was one of many movies made during this period to feature in its narrative the high seas and the men who sailed them. Valentino had recently appeared in *Moran of the Lady Letty* (1922), and other pictures, such as *The Sea Hawk* (1924), followed, indulging the public's fondness for action and romance on the ocean. The film company hired a number of whaling ships based in San Francisco, including the 65-foot *Port Saunders* and an older vessel, the 165-foot *Carolyn Frances*. [110] On several occasions, the camera crew ventured out to sea in search of background footage and would photograph whalers in the act of harpooning the giant creatures. During one such excursion, a near-fatal accident occurred when, without warning, two 20-foot whale-pursuit boats crashed into each other and capsized. Luckily, a tugboat was nearby and successfully rescued the crew members and actor Malcolm McGregor. In typical Hollywood fashion, the cameras kept grinding away, and were able to catch the entire accident on film. [111]

From Freelancing to Stardom

Lon and Hazel continued to stay at the St. Francis Hotel [112] while he worked on the film and they contended with the numerous details of building their new home, located on Sunset Boulevard. [113] Letters from Lon to his business manager shed some interesting insights into Chaney's opinions about the making of this picture and about his coworkers:

> Everything is going along fairly well up here.
> Although we have a dumb bell for a leading man. [114]
> Billy Mong is in the picture doing just a fair part and
> Robert McKim is doing second heavy. The leading
> lady (Miss Dove) [115] is one of those "Blah" sort that
> has all beauty and no brains. I wish by the way you
> could call up Zan the wig man and ask him if he
> received the wigs I sent back to him and explain to
> him that they were too dark and I am doing without.
> Also to send you the bill and you will send check for
> same. We have had exceptionally good weather and
> I hope another week will see us back in
> Hollywood....
>
> I am going out next Wednesday night and sell
> tickets for the benefit ball to be given to get money
> to send to the widowed women in the Jackson Mine
> disaster. [116] But I told the committee that I would
> not make any speech. Aside from what I have told
> you, I know nothing, so will close for this time, so
> will say "so long."

Hazel Chaney said that Lon always had his wigs made by Zan, one of Hollywood's leading wig makers at the time. She said that the two men would spend hours discussing a wig before Lon began a film because he was very particular and took the utmost care that the wig look realistic. [117] The Jackson Mine benefit must have been something that truly moved him. He normally had an aversion to public appearances and avoided them because he felt that movie audiences would quickly become weary of a performer if they came to know him too well. Lon rarely granted interviews, finding his occasional appearances generated more publicity than did the high visibility of those stars who talked to every reporter in town. As it turned out, this was a very smart business move on his part because by cloaking himself in a mysterious aura, he was able to maintain the public's curiosity. The more reluctant Chaney appeared, the more the public wanted to know about him, which translated into ticket sales for his pictures. When Greta Garbo arrived at M-G-M studios, Lon reportedly advised her, "If you let them know too much about you, they will lose interest." [118] This practice also allowed Lon to keep his personal life private and away from the relentless reporters who might have discovered his previous marriage to Cleva Creighton and the scandal of her attempted suicide. Other writers have surmised that Lon's nonattendance at social functions was due to a morose personality, but that simply is not true. According to his grandson, Lon Ralph Chaney, he just didn't care for the adulation and bolstering of one's ego that these events ensured. [119]

Lon noted in another letter to Grasso:

> The weather up here for the past two days has been very miserable. Raining all the time. Am not working today. If it continues will not be home before Saturday or Sunday....

> Have been getting up at 7 o'clock and getting back to the hotel around 7:30 at night. We are working a way out in the bay and it takes a long time to go and come. Yesterday the water was very rough and they wanted me to go in but I refused. They were very nice about it. So "that's that"... Well Al I really don't know of anything else at present so I will close with best regards to you and the Mrs. from the "old man."

As Lon awaited the commencement of production of *The Hunchback of Notre Dame*, Grasso contacted John McCormick, an executive with Associated First National Pictures, in regards to funding a production unit to feature Chaney. This proposal, like the previous ones, would have had Lon producing and supervising four or five pictures a year, and the unit would include several of the personnel from the late George Loane Tucker's company. [120] In a November 18, 1922, letter to McCormick, Grasso outlined four stories that Chaney had selected as potential projects:

> *God's Lighting.* Has tremendous regeneration theme....In this Mr. Chaney will portray a deformed cripple, giving him an opportunity to duplicate his terrific success as "The Frog" in *The Miracle Man.*

> An original story, especially written for Mr. Chaney, by Welford Beaton....This story has a remarkably effective and entirely new treatment of the regeneration theme, based on *Return Good for Evil,* and gives Mr. Chaney wide scope for brilliant acting and characterization.

> An original story by Mr. Chaney. This is an idea never before attempted and will be developed by a famous author. In this story, Mr. Chaney will portray a powerful and impressive character, fighting regeneration, but which finally overpowers him.

> A novelized story by Gouverneur Morris. This is a very unusual and novel theme. In it Mr. Chaney will portray the part of a man who impersonates four or five different distinct characters of the story, giving Mr. Chaney the opportunity of displaying his ability as an actor, and his uncanny power of make-up. [121]

While Paris Sleeps, released shortly after *All the Brothers Were Valiant*, originally was made in 1920 under the title *The Glory of Love*. The plot seems like a perfect Chaney vehicle and was a forerunner to *The House of Wax*, but unfortunately it missed the mark. Chaney portrayed a Parisian sculptor suffering from unrequited love, who seeks the aid of a wax museum owner to kill the girl's lover. This film had enormous potential but failed to live up to its expectations. As the *Film Daily* review noted, "Just to think what Chaney could have done with the madman character certainly detracts greatly from the role he does portray." Adding to this disappointment was the poor direction by Maurice Tourneur, whose work had been praised in such well-received pictures as *The Last of the Mohicans* and Chaney's *Victory* and *Treasure Island*.

In a rare departure from his previous roles, Lon was allowed to win the girl in the final fade out of *The Shock* (1923). Playing a crippled gangster, Chaney regains the use of his legs at the conclusion of the picture after surviving the San Francisco earthquake of 1906. His character is a hardened criminal whose underworld boss sends him to a small town to pose as a telegraph operator and observe the actions of a bank manager. The countryside has a curious affect on Chaney's character, Wilse Dilling, softening his big city toughness. This transformation continues as he falls in love with Gertrude (Virginia Valli), the bank manager's daughter. Chaney applies subtle nuances to his character that give him a realistic appeal, such as in the opening of the film, in which he is drinking tea at a Chinese restaurant. When he burns his tongue while attempting to sip hot tea, Lon winces. It appears he almost curses himself inwardly before blowing into the cup and attempting to drink again. This subtle but realistic touch gives a genuine flavor to his role. In the final scene, following his cure, Gertrude finds him in his wheelchair and asks how he's recuperating. With a slight smile, Lon glances away. When he looks up at her again, his face is void of any emotion as he pantomimes that he's coming along all right. His smile and glancing away indicate that he is hiding something from her, which contributes to the climax when he displays his ability to walk again. Just as Chaney picks up the tip from the table in *Outside the Law* and so instantly establishes his character in one movement, so too, these two examples and many other "bits of business" in *The Shock* contribute to a realistic, tremendously believable character.

Wilse Dilling becomes the hero of the picture when he realizes that Gertrude and her father would be ruined if Dilling's boss carries out his plan. Dilling decides to destroy the bank and its evidence in an explosion, hoping to save Gertrude and her father. Complications arise when Gertrude arrives at the bank unexpectedly just as the bomb goes off. Chaney's grief and anguish are apparent when he learns of her injuries, but he takes care not to overplay the emotions. Later, when he is held hostage in the restaurant by his boss, Chaney's emotional strength comes to the forefront. Cursing his former partners for harming the girl he loves, the actor embraces his character's hatred and elicits a powerful presence, his anger building, while he sits, crippled, on the floor. This disposition of Wilse Dilling is the prelude to the earthquake that envelops the group of villains and ultimately frees Dilling from his crippled body and mind. Only Chaney's performance and the mildly interesting special effects that simulate the 1906 earthquake distinguish this film from the studio's other melodramatic productions.

Lon Chaney's skills, which had been carefully polished on the stage and in his early days at Universal, allowed him to move from the ranks of a supporting player to featured star and noted character actor. While his reputation as a competent performer grew, he was quickly becoming known in the Hollywood community as an actor's actor. In the careers of movie stars, a common thread found in their elevation to stardom is one unforgettable role in which the star becomes synonymous with the part. Generally a performer becomes famous by finding the one role that makes a strong and lasting impression on the public. If he or she is truly lucky, a second role will become equally memorable. But these instances are rare. Luck appears to have been with Lon Chaney because the role of the deaf, one-eyed bellringer of Notre Dame would soon stun film critics and the public alike. The overall scope of the picture would force Hollywood to use such words as spectacle and epic to describe it, giving Universal Studios the industry respect it had long sought. Not only would *The Hunchback of Notre Dame* become the prestige picture Universal needed, but it would also launch Lon Chaney into the realm of international stardom.

Lon made a delicious villain in Maurice Tourneur's *Victory* (1919). Here, he intimidates Wallace Beery as he relates his past deeds.

Lon, Lewis Stone, and Betty Blythe in *Nomads of the North* (1920).

The emotional intensity Chaney brought to the role of Blizzard is evident in this picture. *The Penalty* (1920).

Goldwyn Pictures Corporation of New York

WEEKLY COST REPORT

Star All Star

Director Wallace Worsley

Feature THE PENALTY #98

Week Ending June 25th, 1921.

FEATURE AND ACCOUNT NO.	CLASSIFICATION	TOTAL	
	Started 1/7/20 Finished 4/2/20	THIS WEEK	TO DATE
	48 Days		
500	Salaries, Stars		21257 68
1	Leads		
2	Extra Talent		6823 48
3	Directors		6408 33
4	Assistant Directors		960 00
5	Camera Men		1003 33
6	Assistant Cameramen		300 00
7	Property Men		1552 00
8	Electricians		1083 96
9	Miscellaneous		352 94
510	Editorial Department, Direct Charge		4094 84
1	Scenario		
2	Film Negative		2338 53
3	Film Positive		1605 48
4	Stills		
5	Laboratory		
6	Sets (See Next Page for Details)		9346 35
7	Location Fees		15 00
8	Location Expense		1223 33
9	Travel Expense		1972 73
520	Meals and Lodging Expense		3543 36
1	Props Purchased		35 35
2	Props Rentals		2887 63
3	Wardrobe Purchased		1401 02
4	Wardrobe Rentals		459 43
5	Automobile Hire		1277 04
6	Animal Hire		
7	Telephone and Telegraph Expense		9 75
8	Miscellaneous Supplies and Expense		867 39
9	Electricity		341 94
530	Marine Insurance		110 63
1	Freight and Express		185 42
2	Title Artist Charge		222 49
3	Title Letterers' Charge		272 27
4	Title Insert Man and Title Photographer		105 93
5			
6	Indirect Production Charge		16800 00
	TOTALS		88867 63

A budget breakdown for the film, *The Penalty*.

Alfred Grasso, Lon's business manager from 1920 to 1924, at his office at Universal Studios when he was an assistant to Irving Thalberg. (Courtesy of the Alfred Grasso family)

Lon poses on the Goldwyn Studios lot with the author of *The Penalty*, Gouverneur Morris.

Tod Browning watches noted detective William J. Burns demonstrate how to take a gun away from a suspect on the set of *Outside the Law* (1921). Lon is the unfortunate victim.

As Chin Gow in *Bits of Life* (1921).

Ace of Hearts (1921).

Lon and director Wallace Worsley on the set of *Voices of the City* (1922).

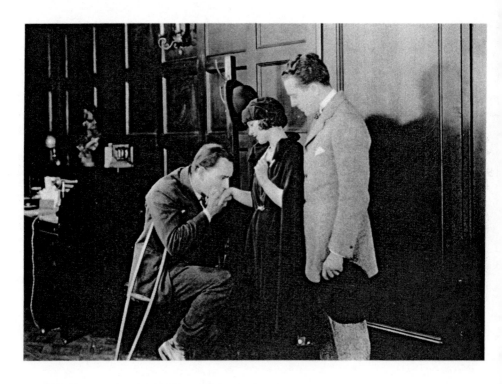

Lon, Edith Roberts, and Jack Mulhall in *Flesh and Blood* (1922).

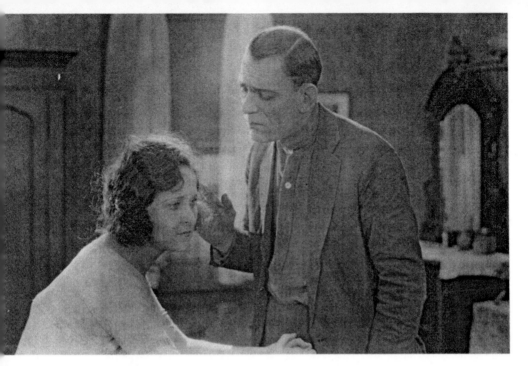

ope Hampton and Lon in *Light in the Dark* (1922).

Lon and Gladys Brockwell in *Oliver Twist* (1922).

Los Angeles, Calif.,
July 15th, 1922.

B. P. Schulberg, Specials, as Producer hereby engages Lon Chaney as artist to play in the motion picture production entitled "Ching Ching Chinaman" and the parties hereto mutually agree as follows:

1.   The term thereof shall commence on or about August 15th, 1922, and end when said part is completed unless sooner terminated as hereinafter provided.

2.   The producer agrees to pay the artist at the rate of Eighteen Hundred ($1800.00) Dollars per week and in computing salary for less than one week, a day's salary shall be one-sixth (1/6) of the weekly rate. Should the artist become incapacitated through any fault of the producer or while on the set or in the studio or on location, etc. the artist shall receive full compensation. The artist shall be entitled to no additional compensation for services rendered at night or on Sundays or Holidays.

3.   The artist agrees to observe all reasonable rules and regulations of the producer in connection with its business, and to perform all services as requested and instructed by the producer.

4.   The artist agrees to furnish all modern wardrobe and wearing apparel necessary in the judgment of the producer for part and the producer agrees to furnish all wardrobe that is not modern.

5.   Should the artist be required to perform services hereunder in any place other than the City of Los Angeles or its environs, the producer shall pay all necessary traveling expenses of the artist, including hotel bills and other charges for board and lodging.

6.   This agreement may be terminated by the producer at any time if the producer conscientiously and in good faith believes that the artist is not satisfactorily performing the required services hereunder or is not suitablemfor the part assigned, or in the event that the commencement, continuation or completion of said production for any reason whatsoever is abandoned, suspended, delayed or interfered with.

7.   The producer shall have the exclusive right to the services of the artist during the term hereof and the right to use the name and likeness of the artist, photographic or otherwise, in connection with the distribution and exploitation of said production.

8.   All notices which the producer is required or may desire to give to the artist may be given by addressing the same to the artist at 1420 N. Berendo Street, Los Angeles, California, or such notice may be given to the artist personally.

9.   The artist represents and warrants to the producer that the artist is fully competent in all respects to enter into this agreement. Executed the day and year above written.

B. P. SCHULBERG SPECIALS

By _B. P. Schulberg_ President

and General Manager.

Lon Chaney

Lon's one-page contract for *Shadows*, under the film's original title, *Ching, Ching Chinaman* (Courtesy of the Alfred Grasso Family Collection)

ank Mann and Lon look over the script on the set of *Quincy Adams Sawyer* (1922). Hank Mann ould later play a comedy waiter in Chaney's 1957 film biography.

Double exposure shot of Lon's two characters, the ape-man and Dr. Lamb. Raymond McKee is in the chair.

Lon and Goldwyn Studios manager Abe Lehr look at the wig Lon would wear as the ape-man in *A Blind Bargain* (1922).

Malcolm McGregor, Lon, Robert Kortman, Ropbert McKim, and William V. Mong in *All the Brothers Were Valiant* (1923).

...on (left, in make-up), scenarist Hope Loring (holding cat), producer B. P. Schulberg, and director ...om Forman (seated) look over the script of *Shadows*. Cinemaatographer Harry Parry stands next to ...he camera. (Courtesy of Bret Wood)

Lon and Virginia Valli in *The Shock* (1923). (Courtesy of George Wagner)

Lon's dog, Sandy, poses with his famous make-up case before it was donated to the Natural History Museum in Los Angeles in 1931. Chaney's name was imprinted on the picture by the magazine that ran this photo.

A Hunchback Becomes
an International Star

(1923)

Serious poses like this helped foster the belief that Chaney was a brooding and melancholy artist.

For years film historians have believed that it was Irving Thalberg's idea to make a film version of *The Hunchback of Notre Dame* for Universal Studios. According to Thalberg biographers, the young studio executive read the book as a sickly child and it became one of his favorites. When he was elevated to production executive at Universal, Thalberg realized that in order to compete with the other Hollywood studios, Universal needed to take the initiative and produce a prestige picture. He was able to persuade Carl Laemmle to approve his idea of producing *The Hunchback of Notre Dame* with a then unheard-of budget of $1,250,000. When the film was released, it received tremendous critical praise and did a brisk business at the box office, and Thalberg's reputation as the "boy wonder of Hollywood" was born.

A scene in Chaney's 1957 film biography has further helped to sustain the theory that *The Hunchback of Notre Dame* was Thalberg's brainchild. The scene shows Thalberg (Robert J. Evans) explaining to Chaney (James Cagney) that the novel was one of his favorites and he wants to make it into a picture. This long-held legend would have remained just that had papers from the Alfred Grasso family not come to this author's attention. The truth is that the idea of making *The Hunchback of Notre Dame* into a motion picture came from Lon Chaney, not Thalberg.

While it is entirely possible that Thalberg read the book as a child and later thought the property would make an impressive motion

A Thousand Faces

picture, Chaney stated that it was his desire to play the title role as early as 1920. [122] Material in the Grasso family collection indicates that Thalberg and Chaney discussed the possibility of Universal's making this picture, and of course it *was* Thalberg who convinced Carl Laemmle to undertake the lavish and extravagant project. However, a March 12, 1921 telegram to H. K. Fly and Co. in New York indicates that Chaney and his business manager, Alfred Grasso, were making inquiries into the ownership of the film rights to the Victor Hugo novel:

> Kindly ascertain and wire my expense whether copyright on *Hunchback of Notre Dame* by Victor Hugo published by Hurst Company has expired and if not who controls world's motion picture rights and at what price could be obtained.

Grasso was told that no copyright existed in America and that they would inquire about world rights. [123] There is no correspondence between Grasso and H. K. Fly and Co. that mentions any other film company or individual inquiring about the novel, suggesting that there was no competition regarding the acquisition of film rights. On March 15, Grasso received the following telegram from H. K. Fly:

> Cable received. $15,000 *Hunchback* world rights outright sale until end of copyright which is 15 years. This work not copyrighted United States but if made, an authorization is asked for later on. For release outside America price will be about 3 times present asking price for punishment damages. Went into matter thoroughly with American agent of French author society. Saw contracts [of] other producers for French works. Consider price reasonable and could not dicker for a lower one.

A Hunchback Becomes An International Star

Grasso replied that he would be in touch soon, and on June 24, he wired the following:

> Please let me know lowest they will accept for 30 day option. If satisfactory will mail you check immediately. Also advise who[m] check must be made out to.

Fly stated that $500 would secure the option for film rights for either thirty or sixty days. After obtaining the 60-day option, Chaney and Grasso went to work to find a producer for the project. On May 22, 1921, Lon received a letter from J. Hoey Lawlor, a set, costume, and title designer in New York, who offered Lon his ideas for the project:

> Regardless of how much advance notice you may give to your plans to produce the *Hunchback*, I can observe from the story that no one would attempt it without you - and without facing complete failure unless they had heavy capital. Again, there are d—-few technical directors who could safely undertake the reproduction of Notre Dame's scenes and atmosphere. In fact, [stage actor Juilan] Greer states that at least some of it must be made in Paris.... There are two scenes at least which cannot be duplicated by any artist in America.
>
> I know the complete story of [Erich] von Stroheim's effort to reproduce Monte Carlo and of how a very large sum could have been saved by a journey to the real location instead of what happened. [124] (I was technical art director of the Universal New York division for many months during the making of *Foolish Wives* and also made the double-animated main title — including von Stroheim's animated portrait.)
>
> However, there is poor comparison of this and

what you contemplate. Your production requires an absolute fifteenth century Parisian atmosphere, and will have it with all its ancient majesty and historical value.

It appears that Universal was negotiating with Lon as early as May 1921, possibly due to Thalberg's interest in the project. In a second letter, dated May 30, 1921, Lawlor advises Lon about Universal's intentions for the project,

> Advise hold off signing any contract with Universal. Information leads me to believe it is their game to secure *Hunchback* for themselves. Hang matter up upon your excuse to visit New York. Also believe they [Universal] are planning Priscilla Dean for Esmeralda. Save this big one for yourself....
>
> Laemmle and Cochrane can't see you taking a big thing like this away from Universal. The possibilities are wonderful, of course, and I'll bet my shirt they'll tie you up in some manner if possible.
>
> George [Cochrane] had the nerve to tell me that your agents have recently offered your services to Universal. This I do not believe....
>
> George added that Priscilla [Dean] would probably be obtained, which means that she would make her part the lead. However, Universal sees a fortune in the picture and will tie you into it if they can.
>
> This production properly staged and with your name at the top is entirely too good for such short skate concerns as Universal, Fox or Metro attempting.
>
> All three of them would jump at the chance, while the most you would receive from it would be a few hundred per week during the making of the picture.

A Hunchback Becomes An International Star

Your reputation is made, and it only remains for you
to cash in for some of the dough these ex-fur
scrapers [125] are spending.

Goldstein and Uffner, two low brows from the New
York slums, but who are now "managers" for
Laemmle, would block any opportunity I might have
with Universal to design for them. They are also
belonging to the class who keep out all art effects in
the above named concerns....

Take it from me that if Universal attempts to film
The Hunchback they will make a huge technical
blunder and produce nothing that can pass the four
leading Broadway houses, to say nothing of foreign
distribution. [126] England and France would laugh
the picture out of their domains.

While negotiations with Universal continued, Lon and Grasso
discussed the project with other producers, even investigating the
possibility of securing funding to produce it independently. During
the negotiations with New York financier H. A. Berg to produce one
or two pictures, Grasso also discussed a plan to finance the Hugo
novel:

While Mr. Chaney is producing said picture, you are
to carry on, at your own expense, a state right
advertising campaign to the effect that Lon Chaney
is to produce *The Hunchback of Notre Dame*.

In the event that at the completion of the first
picture we will have received a sum of money,
either as deposits or sales from state right buyers for
The Hunchback of Notre Dame, amounting to
$200,000 or over, Mr. Chaney is to utilize that
money in producing said picture, he playing the
chief male role, and is to have exclusive supervisory
control over and charge of with reference to all
details and matters pertaining to the production....

A Thousand Faces

> He is to receive $25,000 salary for his services,
> which amount will be charged in as part of the
> production, and paid to him in weekly installments
> pro-rata during the period of producing said picture,
> and in addition to said salary he is to receive 50% of
> the earnings of said picture.
>
> In the event that the sum of $200,000 has not been
> received by us at the above specified time, we are to
> refund all monies received from state right buyers,
> etc. and all obligations between Lon Chaney and
> yourself, other than the agreement covering the first
> picture, will cease and be at an end. [127]

When the deal with Berg failed, Grasso again contacted his friend Hal Layton (who originally had set up the meeting with Berg) to see if another financier could be found. A September 16, 1921, letter from Layton brings some insight into the repercussions of the "Fatty" Arbuckle rape trial, which had recently exploded in the press, and the effects it subsequently had on financing all motion pictures:

> I regret that I have nothing further to report at the
> present time as the damaging effects of the Arbuckle
> affair are making themselves felt very strongly in
> financial circles. Your proposition with others will
> have to be postponed until a more propitious
> moment when I can report something more
> favorable. You will hear from me.

The trial and subsequent scandal ruined the career of popular comedian Fatty Arbuckle and came very close to destroying the entire motion picture industry along with it. Civic groups and leagues of decency across the country were outraged over the allegations against Arbuckle and the surmised "immoral" lifestyle enjoyed by all Hollywood stars.

Studio producers and Paramount Pictures, which produced and distributed Arbuckle's films, decided that the best way to handle the whole situation would be to "sacrifice" the comedian in order to placate the country. Arbuckle was thus banned from motion pictures [128] and the Motion Picture Producers and Distributors of America (MPPDA) was created. It was headed by former Postmaster Will Hays, and was to oversee a strict censorship code, which the producers agreed to follow. [129] In another effort to placate the reformers, a "morals clause" was included in all stars' contracts, binding each to "conduct himself with due regard to public conventions and morals and agree that he will not do or commit any act or thing that will tend to degrade him in society or bring him into public hatred, contempt, scorn or ridicule." [130]

While Lon was working on *The Light in the Dark* in New York City, he held another meeting with Universal regarding their proposed project. Lon detailed the meeting to Grasso in a December 18, 1921, telegram:

> Just returned from meeting with Universal about
> *Hunchback* to be done in Berlin with German
> director. Have another proposition starting at two
> thousand, good story. Universal contract with
> director lasts only two months expiring last of
> March. Wire immediately your advice in the matter.

In a January 1, 1922, interview with the *Colorado Springs Gazette*, Lon mentioned that a German company had offered to make the film in Germany, but he had declined involvement because he felt the three-month shooting schedule would be too short. This telegram is the first hard evidence to reveal that the film was being contemplated for production in Germany, or anywhere else in Europe for that matter. Grasso, in addition to working as Lon's business manager, was also working at the time as an assistant to Irving Thalberg at Universal, and as such he advised Lon to obtain more details (i.e., guarantees of transportation, wardrobe, make-up, etc.). He further stated that unless the Universal offer to do the film in Germany would pay more than the other starring proposition, he should take the starring vehicle. [131]

But the German project fell through, and negotiations with Universal and other production companies continued. Chelsea Pictures Corporation announced in the April 29, 1922 issue of *Motion Picture World*, that they would start production on twenty pictures to be released the following year. They said that Chaney would star in *The Hunchback of Notre Dame*, to be directed by Alan Crosland, possibly to be filmed in Europe. Three other pictures were also announced as starring vehicles for Chaney: *Where's Haggerty?*, *The Thug*, and *The Scar*. Bernard Levy, president of Chelsea Pictures, said in the article that the company was financed by five New York businessmen and bankers. This was the first official announcement that Lon would star in *The Hunchback of Notre Dame*. The deal for all four productions eventually fell apart, and Lon went back to the job of finding a suitable company to produce his project.

Ultimately, Chaney was able to come to terms with Universal, and a contract was signed on August 15, 1922, giving Lon a salary of $2,000 a week. [132] Interestingly, unlike the failed proposals to finance the film as an independent production, Chaney's deal with Universal did not grant him any percentage of the picture's earnings. It is possible that in order to see his project come to realization, Lon may have been forced to give up any hopes of obtaining a cut of the profits. [133] *Motion Picture News* stated in their August 26, 1922 issue that

> Universal has definitely decided to film *The
> Hunchback of Notre Dame*, Victor Hugo's famous
> novel. Word was flashed to the coast this week to
> begin work on the film. The continuity was being
> whipped up into shape, and the location and
> production departments are taking the preliminary
> steps necessary for the construction of the various
> sets.

A Hunchback Becomes An International Star

It's interesting to note that a number of people felt the picture would have to be shot in European locations, instead of building the sets in Hollywood. The primary reason for ultimately deciding not to film in France was that the buildings surrounding the real Notre Dame cathedral were too contemporary and it would be impossible to hide them or cover them with facades. It was during this period that Hollywood gained its reputation for building elaborate sets, and the quality of Hollywood's production skills soon became the envy of filmmakers all over the world. For example, *Ben Hur*, which was originally planned to be filmed entirely on location in Italy, proved devastating to the financial health of M-G-M. [134] The production was eventually brought back to the California studio, where costs and conditions could be controlled. In fact, the famous chariot race was actually filmed on a large vacant lot near the corner of La Cienega and Venice boulevards, not far from the M-G-M studios.

The *Universal Weekly* issue of September 2, 1922, stated that negotiations for "one of the best known stars in the industry" were underway and that an announcement would be made within a week, but *Motion Picture News* became the first industry trade paper to make the announcement that Chaney would star in the production. [135] With Lon's deal consummated, a director and screenwriter had to be chosen.

Lon's association with the production was far more extensive than has been previously believed. He was involved in every aspect of production, and Hazel Chaney said that he was in daily script conferences with scenarist Edward T. Lowe, Jr. and adaptor Perley Poore Sheehan. She said Lon knew the novel so well that he was able to make sure nothing would be deleted that might hurt the progress of the story. [136] Lon's concern that the writer get the story correct is evident in a quote from a letter written to Grasso while Chaney was on location: [137]

> Am indeed pleased to know Sheehan is on the story.
> I only hope he gets the best of it.

Lon was also concerned with the choice of director for the project, and a myriad number of names had been suggested. Erich von Stroheim was considered but quickly rejected for fear that he would increase the film's budget with unnecessary expenditures. In an October 5, 1922, telegram, Grasso told Lon,

> Thalberg would like your opinion on Allan Holubar, Chet Withey, Hobart Henley, Emile Chataud. Please wire me straight.

Lon replied,

> Holubar as expensive as Stroheim. Henley out. Chet Withey not so bad. Chataud might be a possibility. Keep after the others especially Borzage.

Frank Borzage appears to have been Lon's preferred choice for director. He thought that "Borzage would do it nicely" [138] and also suggested Raoul Walsh as a possibility. While Lon was considering some well-known people to handle the directorial duties, Universal had their own ideas, preferring a second-rate director who could shoot the film quickly and fairly cheaply.

Things apparently reached a boiling point, as is evident in this letter to Grasso, in which Lon pointedly stated:

> Now about our dear friends Mr. Universal. Al I want
> to tell you right now that I positively refuse to do
> the picture with any of the directors they have there
> and I want you to go over that contract very
> carefully and see if there is a possibility of getting
> out of it should they be unable to get a satisfactory
> director and cast when it comes time for me to start.
> I will break my contract if they don't. Now I want
> you to be sure and tell Thalberg that and let me

know what he has to say. I am not going to stand
for any of their foolishness or stalling. Now
remember that. Just simply stand "pat" and they will
get busy.

In another letter, Lon reiterates his stance on breaking his contract with Universal:

Now Al I want you to look over that contract
carefully and see if there is a possibility of breaking
it. I feel sure we could take it to Louis B. Mayer and
then [Fred] Niblo would direct it.

A paragraph later, Lon concedes his feelings about Wallace Worsley as a possible director:

Worsley by the way is as good as any of the second
raters or better but for God's sake don't tell them so.

Ultimately the decision was made by Thalberg; Wallace Worsley was chosen as the director. Thalberg may have felt Worsley was the most reasonable choice to helm the project, considering he had previously directed Chaney in four successful films. Supposedly Tod Browning had been announced at one point as the director, [139] but this is highly doubtful because Worsley was chosen shortly after the studio declared Chaney as their star. With Worsley signed as director, attention turned to finding an actress for the role of Esmeralda. In the early stages of production, Universal may have hoped to sign Priscilla Dean for the part, but she was quickly dismissed. While Lon was on location for *Shadows*, he discussed his feelings with Grasso about some of the actresses competing for the role:

Now about [Betty] Compson. [140] I am afraid she
might want to pull some star ideas and you know
how long I could stand for that. However inquire

and find out how her disposition is now. I'll admit
she would be wonderful for the part. What do you
think of May McAvoy? Or Margaret De La Marr or
Mont. I really don't know which it is. However she
is with us in this picture. [141] The one objection I
have to her is, she is inclined to be terribly upstage
and you know I can't stand for that. Can you think
of any other possibility?

Just as with *Gone With The Wind* sixteen years later, almost every actress in Hollywood was considered for the part. Patsy Ruth Miller said that she was offered the role provided that she be available when production started, or she would forfeit her chance. She said Lon was extremely upset when he learned that she had not been put on the payroll directly after his approval of her. [142] It was not an uncommon practice for studios to offer a prize role to a young performer with the provision that they be readily available without any advance remuneration. Lon not only approved of casting Patsy in the lead role but was also concerned about her being signed, as is evident in a letter to Grasso, in which he inquires, "Have they gotten in touch with Patsy Ruth Miller for Esmeralda?" [143]

It must have been a trying time for Lon, waiting for the film to begin while engaged in another production on location in San Francisco. In the letter to Grasso quoted above, Lon also inquired about the construction of the sets, asking, "Have they started on the sets yet and if so how do they look?" [144]

Chaney's involvement in the production was extensive. Patsy Ruth Miller said that when she came out to the studio to test for the role, she didn't remember meeting the director, but vividly recalled meeting Lon, who came down to the set and quietly explained the role of Esmeralda. [145] For years, stories have circulated that Chaney helped direct many of the scenes in the picture, including the scene where Esmeralda is tortured into confessing that she killed Phoebus. It was often dismissed as Hollywood publicity. However, with the new proof that Chaney was thoroughly involved in all aspects of production, it is very probable that he could have directed many scenes, especially if he felt that Worsley was not obtaining the desired results. Patsy Ruth Miller said that Lon was on the set daily, even on his days off, occasionally making suggestions to Worsley regarding certain scenes. She said they often discussed the script over lunch, yet she never recalled any friction between the two men. 146

While Lon was finishing *All the Brothers Were Valiant* and preparing to start *Hunchback*, producer Arthur Sawyer inquired about his services for *The Shooting of Dan McGrew*, based on the poem of the same title. Grasso notified Lon in an October 9, 1922, telegram:

> Sawyer wants you for *Shooting of Dan McGrew*
> starting after completion *Hunchback*. Guaranteeing
> three weeks. Am trying to get twenty-two hundred
> weekly. Wire me your opinion and if you want any
> rest after *Hunchback*.

Lon replied that he needed two weeks' rest after finishing *Hunchback* and demanded a four-week guarantee. He also wanted to know what director they had in mind for the project. Arthur Sawyer, who had produced *Quincy Adams Sawyer*, had Lon in mind for the role of Jim. In a March 6, 1923 letter to Lon and Grasso, Sawyer relates his ideas for Chaney's role in the film,

> Everybody in the "know" thinks that in *McGrew* we
> are going to make one of the masterpieces of the
> screen and I want to have this characterization
> begin "cooking" in your mind as this picture will be
> a composite and I want you to have as big a hand in
> the preparation as any of us.
>
> Referring to the question as to whether you were

117

the best selection for the "sympathetic husband," I called the attention of these people [industry insiders and theatre owners] to *Shadows* and *The Trap*, in both of which pictures you certainly brought "tears" and "sympathy" from the audience.

My little organization knows perfectly well that you are going to "put over" a new characterization in the part of the husband and I know very well that you are going to show them "something" that they did not know you possessed.

I know you will get all the "tears" and "sympathy" that we will need and I have a very clear visualization in my mind of your wonderful scenes with your little baby after you have been deserted by Lou....

Bearing all the above in mind, will you please begin to mull over the possibilities of climaxes and situations on McGrew. I sincerely trust that *The Hunchback* is living up to all you have hoped and I trust it will be your greatest achievement to date. [147]

This letter indicates that producers and theatre owners still entertained doubts that Chaney could play a believable sympathetic part, erasing the memory of his many villainous roles. It was a hurdle many actors faced in their careers, including James Cagney, who was considered by most to be only a "tough guy" until he proved the naysayers wrong when he sang and danced in *Footlight Parade* (1933). Because of Chaney's schedule on *Hunchback*, he had to drop out of *The Shooting of Dan McGrew*.

Lon's starting date for *The Hunchback of Notre Dame* was pushed back from October 2 to October 28, 1922, which evidently caused some concern at the New York office of Universal. On October 20, Lon sent a terse wire to Thalberg:

A Hunchback Becomes An International Star

Will finish picture about October 28. If this is
satisfactory kindly call Milton Hoffman and state my
salary to them is the same as with you or have
Grasso see him. You can explain situation to Grasso.
Notify me at earliest possible moment so I can act
accordingly. Proposition lies entirely in your
hands.[148]

Universal was understandably nervous as the costs for sets and costumes rose while their leading star was busy on another picture. Thalberg wired Lon that he had "informed Grasso and Milton Hoffman OK with me if you finish October 28." Chaney's official starting date was November 10, with principal filming beginning on December 16, 1922.

Probably the single most difficult obstacle facing the production was the enormous number of costumes to be issued not only to the stars and the supporting and bit players but to the thousands of extras as well. A Colonel Gordon McGee was hired as costume supervisor, and the logistical problems were remedied. A building was constructed near the massive Notre Dame cathedral set on Universal's back lot, from which the costumes would be issued.[149] It was 120 feet in length and had eighteen numbered windows. When an extra received his daily voucher from the studio casting office, a number on the paper directed the person to the proper window to get his costume. Extras were sent to the same window each night, keeping the issuance of costumes as orderly as possible.[150]

The large building was expanded when the company started filming its night sequences, which involved almost two thousand extras in February and March, 1923. Rather than being continually recast, these extras were kept on the payroll, thus ensuring that each had an already-fitted costume ready to wear.[151] Chaney, Worsley, and writer Perley Poore Sheehan were all involved in approving the casting of the extras for the various scenes.[152] At one point during production, more than two hundred people were maintained on the studio payroll just to handle the extensive wardrobe duties involved with this production. [153]

Another problem facing the filmmakers was how to light the massive sets for the nearly two months of night work. The cathedral set and the square, known as Palace du Parvais, covered an area measuring 600 by 900 feet. Staging the "Festival of Fools" sequence required the use of 37 sunlight arcs, 5 General Electric high-intensity spotlights, 154 Winfields, 47 overhead spots, and 62 practical arc lights. [154] The scene in which the gypsies storm Notre Dame to save Esmeralda could go down in Hollywood history as the one scene to use the largest number of electricians, lights, and cable of any one production. Fifty-two sunlight arcs, 21 General Electric spotlights, 30 120-ampere spots, 47 overheads, and 259 Winfields were required to light the large square and cathedral, while 230 electricians manned the seven motor generators and five miles of cable that supplied the power. In addition to the *Hunchback*, Universal had 17 other companies shooting on the lot, which required additional manpower and equipment. [155] Trucks would depart Universal in the late afternoon, headed for every studio and rental facility in Hollywood with the objective of gathering every available light, to be taken out to the back lot and placed in its designated spot. When the night's filming was done and the sun was rising over the hill behind the massive set, the electricians would once again load the lights onto trucks, and return them to the various studios for use in the morning. This routine was repeated every day for nearly two months. [156]

This massive amount of lighting was absolutely essential because the nitrate film stock had a slow exposure rate, necessitating additional illumination for proper exposure. Movies of this period often shot night sequences during the day and, to simulate nighttime, simply tinted the scene blue in the developing lab. Later a filter came to be used on the camera lens which gave the same effect as the tinting. But in order for the fiery torches to register properly and the sets to resemble fifteenth-century Paris, shooting night at night was required. Any crew member will tell you that night shooting is one of the toughest shifts to work, especially on Universal's backlot where, even in the summer months, it gets notoriously cold after sundown. In the eighty years that Universal has occupied its present location, this is the one thing that has not deviated in an ever-changing industry. So it is easy to imagine that the two months of night shooting for *The Hunchback of Notre Dame* must have been rough-going.

Carla Laemmle, the niece of Universal's founder Carl Laemmle, recalled visiting the huge set both at night and during the daytime:

> The set [the cathedral and square] was just enormous. It was the biggest set I had ever seen, I remember being on the set while they were filming where Lon rescues Patsy Ruth Miller in front of the church. It wasn't a very easy scene [for Chaney], but he was very agile and had great control of his body. His make-up was really remarkable, very moving. It was gruesome, yet pathetic. Your heart went out to him.
>
> My family was living in a bungalow on the studio lot and I remember one night seeing this very bright light coming from over the hill. We all went out to the back lot and the set was lit up. I had never seen anything like it before. [157]

In order to communicate with the numerous electricians, assistant directors, and extras, the company employed the Western Electric Public Address System. Speakers were placed all over the Palace du Parvais set, allowing Worsley to address the extras as well as to direct the electricians in placing their lights. Prior to using this system, a director would use a large megaphone to shout his orders, hoping he could be heard. Lighting director Harry D. Brown recalled that during lunch, the radio would be played over the speaker, not only providing some entertainment but also keeping the extras from wandering away. [158] A one-hundred-foot-tall camera tower was erected above the cathedral set for the numerous shots of the square as well as for Joe Bonomo's stunt in which (doubling for Chaney) he slides down a rope to rescue Esmeralda from her near-execution. More than two acres of cement and one acre of cobblestones were used to pave the huge square and the other streets simulating fifteenth-century France. [159] To ease the arduous schedule of night shooting and lift morale on those long nights, several crew members took it upon themselves to write, print, and distribute a publication called *The Hunchback Illuminator*. This little newspaper was distributed among the crew to keep them apprised of events during production and to provide some inside jokes. [160]

In *Lon Chaney: The Man Behind the Thousand Faces*, I explained how Chaney made himself up as Quasimodo, debunking the often-told myths other writers have perpetuated for years. [161] In an article originally written for the trade journal *Oral Hygiene* published shortly after Lon's death, James L. Howard, D.D.S., explained how he created several of the sets of the teeth that Lon used in his films. In his article, Dr. Howard explained how he helped Chaney make the intricate dentures for his role as Quasimodo:

> One of his [Chaney's] first considerations was his teeth, and in the use of teeth as a vital part of characterization he was not only a master, but a pioneer. On numerous occasions, through practically a decade, I was called upon to design dentures peculiarly expressive of his different roles... the enormous number of dentures that he tried for various effects before securing just the right thing....
>
> Soon after he received this terrific assignment [the role of Quasimodo] Lon came to me. He had a vast

idea in his mind — vaguely. He seemed depressed for fear he could not live up to his own hopes for the part. For the first time, he had no clear-cut, definite idea of the sort of teeth he wanted. Instead of telling me, he asked me what I thought he should have in the way of dental fixtures. Well...I thought it over, and advanced, as a result of long observation, that from what I had seen, hunchbacks had a large lower jaw. He instantly agreed with me. In the next breath he asked how I could make him an over-developed mandible [bone of the lower jaw] — and in less time than a breath I told him I didn't know. But he insisted that I scheme some way to get the desired effect.

I made an upper plate to fit over his own teeth, but left the molars [back teeth] off. In the lower jaw I made a plate to go over his own teeth and extend well down on the buccal sides [the sides of the mouth facing the cheek], forcing his cheeks down half an inch, or perhaps three quarters of an inch. I put no teeth in the lower plate, but cut the front out, letting the natural anterior [lower front teeth] show. The effect was exactly what he wanted, but the problem was how to hold the lower contraption in his mouth.

I first got a set of small coil springs, such as those we are told held the historic ivory dentures of George Washington in place. These were by no means strong enough. Then I took two pieces of alarm clock spring, each about two inches long, vulcanizing [hardening] one end of each spring to the upper plate in the molar regions and letting the lower ends slant down and rest on the occlusal [top] ridges of the lower appliance. This caused strong pressure on the lower, and permitted the mouth to open and close, at the same time forcing the muscles of the cheeks down, thereby accomplishing the purpose of characterization. [162]

A Thousand Faces

During the final months of production, the Chaneys' household was increased by one. During one of their trips to San Francisco, Lon and Hazel had met a man who owned a wire-hair terrier and had inquired whether it was for sale. The owner declined to part with the dog because he planned to exhibit him in a New York show. But in a March 27, 1923, letter, the owner of Humberstone Kennels in San Francisco wrote that the dog was indeed for sale if the Chaneys were still interested, noting, "He has grown to be a very trappy and intelligent chap with lots of pep and very attractive." Grasso, replying on Lon's behalf, asked for a picture of the dog and stated that if the Chaneys did not take the dog, they were certain they could find a buyer. The terrier, then called "Roscoe," [163] was shipped for approval to the Chaneys and, in a May 11 letter to the kennel owner, Grasso stated:

> Mrs. Lon Chaney asked me to write you and inform
> you that they like "Sandy" very much and would like
> to keep him, but as they are living in an apartment it
> is impossible for them to have two dogs.
>
> However, if you are willing to take "Tuffy" [their
> present dog] back and $75 for "Sandy," they would
> like to make the exchange. [164]

The exchange was made, and Sandy became part of the Chaney household, traveling with them to Colorado Springs that June and often accompanying Lon to the studio. A touching picture was taken after Chaney's death when his make-up case was placed on the back porch of his home before being donated to the Natural History Museum in Los Angeles. Sitting next to Lon's make-up case is Sandy with a wistful look on his face.

Another piece of correspondence in the Alfred Grasso collection came from pugilist Jack Dempsey, who offered Lon a chance to buy stock in Dempsey's Great Western Coal Mine Company:

124

A Hunchback Becomes An International Star

My Dear Lon:

Well here I am down to hard work both in
connection with my coal company and training for a
Fourth of July battle. I am off today for Dempsey
City, which is the mining town located on our coal
properties, to get down to hard work. Joe Benjamin
with me and "Doc" Kearns, who left yesterday for
New York, is sending me back a bunch of big
fellows to slam me around, or get slammed.

Before leaving I want to get this line off to you to tell
you to take some of the stock of our company
before it is offered for public subscription. We have
a wonderful proposition that is going to be a very
big money maker and the limited amount of stock,
that will be offered in a few days, will be quickly
over-subscribed. So I have set aside a certain amount
to be sold at par, for friends of mine, like yourself....
I would not like to see you miss the opportunity of
becoming a stockholder with me....

Bestest [sic] regards,

Always Sincerely,

Jack Dempsey [165]

Now that Lon was quickly becoming one of the top stars in
motion pictures, it seemed that everyone wanted him to invest in
some type of business or looked to him for a helping hand. The latter
is obvious in a December 5, 1922, letter to Lon from Joe Murphy, an
acquaintance from his theatrical days:

I was out to see you both yesterday and to-day but
found you too busy for to have a few words. I am
glad to see you started as a matter [sic] all of us old
timers are glad to see you go, such as Horace Davey,
Gene Walsh and myself.

A Thousand Faces

> I just finished a five reeler with Jack Nelson as his
> asst. Your nephew Geo[rge]. [166] was also with me.
> Now Lon, Xmas is coming and I have a little 7 yr. old
> girl to support. Of course I am not doing anything
> now, have lots of promises but was in hopes that
> you could place me if it was 2nd asst. with your
> co[mpany]. I know you'll do what you can for us old
> boys as we are a big help sometimes. So trusting you
> will be able to place me... So here is all of the best
> wishes in the world to you Lon. I hope to hear from
> you if possible.
>
> P.S. You said hello yesterday and gave me the wink.
> I was going to stop you then but you had too many
> bothering you so I thought best to drop you a line.

Lon diligently avoided people who hung around in hopes of obtaining something or who found some personal satisfaction being in the presence of a celebrity. He believed these types of people were parasites, fawning over stars and telling them how wonderful they were. Lon felt that feeding one's ego went a long way toward damaging talent and could eventually ruin a career. [167] Yet he had a soft spot for old stage performers and technicians, and he would try to find them work whenever possible, including Joe Murphy. [168]

When production on *Hunchback* was completed, the Chaneys, with Sandy in tow, left for a two-week vacation in Lon's home state of Colorado. They arrived in Colorado Springs on June 19, 1923. His return was big news in the local papers, which emphasized Lon's strenuous work while making *Hunchback*. Lon and Hazel left his hometown three days later, heading for Glenwood Springs. During his vacation, Lon wired Grasso regarding his father's fragile health:

> I want you to show the following to Dr. Commons.
> Dr. Commons, keep father in hospital as per my
> instructions regardless of others' orders. They don't
> understand conditions. [169]

A Hunchback Becomes An International Star

Grasso replied the same day:

> Saw Doctor Webster who attends your father while
> Commons away and showed him your wire. [170] He
> informs me father doing nicely.... Will follow your
> instructions keeping father at hospital until you
> instruct otherwise. I see father often and attend his
> wants. Without exaggerating he looks and feels very
> much improved. In fact Doctor advised taking him
> out in car for a short ride during day from next week
> on. I will see that John [Jeske, Chaney family
> chauffeur] does so in closed car. Do not worry any
> more about him as whatever instructions you wire
> me will be carried out explicitly. Your new house
> coming along well. Business matters look very
> promising but will not bother you until something
> very definite develops. Arranging for Creighton
> leave Thursday. Wire me where I can reach you
> after Tuesday as will wire you as soon as
> reservations are made. Everybody sends love [to]
> you both. That's that now go on your way and enjoy
> yourselves. [171]

Hazel caught a cold while in Glenwood Springs and returned to
Colorado Springs on June 30, staying with the family of Lon's
childhood friend, Harry Hughes. Creighton joined his father in
Glenwood Springs, where the two went hiking and fishing for several
days. Hazel wired Grasso that Lon and Creighton were due to return
the following Wednesday and that they would leave that Friday or
Saturday. Before the Chaneys departed, they took in some of the local
sights around Colorado Springs, including Seven Falls, Garden of
the Gods, and Lon's familiar terrain of Pike's Peak.

Irving Thalberg left Universal in February 1923 after a falling-out
with Carl Laemmle. He joined Louis B. Mayer's company as vice-
president and production assistant, a move that would soon make
both men Hollywood legends. Thalberg recognized Lon's unique
talent and signed him to appear in *Span of Life*, based on the stage

play by Sutton Vane, to be produced by Mayer's company in May 1923. Lon was to star as Derringer, an ex-convict clown, and the picture was scheduled to begin production between July 2 and July 9, 1923, but it never materialized. [172] *Span of Life* was later announced as a Chaney project for M-G-M in 1926, two years after Mayer and Thalberg took over operation of that studio. Unfortunately, the film became one of several proposed Chaney vehicles that never came to fruition.

While Lon awaited the start of his next picture, Universal was busy preparing *The Hunchback of Notre Dame* for its New York première. Word throughout the industry was that Universal had a major hit on its hands and a first-rate prestige picture. In planning the New York event, executives discussed the possibility of having Lon make a personal appearance. Universal executive James V. Bryson contacted Chaney after William Koenig, the studio's assistant general manager, indicated the reclusive actor might consider attending the première. In an August 2, 1923, telegram to Lon, Bryson did not soft-peddle the effect his appearance would have at the big event:

> Bill Koenig wires there's big possibility you visiting New York during *Hunchback*'s initial week's opening. News received here by everybody with great enthusiasm. Certainly would mean opportunity of lifetime for you to satisfy your millions of admirers from coast to coast by giving them chance of paying you their personal respect as well as proving that you think well enough of them to lose a couple of weeks' salary.

> Your appearance in New York at the opening of the screen's most gigantic achievement besides your supreme effort would mean a riot. If [Douglas] Fairbanks, Chaplin, [Mary] Pickford, Jackie Coogan...can afford it why can't you? Everybody here wild about *Hunchback*.

A Hunchback Becomes An International Star

Apparently the telegram persuaded Chaney, for he agreed to attend the première. On August 7, William Koenig wired Bryson at Universal's New York office:

> Chaney agrees [to] go to New York. Would like to
> leave about August 20 arrive 25 or about a week
> before opening. Might help you should you desire
> re-cut picture. Think this good idea as Lon has
> watched picture very closely. Could probably
> improve it. [173] This gives splendid opportunity.
> Press entertain, interview him. Get out plenty good
> publicity. Arrangements made [by] Grasso, Lon's
> manager. Universal [to] pay all expenses [for] Lon
> and companion entire trip. Wire immediately
> [whether] this arrangement meets your approval.

Bryson's enthusiasm about Chaney's attending the première is evident in an August 10 telegram to Lon:

> Koenig tells me the glad news. This is no place to
> tell you what Carl Laemmle and Universal executives
> think much less personal feelings. Intend bringing
> you across America as no notable ever received.
> Quicker you get here the better. Until then all I can
> say, thank you Mr. Chaney.

With Chaney's departure from Los Angeles imminent, the studio's New York office was hastily compiling plans to capitalize on his appearance. Carnegie Hall was chosen for the benefit premiere on behalf of the American Legion's Veterans Mountain camp, prior to the official première at the Astor Theatre. Bryson's telegram to Koenig on August 10 displays the company's excitement over the entire event:

> Congratulations upon Chaney achievement. Greatly
> appreciated. Want [to]bring him across continent in
> showmanship style. Stopping over at Salt Lake,
> Denver, Omaha, Kansas City, St. Louis, Chicago,

A Thousand Faces

> Cleveland, Toledo, Pittsburgh, Philadelphia. Strongly
> represented all cities. [174] Pike should assist with
> organization otherwise will send our own man if
> nothing else possible. Have arranged premiere
> showing of *Hunchback* [at] Carnegie Hall for
> benefit [for] veterans mountain camp American
> Legion and offered Chaney's personal appearance if
> Chaney agreeable....
>
> Our story Chaney leaving present work [to] come
> [to] New York assist Legion with their new two
> million five hundred dollar drive. This is telegraph
> news which will bring veterans and publicity
> everywhere. Such news will make Chaney idol
> of America. Working twenty four hour shifts
> reediting. [175] If any suggestions develop wire
> immediately.

While Universal may have mapped out a detailed schedule for public appearances, Lon was not at all happy with the idea. He disliked personal appearances so much that he canceled many of the cities on the itinerary, stating that he had agreed only to the New York event because it would help the American Legion. [176] At first it was thought Hazel would be accompanying Lon on the trip east, but she elected to stay home to attend to the details of their new home. Instead, Alfred Grasso accompanied Lon on the New York trip, leaving Los Angeles on August 15 instead of the often-believed date of August 30. [177] Lon was given a hearty send-off by members of the American Legion as well as by Hazel, Creighton, and his brother John Chaney. In Salt Lake City, he appeared at a fund raiser for disabled veterans of the World War. [178] Shortly after he left that city, newspapers falsely reported Chaney had been killed in a train accident. [179]

In some cities, Chaney's arrival was hardly noticed due to train schedules. While waiting to transfer to his 11:35 p.m. train in Cleveland, Ohio, Lon chose not to sit, but to walk around and see some of the city, as well as get a bite to eat. Accompanying him on this walk through the city was Billy Leyser of *The Cleveland News*. In an article entitled, "Lon Chaney Is Regular Fellow," Leyser noted that:

> Mr. Chaney is enroute to New York, where he is to have a hand in cutting his recent starring vehicle, *The Hunchback of Notre Dame*...
>
> If ever Lon Chaney does make a personal appearance before an audience, it will be a decided success. He does not impress you as a screen player, but rather as an executive of some large industrial organization. He has an exceptionally forceful personality, a keen insight into that which is known as "human quality" and is a convincing talker, a real friend and a gentleman. [180]

Lon Chaney was greeted at Grand Central Station in New York City on September 1 by a brass band and a large public turnout. At the train station, Lon posed for a picture with a youngster who had to be one of the luckiest boys in all of New York, twelve-year-old Herman Eisenstadt. Elliott Stuckel, the director of publicity for Universal, sent Lon the following letter on September 19:

> I am enclosing herewith the letter you received in New York from Herman Eisenstadt, the little boy you picked up at the train station and also a copy of my reply to him. It would be a great event in the boy's life if you would write him the letter he asked for from the Coast.
>
> Jim [Bryson] and I have just returned from Boston where we opened to capacity business Monday night at the Tremont Temple. I am going to get a copy of each criticism from that city and send it to you. From all indications we are going to duplicate the New York success there. At the Astor Theatre,

we are now sold out for the next two weeks. We are
going to open at the Pitt Theatre, Pittsburgh, Pa., on
September 24 and at the Chestnut Street Opera
House in Philadelphia on October 1.

I trust you landed back in your beloved California
safely and the next time I see you, you will have
forgotten all about the brass band. [181]

The touching letter from young Herman Eisenstadt
read:

Dear Mr. Chaney,

Well how do you like our picture? Believe me, I
never had such a pleasure in my life as seeing the
picture in the paper. And Oh! Boy, talk about
popularity. Why all the kids in my block came to see
me to find out if it really was me.

They couldn't believe it, but I told them that they
shouldn't be surprised if they saw me in the movies
with you. And they all fell for it and asked for passes.
Ha! Ha!

Well, Mr. Chaney, I know you are a very busy but I
would be pleased to have another remembrance
besides this picture so if you have the time write me
a letter and I will keep it forever.

Your little friend,

Herman Eisenstadt

P.S. I will try and go to see you in the picture *The
Hunchback of Notre Dame* if the price is not to[o]
much. [182]

Lon not only sent the boy a brief letter but also arranged for two
tickets for him to see the picture. [183]

A Hunchback Becomes An International Star

After the reception at the train station, Lon was the guest at an informal luncheon at the Hotel Astor. Chaney was a big hit with the reporters, who noted that he was just a "regular fellow" compared with other stars. *The Exhibitors Trade Review* noted:

> No one can sit with this player at a table for an hour, as has been the privilege of this writer, without feeling an abounding respect for the man Chaney and a still larger admiration for his ability to study and to absorb the ways and the peculiarities of mankind.
>
> Much was said in the course of that short hour, but the impression left by the actor was that of a man filled with an understanding of humans, weak as well as strong.
>
> One thing may be set down at the beginning, and that is Mr. Chaney's unalterable opposition to personal appearances or to letting the public into the studio—or any other proceeding which tends to lessen the illusion of the person out in front of the screen. [184]

The reporter for *Moving Picture World* echoed similar opinions:

> Lon has set opinions against personal appearances, but we are here to tell him that he can travel the country over meeting newspaper folk without a bit of damage to his laurels. You can't say that about all of 'em.
>
> Chaney personifies sincerity intelligently directed; and it is a first impression that grows with each moment of conversation. Not merely a few pat parrot-like phrases, but real evidence of a deep love of his art, wholehearted desire to play fair with it, and boundless ambition for its betterment. [185]

A Thousand Faces

While Lon may have been comfortable with the reporters at the luncheon, quite the opposite was true of the official opening of the picture at the Astor Theatre on September 2. Alfred Grasso said Lon was extremely nervous at the opening, and during his entire trip he would regularly call his wife at midnight to relay the events of the day. [186] If Lon was nervous about the film's reception, his fears were quickly allayed when the final fade-out flashed on the screen and the lights came up with

> round after round of cheers and deafening applause.... The unusual make-up of the audience emphasized all the more their outburst at the end— an outburst which did not lessen until Lon Chaney, the star, had been half pushed, half dragged to the stage that he might stutter his thanks in the din of hundreds voicing their approbation of his marvelous portrayal of Quasimodo. [187]

The Hunchback of Notre Dame was hailed as a masterpiece and audiences flocked by the thousands to see this epic production. Yet when a scratched and less-than-pristine print is presented today, it is difficult to understand why so many moviegoers were affected by this picture in 1923. [188] To equate *Hunchback*'s popularity in terms the present-day moviegoer can understand, compare it to *Jurassic Park*, which similarly promised audiences things never before done on a motion picture screen. Alas, viewing *The Hunchback of Notre Dame* today, only Chaney's masterful performance sustains the epic grandeur of the picture. The crowd scenes are admirably handled but lack the panache De Mille or Griffith might have brought to the screen. Also, after its New York run, the picture was trimmed from twelve reels to ten so that medium-sized and small theaters across the country could accommodate it. Some scenes appear to begin or end abruptly, giving the film a certain unevenness — a problem pointed out in *Film Daily*'s review:

A Hunchback Becomes An International Star

Far too much material in the book and director
made an effort to get too much in with result that
some sequences are far too short and choppy, but in
the end there is a real thrill. [189]

The epic film also proved to be helpful to investigators of the Burns International Detective Agency. While watching the movie, one of the investigators noticed an extra in a crowd scene who was wanted for forgery. They notified the police in Hollywood, and the man was arrested and sent to prison. [190]

The Hunchback of Notre Dame by Victor Hugo tells the story of several characters, including Quasimodo. In many respects it could have been two separate novels, one dealing with Quasimodo and his love for Esmeralda, the second following Esmeralda and the other three men who love her: Gringoire, Phoebus, and Jehan. Other versions translated to the screen have either omitted one or two of the male love interests or combined them into one. In Chaney's version, Gringoire serves as comic relief while Phoebus is presented as Esmeralda's main love interest. Jehan's character remains true to the novel, as the villain who longs for the gypsy girl. The ending of the picture, however, is completely different from Hugo's novel in which Esmeralda dies by hanging. Years later, two skeletons are found in the dungeon, one with a pronounced curve to its spine embracing the other. When the two are separated, the skeleton with the curved spine crumbles to dust. In Chaney's film, Quasimodo rescues Esmeralda from the clutches of Jehan but, before the hunchback can throw the villain to his death, he is stabbed. Mortally wounded, Quasimodo sees Esmeralda and Phoebus reunited and realizes that the woman he loves is truly happy. The hunchback struggles to his beloved bells where he rings his own death knell before expiring.

Lon Chaney was the quintessential Quasimodo. Alfred Grasso found a rare copy of Hugo's novel that contained several sketches of the hunchback by the author. It was from these illustrations, along with Hugo's vivid description, that Lon conceived his make-up for the role. [191] Of all the other actors who have undertaken this character, Chaney's performance remains the most impressive. His Quasimodo is a lonely figure, shunned by humanity. In return, he greets society with contempt. The hunchback's one true friend is Dom Claude, the priest, who gives him the love he has never otherwise had. Quasimodo is devoted to the priest, and follows him around like a dog follows its master. Society shuns the hunchback because of his physical deformities and deafness (something that Chaney could easily understand), so Quasimodo withdraws into the solitude of ringing the church bells which caused him to lose his hearing in the first place. The bells provide the hunchback with his only source of joy, and allow him a way to express himself. Chaney displays this when, before ringing the bells, he gently pats the rope before pulling it, much like greeting an old friend. After rescuing Esmeralda from the king's guard in front of the cathedral, he climbs into the rafters to push the giant bell, approaching it with great anticipation, much like a child waiting to see Santa Claus. As the bell begins to make its large echoing noise, Chaney smiles gleefully, clapping his hands and jumping up and down. Thus he imparts to the audience Quasimodo's childlike enthusiasm, building sympathy for the character despite his unsightly appearance. As the huge bell gains momentum, Quasimodo cannot contain his exuberance; he jumps on the bell, riding it as if it were his trusty steed.

The hunchback blindly follows the orders of Jehan, who intimidates him with threats of physical harm. His loyalty is put to the test when Quasimodo is captured by the king's guards while trying to kidnap the gypsy girl for Jehan. As he is tied up by the guards, Chaney looks around for Jehan to intercede; his expression is that of a lost child looking for its mother. He slowly realizes he has been betrayed by the one he trusted and shakes his head. His

A Hunchback Becomes An International Star

bewilderment and hurt propel the touching scene in which Esmeralda, who once rebuffed Quasimodo, comes to his aid by giving him water while he is on the pillory. In the hands of another actor, Quasimodo could easily have become something of a monster, eliciting no sympathy at all from the audience. Yet Chaney was able to fashion a moving performance that overshadowed the admirable work of the other actors, turning the Hugo novel into his own starring vehicle. It is Chaney's performance alone that has enabled the film's popularity to endure for the more than seventy years since its release.

When he returned from the movie's New York première, Lon Chaney was no longer Hollywood's leading character actor—he had become Hollywood's leading character star.

UNIVERSAL FILM MANUFACTURING COMPANY, a New York corporation, as "producer", hereby engages LON CHANEY, as "artist" *and he started in the part of Quasimoto the hunchback — L.C.* to play in the motion picture feature production entitled "THE HUNCHBACK OF NOTRE DAME", and the parties hereto mutually agree as follows:

1. The term hereof shall commence when the artist is actually required to first appear before the camera, or in the event that the first photographing is done outside of Universal City, California, then said term shall commence on the day the artist leaves for location. It is the understanding of the parties hereto that said term will commence on or about October 2, 1922. ~~Said term shall end when the part is completed.~~ XX
Said term shall end when the part is completed.

2. The producer agrees to pay the artist a weekly salary of Two thousand *American — L.C.* dollars ($2000.00) during the term of this employment, in full for his services hereunder, and guarantees that the term of this agreement shall continue for a period of at least *Consecutive — L.C.* ten weeks.

3. The artist agrees to observe all reasonable rules and regulations of the producer in connection with its business and to perform all services as requested and instructed by the producer.

4. The producer agrees to furnish the artist with all costumes, wardrobe, wigs and special make-up material.

5. Should the artist be required to perform services hereunder in any place other than the city of Los Angeles or its environs, the producer shall pay all necessary traveling expenses of the artist, including hotel bills and other charges for board and lodging.

6. The producer shall have the exclusive right to the

1.

services of the artist during the term hereof, and the right
to use the name and likeness of the artist, photographic or otherwise, in connection with the distribution and exploitation of
said production.

7. Should the artist suffer any physical incapacity or
disfigurement materially detracting from his appearance as a
motion picture actor, or interfering with his duties hereunder,
the producer need pay him no compensation during the period of
such incapacity or disfigurement, and in the event that such
incapacity or disfigurement continues for a period of more
than one week, the producer at its option may terminate the
employment herein provided for.

8. All notices which the producer is required or may
desire to give to the artist may be given by addressing the
same to the artist at Universal City, California, or such
notice may be given to the artist personally.

9. The artist represents and warrants to the producer
that the artist is fully competent in all respects to enter
into this agreement.

IN ITNESS WHEREOF the parties hereto have executed
this agreement the 15th day of August, 1922, the producer by
its general manager thereunto duly authorized.

UNIVERSAL FILM MANUFACTURING COMPANY

By _____
General Manager.

_____

2.

haney's two-page contract for *The Hunchback of Notre Dame*, signed by both Lon and Irving
halberg. Note the corrections Lon added to the contract, which were initialed by both him and
halberg. (Courtesy of the Alfred Grasso Family Collection)

Wallace Worsley, Lon, and Norman Kerry discuss the script.

Wallace Worsley, writer K. C. Beaton, Carl Laemmle, and Lon on the set of *The Hunchback of Notre Dame* (1923).

Construction begins on the cathedral and large square sets.

A picture from a deleted scene in which Quasimodo exchanges candles for some clothes for Esmeralda.

This ad was placed in the Hollywood casting directory to notify producers and directors of Lon's availability for work. (Courtesy of the Alfred Grasso Family Collection)

Rare picture of Lon, holding his traditional cap. (Courtesy of Loren Harbert)

ter completing *The Hunchback of Notre Dame*, the Chaneys went to Colorado Springs for a much-
eserved vacation. Here, Lon points to his old home from the top of Pike's Peak. (Courtesy of Loren
arbert)

on and Hazel atop Pike's Peak. (Courtesy of Loren Harbert)

Leaving for the New York première of *The Hunchback of Notre Dame*, Lon shakes hands with his son, Creighton. Chaney's business manager, Alfred Grasso stands behind him. Chaney's wife, Hazel, is to his right. (Courtesy of the Alfred Grasso Family)

...n poses with an unidentified woman as his train stops in Chicago, prior to his arrival in New York ...r the première of *The Hunchback of Notre Dame*. Alfred Grasso (left, with straw hat and overcoat, ...anding next to train conductor) discusses transportation details with a Universal employee. (Courtesy ...the Alfred Grasso Family)

...topping in Pittsburgh en route to New York, Lon (center) poses with members of the press. Alfred ...rasso is seated far right. (Courtesy of the Alfred Grasso Family)

Lon poses with twelve-year old Herman Eisenstadt upon his arrival in New York City's Grand Central Station.

A Phantom
Before Stardom
at M-G-M

(1924-1928)

This rare photo illustrates the simplicity and effectiveness of Chaney's *Phantom of the Opera* make-up. This photo is the only known picture to feature Chaney in a character make-up with his famous make-up case. (Courtesy of Seaver Center for Western History Research, Los Angeles County Museum of Natural History)

An actor who brings a particularly vivid portrayal to the screen will often find himself in the unenviable position of having to follow that role with another performance of equal or greater quality. Lon Chaney was no different, but unfortunately his next choice was less than stellar. On September 25, 1923, Lon signed a contract to appear in *The Next Corner*, a romantic melodrama for Paramount Pictures, which was greeted with negative reviews. One has to wonder what could have possessed Chaney to undertake such a deficient role. [192] This was the question many trade journals echoed in their reviews, including *Exhibitors Trade Review*, which commented, "Why Lon Chaney, an actor of rare parts, consented to appear in such a foolish role as that of foster-brother Serafin remains an unsolved problem."

For years it has been accepted as fact that Thalberg, who was then in charge of production at M-G-M in 1924, lent Chaney to Universal for *Phantom of the Opera*, despite the protests of Louis B. Mayer. Hollywood history maintains that Thalberg's reasoning for this loan-out was that Chaney's future box office appeal would be enhanced by his appearing in this picture. Once again, myth has taken precedence over truth. In my biography, I stated that Chaney agreed to appear in *He Who Gets Slapped* as a one-picture deal and that he did not sign a long-term contract with M-G-M until February 15, 1925. In that contract, there was no clause stating that there had been a previously signed agreement with the studio, thus strengthening the belief that Lon was still freelancing at the time.

In the Alfred Grasso collection is new evidence that leads us to believe that filming *Phantom of the Opera* was originally Chaney's idea, not Universal's. In a November 23, 1923, telegram to Bobbs-Merrill Company, Lon requested,

> Please wire me...whether or not the world's motion picture rights to Leroux's *The Phantom of the Opera* is available and if so at what price and terms. [193]

An October 14, 1923, article in the *New York Morning Telegraph* stated that Lon was considering two contract offers, one from Universal and the other from the Carl Anderson Company. The terms offered by Universal remain unknown; however, one speculation is that they could have offered Lon an opportunity to star in a production of his choice. This theory becomes more probable when one considers that Chaney sent the telegram regarding the status of the film rights to *Phantom* just six weeks later. The deal with Carl Anderson Company was to be financed by the Motion Picture Theatre Owners of America. The essence of the agreement was to provide much-needed pictures for their theatre exchanges. Because a typical movie in the 1920s would play for only two or three days at a local theatre, the enormous turnover of product required an abundance of motion pictures.

In addition to *Phantom*, Lon contacted Gouverneur Morris (author of *The Penalty*) regarding the rights to his story, *Simon Louvier*. [194] It appears that Lon was lining up a handful of projects before he and Hazel traveled to New York City to meet with Universal and Carl Anderson's company on January 16, 1924. [195] A few days after arriving in New York, Lon sent Grasso a lengthy letter detailing the recent meetings:

A Phantom Before Stardom at M-G-M

Well now Al I went at once to see Cohn and
showed him the correspondence with Anderson
and he did not seem very pleased. He says the
whole thing was terribly bawled up and finally let it
drop for the lack of correct information. [196] Well
things were dropped right there about that and he
wanted to know if we wanted to shoot with him on
his <u>own</u> money to the extent of $75,000.00. He
wanted to know if I had a story that I thought I
could do for that amount. He said he would be
willing to go 50/50 on the profits but did not
mention salary.

Now he is anxious to get my answer by the first of
next week and I said I would do everything in my
power to give him a definite answer yes or no by
that time. Now he says I can make the picture in
California if preferred. What I want you to do is give
me an approximate cost of production on that
Italian story of mine and also where we would make
it. I am going to see him again and ask him just
what salary he expects me to receive out of that
and about cast, director, cutting, etc. I will wire you
tomorrow the 27th how I come out.... [197]

Things do not look so prosperous here. I was up to
Universal and they wanted me to do *Phantom of
the Opera* for $100,000.00. Can we do it? Look into
it at once and give me all the dope and data on that
also.

Hunchback closed last Sunday but they are going to
bring it back. Perhaps at the Capitol. [198] So far they
have taken over $800,000.00 since it has opened.
That is of course from all over. But that is very
wonderful I think.

I am going to try and find Schulberg tomorrow and
see what he is going to do. Also some of the other
birds. If anything turns up I will wire at once. I
don't know of anything else excepting we are
taking in all the shows and trying not to worry.

A Thousand Faces

It appears from Chaney's letter that Universal wanted to make *Phantom*. But a budget of $100,000 was too meager, even in those days, for a picture of this magnitude. The budget for an average picture in 1925, featuring one major star and without any elaborate sets or costumes, could run about $75,000 to $125,000.

Film historians are obliged to speculate about why Lon became interested in the Gaston Leroux novel. One can't help but wonder whether Lon read the novel's serialization, which had appeared in the *Los Angeles Examiner* in 1911, while he was performing with the Ferris Hartman troupe.

One phrase in his letter to Grasso is very revealing. Despite his popularity, Lon notes that he's, "trying not to worry." It's hard to believe that he would have had to worry about any project, given the success of *The Hunchback of Notre Dame*. Then again, at the time he had no one like Irving Thalberg to look after his interests, although that would change within a few months. After the collapse of negotiations with Anderson, Chaney continued to discuss an agreement with Universal regarding *Phantom of the Opera*. Unfortunately, without the supervising talent of Thalberg, this picture would suffer considerable problems during production. While the script and other production logistics were being worked out, Lon appeared as the demented surgeon in *The Monster* for Roland West Productions and Tec-Art, although the movie would not be released until early 1925.

The studio system had been operating for several years, but it did not become the paradigm of the industry until the merger of Metro Pictures, Goldwyn Pictures, and Louis B. Mayer Productions on April 26, 1924. Metro-Goldwyn-Mayer studios, or M-G-M as it was often called, became the greatest and most impressive studio in Hollywood. Whereas other studios over the years have been admired for their various productions, nothing could beat an M-G-M picture because the studio boasted some of the top stars, directors, and writers in the industry. Its slogan, "More Stars Than There Are in Heaven," was adopted shortly after the merger to signify the studio's impressive roster of talent. The quality of its sets, costumes, and overall production enabled an M-G-M film, even the program pictures, to surpass the best that the other studios had to offer. In addition, M-G-M had the huge Loew's Theatre chain through which to distribute its movies, helping them to dominate the industry.

Universal Pictures disclosed on May 17, 1924, that Lon had been signed for a picture, the title to be announced at a later date. [199] The news was warmly received by theatre owners and distributors even though no definite picture was mentioned. Actually, Universal was busy finishing the script for *Phantom of the Opera*, trying to come up with a reasonable scenario to equal the success of *The Hunchback of Notre Dame*. As work on the script progressed and the elaborate sets were being constructed, Lon began production on *He Who Gets Slapped*.

The film version of Leonid Andreyev's *He Who Gets Slapped* was M-G-M's first official release. Thalberg, in charge of studio production, chose Chaney for the role of the disenchanted scientist who joins a Paris circus to become a clown. Hazel Chaney said that Thalberg promised Lon that if he made good in this picture the studio would offer him a long-term contract. [200] *He Who Gets Slapped* is one of the finest pictures made during the silent era, a combination of poetic imagery and refined moods. Directed by Victor Seastrom, the movie was a risky venture; its esoteric subject matter, frequently presented in symbolic scenes, could have alienated the average movie-goer. Instead, audiences heartily embraced the picture, and it still makes an indelible impression. The movie succeeds in its storytelling as well as in its technical aspects; the numerous dissolves and superimposed images add an almost mystical touch. [201] *He Who Gets Slapped* was a critical, artistic, and box office success for the newly formed studio.

A Thousand Faces

Chaney's performance is tremendous and in many ways surpasses his work in *Hunchback*. [202] He is extremely restrained in his gestures, never overemphasizing his character's delicate emotional state. As scientist Paul Beaumont, his focus is completely on his life's work. This single-minded dedication, as well as his emotional dependency on his wife (Ruth King) and his benefactor, Baron Regnard (Marc MacDermott), bring about Beaumont's emotional downfall. When he learns that the baron has stolen his thesis, Beaumont confronts his patron; Regnard mockingly slaps him in front of a crowd of distinguished scientists. Crushed and defeated, he turns to his wife for solace only to learn that she is in love with the baron. When Beaumont pleads with her, she waves a hand at him — and inadvertently slaps him in the face. As the baron quietly laughs at Beaumont's tragedy, the struggling scientist begins his emotional downward spiral. Chaney conveys this unravelling by rolling his eyes like a madman, yet he never takes the gesture beyond the limits of believability. He returns to his library, where he laughs at himself, recalling the words of his wife: "Fool! Clown!"

Beaumont forsakes the world he has known and joins a circus. As the clown known simply as HE, he is slapped for saying foolish things. HE becomes the circus's most popular performer, hiding his broken heart behind the mask of a clown — a theme found in many of Chaney's characterizations. As HE, Chaney is remarkably restrained when away from his audience, in contrast with the performing clown who is always jovial. This further enhances Beaumont/HE's confrontation with Baron Regnard when he learns that Regnard now desires the one woman HE loves, Consuelo, the bareback rider (Norma Shearer). HE is the paradox of the circus clown: while performing, he makes others laugh, yet away from the crowd, he is unhappy, still suffering from the slaps of life's reality. Consuelo revives his feelings of love, but when HE confesses his feelings to her, she playfully slaps him and laughs. Again he is crushed. But when Consuelo's virtue is about to be compromised by her despicable father and Baron Regnard, HE willingly sacrifices his life for her happiness.

The film is rife with symbolism, from the laughing clown that spins the globe throughout the picture to Chaney's death scene, in which he clutches a stuffed heart to his bleeding wound. In HE's act, an audience of clowns sits in rows, just as the distinguished scientists had sat earlier in the film. When the clowns laugh, the image dissolves into the faces of the scientists, wearing clown hats and laughing, dissolving again into the clowns. One of the most poignant scenes in this picture takes place after Chaney has been mortally stabbed by Consuelo's father. HE turns a lion loose to attack the girl's father and Baron Regnard. After witnessing their deaths, HE looks at the lion, expecting to be attacked next, and says, "Come, my friend — give me the last slap." But the lion tamer intervenes, and HE, hearing the introductory music for his act, struggles to his feet. HE proclaims to the audience, "The world must have its love — the world must have its tragedy — but always...the clown comes out to make people laugh." Collapsing to the ground, HE dies in Consuelo's arms. The film ends with the spinning globe. Surrounding it is a ring on which a group of clowns stand. In the middle of the group lies the still, lifeless body of HE. The clowns gently pick up the body and toss it over the side of the ring, watching as it disappears into oblivion.

(A struggling actor in Hollywood, Bela Lugosi worked as an extra in this picture, playing one of the circus clowns. Three years later, Lugosi would be starring in *Dracula* on Broadway, and later in the film version that many fans and historians had mistakenly thought Chaney would essay.) [203]

When production of *He Who Gets Slapped* was completed, Lon turned his attention to creating the make-up for the *Phantom*. Hazel Chaney has said that the concept of the Phantom's appearance was so vague in everyone's mind, including those of the producer and director, that they left it entirely up to Lon. [204] Chaney's make-up was so startling and effective that it has not only been an inspiration for many make-up artists but it also influenced the creator of Batman. Bob Kane said his conception of the Joker came from a combination of Chaney's make-up in *Phantom of the Opera* and Conrad Veidt's in *The Man Who Laughs*.

The August 1 starting date for *Phantom of the Opera* was pushed back because of delays in set construction, not to mention Universal's inability to find a suitable ending for the film. [205] The original script by Bernard McConville and James Spearing was discarded when Elliott Clawson was brought in at the request of director Rupert Julian. Clawson, in his script, followed the Leroux novel more closely than had the previous scenarists, yet he was unable to contrive a viable ending. In one version, the Phantom and Christine escape the pursuing mob by commandeering a coach and driving wildly through the streets of Paris. [206] When the coach crashes, the Phantom tries to escape by climbing a building but is shot by the leader of the mob. Another ending retained the coach chase, but when it crashes, Christine and the Phantom find refuge in her home where he dies, as Raoul, the Persian, and the mob leader break in. A third ending had the Phantom freeing Christine and Raoul after she gently kisses him, and the mob finding him dead at his organ later. This was the original ending actually filmed by Julian; however, it later was cut in favor of the carriage chase through the streets of Paris. [207]

Rupert Julian, who had been a fixture on the Universal lot since the early teens, was chosen as the director primarily because he had been able to step in and finish the directing chores on *Merry-Go-Round* after Erich von Stroheim had been fired. Julian, who had worked at the studio as both an actor and director, was a mediocre director at best. But to Universal, he was a hero when he delivered *Merry-Go-Round* close to its original budget; also, it was included on many Top Ten lists of movies released in 1923. Many of his co-workers felt that Julian tried to emulate the von Stroheim demeanor by wearing riding boots and sporting a waxed moustache. And, like von Stroheim, Julian succeeded in antagonizing most of the cast and crew during the production of *Phantom*. Lon and Julian quickly fell into disagreement over the portrayal of the *Phantom*, and relations between the two men escalated to the point where Lon refused to speak to or take direction from Julian. Cameraman Charles van Enger acted as an intermediary between the two, relaying Julian's direction to Lon and returning Lon's usual reply: "Tell him to go to hell." [208]

As with *Hunchback*, a massive casting search was launched to find an actress to play the role of Christine. This effort may have been a publicity ploy on the studio's part because the studio settled on Mary Philbin, who had appeared in their production of *Merry-Go-Round*. As casting continued for the other roles, Hollywood's first steel-and-concrete stage was built on the Universal lot expressly to house the interior of the Opera House as well as the Grand Staircase set. [209] The stage still stands, although only the opera box seats remain untouched. [210]

Eleven sculptors and scenic artists were hired to design the elaborate interior of the Opera House, the Grand Staircase, and a full-scale version of the Apollo statue for the roof of the Opera House. The chandelier, which the Phantom cuts loose upon the unsuspecting audience, was an exact replica of the one in the actual Paris Opera House. Weighing in at 16,000 pounds and measuring 40 feet in diameter, the chandelier was an impressive sight and, no doubt, probably caused a few extras in the audience to question the strength of the chain which held it in place (the set could seat up to 3,000 extras). When it came to filming the crash of the great chandelier, Universal was obviously not thrilled with the prospect of letting a very expensive set decoration be destroyed, not to mention the potential hazard to the extras seated below. Cameraman Charles

A Thousand Faces

van Enger solved this problem by having the chandelier lowered to just above the extras' heads. While the cameras started cranking away at a very slow speed, the chandelier was pulled back up to the ceiling. The shot was reversed in the developing lab so that when it was projected at the proper speed, the chandelier appeared to be crashing down upon the audience, yet the extras and the huge ornament emerged without a scratch. [211]

Carla Laemmle was chosen by choreographer Ernest Belcher to play the role of the prima ballerina in the film. Seventy years later, she recalled her experiences during the making of the picture:

> I was a student of Mr. Belcher's and he chose me as the prima ballerina. We rehearsed the ballet on the *Phantom* stage for at least a week or two. I remember we spent a lot of time practicing the dances before we filmed them. It [the interior of the opera house] was a very impressive set; you felt like you were actually in a real theatre. When we filmed the ballet numbers, the orchestra played for us. We didn't have anything like a playback system. They had extras in the audience, and when we finished our number they would applaud. It was like performing in real opera.
>
> I remember seeing Lon in his make-up and it was pretty scary. I'd say ghastly. I don't know how Mary [Philbin] was able to work next to that face every day. It [Chaney's make-up] probably helped her when she was to look frightened! As I recall, the color of his make-up was a chalky white. I find it kind of amusing that so many people thought this film was scary, especially when you consider the type of films that are produced today. I had no idea that it [*Phantom of the Opera*] would still be such a popular film all these years. [212]

Filming began on October 29, 1924 and lasted for ten weeks.

Lon completed his scenes by mid-November and prepared to return to M-G-M to start work on *The Unholy Three*. [213] When *Phantom* finished production shortly after the new year, film editors began assembling the 350,000 feet of exposed film. Universal's publicity department formulated their plans for the picture's February première in New York. Red Phantoms (in the Red Death costume) started appearing on blank billboards throughout the city, and two of Broadway's largest electric-light signs proclaimed the upcoming event. [214]

Phantom of the Opera was a twelve-reel picture and ran slightly over two hours, like its predecessor, *The Hunchback of Notre Dame*. In order to gauge audience reaction, the studio arranged a sneak preview at a Los Angeles theatre in early January 1925. For the most part, the advance audience felt there was too much suspense in the picture; some preview cards suggested that the producers add some comedy to ease the tension. Instead of realizing they had a successful suspense film, the studio panicked and started to fix the "problems." While executives discussed possible solutions, the New York première was quietly cancelled and *Phantom of the Opera* was temporarily shelved.

By March, a new ending had been shot, retaining the carriage chase, but having the Phantom meet his demise at the hands of the mob. Chester Conklin was hired for comic relief and new title cards were added. Edward Sedgwick, who had directed many of the studio's Hoot Gibson westerns and several of Buster Keaton's M-G-M comedies, was brought in to direct these additional sequences. Universal desperately needed to find another theatre for the screening of their picture, but unfortunately all the New York theaters were booked, as were the major theaters in Los Angeles. The studio finally reached an agreement with the Curran Theatre in San Francisco, and the film premièred there on April 26, 1925. (At the time, the Curran was primarily a legitimate theatre.

A Thousand Faces

Interestingly, Andrew Lloyd Webber's musical version of *Phantom of the Opera* played at the very same theatre in 1993.)

"Tonight! Hollywood Comes To San Francisco!" exclaimed the full-page ad in the *San Francisco Chronicle*. Mary Philbin, Norman Kerry, and other Universal stars attended the heralded event, but Lon, much like the Phantom himself, was nowhere to be seen. An elaborate ballet number preceded the screening of the picture, which was accompanied by a full orchestra. Universal executives were certain that they had resolved the picture's problems and had another hit on their hands. The proclamation that the picture was "proving a sensational success...playing twice daily to exceptionally large audiences at prices ranging up to $1.50 per seat," [215] was mostly wishful thinking on the part of Universal. The studio was trying to downplay the dismal attendance at the film. In one week, the film took in a paltry $5,000, while films at other San Francisco theatres were earning three or four times that amount. The managers of the Curran Theatre wished they could wash their hands of this albatross, but they were locked into a four-week contract. *Phantom* limped along, finishing its engagement on May 23.

The biggest complaint, from both critics and the public, was that the inclusion of the new subplot (featuring a rival competing with Raoul for Christine's affections) and the comedy scenes made absolutely no sense. The studio pulled the picture after its San Francisco run and ordered the comedy scenes and subplot junked. A new set of title cards was written to explain the many holes then left in the film's story. (Unfortunately, many of the ballet sequences, shot in the two-strip Technicolor process, were discarded along with the other scenes during this editing session.) Studio executives seemed satisfied with the changes and soon began to rebuild the publicity momentum they had lost, scheduling the picture's New York première for early September at the Astor Theatre.

Phantom of the Opera contains all the elements needed for what should have been a marvelous picture. Instead, we are left with a mediocre melodrama that holds up today solely due to Chaney's riveting performance. The picture lacks style and the lighting fails to create the necessary mysterious mood. Universal clearly proved its lack of leadership by assigning a second-rate director to the production, one who failed to grasp the fact that they had a genuine thriller on their hands. The female lead, Mary Philbin, delivers the most glaringly inferior performance in the film; her broad and overdramatic gestures are what current audiences think all acting was like in silent pictures. This lack of a strong and supportive performance by the leading lady weakens the entire picture. Norman Kerry, as Raoul, is reduced to a stereotypical leading man and, with the numerous additions and deletions made in the picture, he is left with little upon which to build his role. Only Arthur Edmund Carewe (playing Ledoux), Gibson Gowland (as Simon Buquet), and Snitz Edwards (as Florine Papillon) were able to breathe life into their performances.

Equally disappointing is the presentation of the crashing of the great chandelier. Other than some flickering lights from the chandelier, there is absolutely no build-up of suspense prior to the big moment. We are presented with a title featuring a shadowy figure that is supposed to be the Phantom (the gestures certainly are not Chaney's), over which is superimposed the well-known phrase, "Behold! She is singing to bring down the chandelier!" Suddenly it crashes down upon the audience, and the potential for a wonderful suspenseful moment is entirely lost. However, the chase at the end of the picture, directed by Edward Sedgwick, does manage to build suspense just before the climatic death of the Phantom. As for the unmasking scene, one can't help but speculate that Chaney may have had a forceful hand in directing it especially if he felt that Julian wasn't grasping the emotional impact.

But despite the shortcomings of Julian's direction and Universal's

A Thousand Faces

lack of leadership, Chaney's performance was what people came to see. It's hard to imagine another actor who could have played this role with equal amounts of fearsomeness and pathos as did Chaney. Had he followed Julian's inept direction, the Phantom would never have gained an ounce of sympathy from the audience. Yet Chaney was perceptive enough to understand the character and to obtain a proper blend of terror and empathy. Chaney's Phantom is not a monster. His facial disfigurement is a defect with which the character was born. Because of his deformity, his family turns him out and he is rejected by society, which forces him to seek solace in his music in the subterranean cellars of the Opera House, much the same way as Quasimodo sought his consolation in the bells of Notre Dame. By training the beautiful singing voice of Christine, he hopes she will look beyond the mask and fall in love with him. The "monster" in the Phantom is unleashed when society interferes with his intentions. It is then that the darker side of the Phantom, as with many characters who are rejected or misunderstood by society, comes to prominence. Because so many scenes were deleted, the film lost its ability to give the audience an insight into the Phantom's love for Christine, showing that his despicable actions are, like those of many of Chaney's characters, blinded by his devotional love for the girl.

When the Phantom first encounters Christine, he treats her with the utmost tenderness. His gentle manner is readily apparent as he lifts her onto a horse to take her to the subterranean lake. And when she accuses him of being the Phantom, he bristles, conveying this emotion entirely by body gestures, his face covered by his mask. His confidence in himself appears strong now that Christine is with him. Yet we see all that strength and self-confidence shatter when Christine rips away his mask and exposes his hideous face. This, of course, unleashes his suppressed anger. At first he appears to savor her fear, resentful of her treasonous act, but, realizing that his darker side has been exposed, the Phantom expresses great anguish. His chances of winning her love are forever lost. Despite this character's hideous visage and evil deeds, at this moment the audience cannot help but sympathize with the Phantom. When he learns that Christine has broken her promise not to see Raoul, he becomes enraged at the betrayal. He kidnaps her in the middle of her performance, accuses her of lying, and demands her love. Discovering that her lover and the secret police officer, Ledoux, have tracked him and are hiding in the room of many mirrors further inflames his rage and totally obstructs any reasonable thinking. After the carriage chase, when he is finally cornered by the mob, the Phantom displays one last act of contempt toward the society who he feels has shunned and mocked him. He holds them at bay, pointing to his closed fist above his head, signifying a potential bomb. As the mob closes in on either side of him, he wards them off one last time, then laughingly reveals that his hand holds — nothing. The mob kills him. The original ending, however, as previously mentioned, was quite different: the Phantom realizes he must let Christine and Raoul escape, and he releases her after she has gently kissed him. Unfortunately, none of this footage exists, but it would be interesting to see how Chaney executed the scene, given his ability to express this emotional range. The prints of the film available today do not include this scene, of course, and most viewers are quick to assume that the Phantom is either a complete madman or a monster.

Phantom of the Opera opened to mixed reviews and outstanding business at the box office. Chaney's performance was highly praised, as were the sets and costumes but the months of adding and deleting scenes were painfully obvious. Critics were quick to point out the uneven storyline. Reporting on the September 6 première, *Moving Picture World* noted:

> Despite a continuous rain, traffic was halted in
> Times Square by the thousands who crowded
> around the front of the Astor. Police reserves called

from the West 47th Street police station had little effect in clearing the situation. The quota of seats allotted to the public for the opening performance soon was used up, but still hundreds pushed their way to the theatre front, seeking admittance...

Everything about the presentation of *The Phantom of the Opera* was in keeping with the "spirit." Entering the lobby, the guests were initiated into the weirdness and mystery.... The walls were covered with plaster "stone" and from the low ceiling hung wrought iron lamps giving forth an eerie glow. Above the entrance, lying in a niche, was the full length figure of the "Phantom," robed in the red silk of the Bal Masque scene. His skeleton face grinning at the throng below sent cold shivers up and down the spines of those who caught sight of him for the first time....

The curtain rose upon a group of ballet dancers, trained by the internationally famous Albertina Rasch.... As the ballet came to an end the lights were slowly dimmed, and the girls suddenly started across the stage with a shriek of terror to huddle in a frightened group on the opposite side. In the darkness of the stage a pale light began to appear in the center stage back. As the audience sat tense, not knowing what to expect, a full-length figure in white robes emerged, seemingly poised in mid-air. It was the "phantom" produced by the great magician, Thurston, as his answer to Universal's $1,000 challenge for such an apparition. [216]

The film enjoyed a healthy and lucrative run at the box office and, despite the mixed reviews, was placed on many Top Ten lists of 1925 movies. Although Lon did not attend the New York première, he and Hazel were in attendance at the Los Angeles unveiling at the Rialto Theatre. *The Los Angeles Record* noted:

A Phantom Before Stardom at M-G-M

> Mr. and Mrs. Lon Chaney...oh, what a wild burst of
> applause. The house fairly shook with greetings. [217]

In Colorado Springs, Lon made arrangements with the Liberty Theatre for a special screening of the film for the students of his grandparent's school for the deaf. [218]

(In 1993, *Phantom of the Opera* returned to Broadway in a rather big way on Halloween night. Arrangements were made by Kino Video to screen the film on the Sony JumboTron screen located in Times Square. It marked the first time any motion picture was shown in its entirety on the large Sony screen.) [219]

Although the film finally proved to be a success in America, the same cannot be said of its release in England. First of all, bad feelings were created when Carl Laemmle, fearing that some reels might be stolen, requested the help of Scotland Yard to guard the movie. They turned him down. A similar request made of the British War Office was denied as well. Then a Universal employee in London dreamed up a publicity stunt that backfired. He contacted a local army regiment conducting a recruiting campaign in Southampton and told them that, if the troop would accompany Universal executive James Bryson, who was arriving with a copy of the movie, the regiment would be filmed for a Universal newsreel. And so, Bryson and the print, with cameras rolling, were greeted with the kind of fanfare usually reserved for royalty. The film, escorted by the regiment on the train, was to have been met by an armored car detachment for the final journey to London, but this detachment was canceled. The regiment from Southampton proceeded on foot with the camera crew detailing the march. While Universal was thrilled with the publicity, the English press and government were less than enthusiastic after discovering they had been duped. Calls for an inquiry and boycott were quickly dispatched, and Universal was forced to pull *Phantom of the Opera* from the English market, costing the company tremendous revenue. In 1930, the film was

A Thousand Faces

allowed to be presented in England in its part-talking version, but by then it had lost most of its appeal. [220]

In Lon's next movie project, *The Monster*, he did play a madman, a once-famous surgeon who overtakes the asylum in which he is confined. *The Monster*, released in February 1925, was not produced by M-G-M. It was an independent production of Roland West Productions and Tec-Art, and M-G-M negotiated the rights to distribute the picture under their studio logo. [221] (In 1927, M-G-M purchased the rights to the picture from Roland West Productions, which led to the assumption that the film was an original M-G-M production.) While Lon received top billing, he does not make an appearance until midway through the picture. [222] *The Monster* does not hold up well today as a chiller-comedy. The sets and lighting provide a wonderfully moody and suspenseful atmosphere but the supposed comedy angle causes the film to drag and ultimately to suffer comparisons with similar genre pictures. Had the film been geared toward a straight suspense theme, like Roland West's production of *The Bat* a year later, it might have been a better picture. The supporting cast, particularly Johnny Arthur, is inadequate in portraying either fear or comedy, and relies on broad gestures and overacting to express any emotion. The comedy is neither funny nor original, and whatever suspense that might have been created fails to reach the apex needed to hold the interest of the audience.

The role of Dr. Ziska certainly had its limitations, for there was not much for Chaney to build upon. We see Dr. Ziska as a charming but strangely off-beat character, with his friendly smile quickly changing to a sneer behind the backs of his unsuspecting victims. In the scene in which he plans to transfer the soul of one of his unwilling victims into the body of a woman, Chaney displays such a frenzied delight that it provokes laughter. However, Lon's overall demeanor is limited to sneers or scowls in an attempt to appear frightening. Overall, the picture is unsatisfying and makes one wish the plot had taken a more serious approach rather than playing for attempted laughs.

Regardless of the discrepancies of *The Monster*, Thalberg made good on his promise: the studio executive signed Lon to a one-year contract, with two additional one-year options, starting at a weekly salary of $2,500. [223]   M-G-M announced in June 1925 that Chaney, along with Norma Shearer, John Gilbert, and Roman Novarro were being promoted to stardom. In Chaney's case, this seems a bit redundant because his performance in *The Hunchback of Notre Dame* had already launched him into that stratosphere. What the announcement really indicated was that Chaney and the others would be pushed by the studio as their major stars and that projects would be developed especially for their talents. For Lon, that meant new and exciting characters and the opportunity to collaborate once again with director Tod Browning. Chaney's previous work with Browning revealed only a little of the potential these two men would later exhibit. But with *The Unholy Three*, they cemented a collaboration that would prove to be successful at the box office and with critics. How this project came to the screen has become a Hollywood legend.

Tod Browning had been peddling the story for some time. The plot concerns three sideshow performers who commit robberies after hours. The ventriloquist masquerades as an old woman, Mrs. O'Grady, and runs a bird store, while the midget pretends to be a baby. When a parrot sold to a wealthy customer refuses to speak, Mrs. O'Grady and her baby grandson (the midget) appear at the house to solve the problem. She induces the bird to "speak" by means of ventriloquism, while the midget cases the house for a future burglary. Studio executives passed on the project, claiming the story was weak; however, another possible reason for its rejection might have been Browning's problem with alcohol. He had been one

A Thousand Faces

of Universal's most popular directors, turning out picture after picture with positive results at the box office, but his drinking eventually eclipsed his talent. Directing films for low-budget production companies such as Gothic Pictures and Co-Artists Productions did nothing to help his reputation, either. Fortunately, admirers of Lon Chaney and Tod Browning have Irving Thalberg to thank for rescuing *The Unholy Three* from the potential graveyard of never-produced scripts. Thalberg had a strong belief in the story and no doubt in Browning's ability, and he gave the floundering director a chance. And, as luck would have it, Browning recently had managed to dry himself out and had begun the arduous task of redeeming his reputation.

In Lon Chaney, Browning found an actor who could play roles no other actor could or would have dared to attempt, and their collaboration allowed him to invent unconventional scripts and characters. The roles he created for Chaney were neither completely protagonistic nor antagonistic but rather a mixture of both. One moment a character is a likable person, despite any physical deformities, but then just as quickly he turns into something of a fiend. Yet by the end of the picture, the fiend has regained his sensibilities and usually has sacrificed his own life to save his loved one from the evil plans he has unleashed, thus restoring himself to heroic stature. This type of character can be found in most of the Chaney-Browning pictures, especially *The Unknown*, *West of Zanzibar* and *Road to Mandalay*. The success of taking a role from one extreme to the other and being able to redeem the character, meanwhile maintaining the audience's sympathy, can be directly attributed to Chaney's unique talent.

However, Browning's success in direction was not always consistent. Most of his pictures with Chaney have a strong opening or first half but a muddled second half, in which the actions of Chaney's character clash with the redemption of one of the lovers. In some films, such as *The Unholy Three*, *The Blackbird*, *The Unknown*, and *West of Zanzibar*, these clashes helped to propel the story; but, for the most part, the confrontations tended to slow down the pacing and ultimate success rested almost entirely upon Chaney's performances. The unique mood Browning created in the beginning of his pictures was rarely carried through to the conclusion. For instance, in *The Blackbird*, Browning establishes the Limehouse district with a wonderful ambiance of characters and fog-shrouded sets. But once West End Bertie is framed for murder, the action is reduced to taking place in a few rooms at the mission, and the flavor of the earlier scenes is forgotten. Only in *The Unknown* and *West of Zanzibar* does the director manage to maintain the atmosphere with which he begins.

Browning also disappoints his audience by minimal use of camera movement. Unlike the camera work in Chaney's *Tell It to the Marines*, *Mockery*, and *While the City Sleeps*, Browning's pictures rarely utilize a tracking or "dolly" shot. [224] Occasionally this lack of movement enhances a scene by causing the set to become claustrophobic, as in *The Blackbird*, when West End Bertie is hidden in a small room. Exceptions aside, however, the lack of camera movement does not induce one to become caught up in the action but rather to remain a passive viewer.

The Unholy Three, blending elements of a circus sideshow, criminal melodrama, and off-beat characters, helped reestablish Tod Browning as a successful director. No other director has been able to capture the realistic and mystical environment of the circus sideshow as Browning did in *The Unholy Three*. His early years in carnivals and sideshows were put to good use in this film as he introduces the viewer to the various performers. We see the sword swallower, the thin man, the Siamese twins, and others. Finally we come to Hercules (Victor McLaglen), the strongman. A mother admonishes her young son not to smoke so he'll grow up to be as strong as Hercules. After

A Thousand Faces

completing his act, Hercules sells his pamphlet on physical development to the crowd, and the young boy eagerly buys one. As he and his mother turn away, looking over the book, Hercules lights up a cigarette behind their backs. This scene illustrates just how deftly Browning could inject reality into the fantasy world, an element found in many of his pictures.

After the midget, Tweedledee (Harry Earles), and the strongman commit a murder, Browning increases the dramatic tension, most notably when the police detective comes to question Mrs. O'Grady (who is really Echo in disguise). While Echo is being questioned, Tweedledee (dressed as the baby) places the stolen jewelry into the belly of a toy elephant on the floor in front of the detective. The policeman's attention is inadvertently drawn to the toy elephant when he accidentally hits it with his foot. Continuing his questioning, he picks up the toy and plays with its bobbing head, while Echo gestures to the midget to retrieve it. Tweedledee beckons for the toy and the detective pretends to throw it to him, causing the jewels inside to rattle. As he begins to examine the toy, the tension is further heightened by the reaction of the trio, who (along with the audience) expect the officer to open the toy and discover the jewels. Only when Hercules intervenes by taking the elephant from the officer and giving it to Tweedledee, is the suspense relieved. Although they work as a team, each member of the criminal trio displays his own idiosyncrasies. Tweedledee is coldblooded and without a shred of remorse for his deeds. Despite his strength, Hercules is basically a weak and easily-deceived man. Only Echo has any sense of conscience and is the solitary member of the trio to express concern regarding the murder.

Playing the character of Echo allowed Chaney to give a tour de force performance, essentially playing two characters in one. Mrs. O'Grady stands apart from Echo except in the scenes depicting the transformation from one role to the other. This is especially true when Echo, hiding behind a door, calls Rosie (Mae Busch) in the voice of Mrs. O'Grady. This same scene was repeated in the sound version, but the silent picture allowed Lon to display his pantomimic talent. To convey to the audience that he was mimicking the voice of the elderly lady, Lon employed the facial and body gestures used for that character. Despite the lack of sound — not to mention that Echo is not dressed in the old-lady disguise — the effect is believable. Echo's conflict between his selfish desire for Rosie and his conscience is the emotional backbone of his character. This struggle comes to the fore not only in the dramatic climax in the courtroom but also at the end of the film. Rosie has promised Echo she will forget Hector (Matt Moore), if Echo will help clear him of the charges brought against him. (The trio have framed him for the murder.) At the end of the film, both Echo and Hector are acquitted, and Rosie keeps her promise to the ventriloquist, who has returned to performing. When she reminds Echo of her bargain, he hesitates, pitting his selfish desires against what he knows to be the right thing to do. He laughs off her offer and urges her to go to Hector. As she leaves, Echo uses the dummy to say good-bye. When she turns around, he yells, "Good-bye, old pal," and waves to her with the dummy's arm. Then Echo lets the dummy rest against him, giving the prop a life of its own. As the crowd gathers around his platform, he begins his act and the camera fades out. By using the dummy as an extension of his own feelings, Chaney touchingly gives the moment emotional impact without overplaying the sentiment.

Lon's final release of 1925, *Tower of Lies*, directed by Victor Seastrom, is one of four M-G-M pictures now considered lost. Chaney plays Jan, a Swedish farmer, whose daughter goes to the city to earn money to help pay off the family farm. Glory (Norma Shearer) promises to return in a few months but does not. Jan becomes despondent and eventually suffers an emotional breakdown over her departure. He withdraws into the fantasy world he often created for her as a child, imagining himself to be the emperor of that fictional kingdom. When Glory does return, it is to rumors that she managed to pay off the farm debt by becoming a prostitute. This gossip is too much for her to bear and she takes a boat back to the city. Her father frantically follows her but falls off the dock to his death. When the captain of the boat on which Glory is sailing sees Jan's accident, he reverses course, which causes Lars (Ian Keith), the man who led Glory to prostitution, to fall overboard and drown, as well.

The film opened to mixed reviews, many of which claimed that the symbolic montages in the movie were too sophisticated for the average movie audience. An example of this effect is found in the April 18, 1925, script, although it was later changed in the final print. After Jan learns that his daughter has paid off their mortgage but is not coming home, he wanders into the forest in a daze. He sits alone on a stump as his mind slowly begins to fall apart. The scene dissolves into four visions: the baby Glory in Jan's arms; crowning his daughter with a wreath of pine cones; his daughter saying she is leaving for the city; and a girl standing on the boat. It then dissolves to a title card: "Through the fading years old Jan untiringly waited for Glory Goldie's home coming!" Next we see a close-up of Jan and then the bow of a boat making its way down a river. Superimposed over Jan's face is the title, "Each day's disappointment only added fresh vigor to his faith in tomorrow." The title then dissolves from a close-up of Jan to the stern of the boat going away. [225] This montage sequence was not only symbolic but also depicted the progression of several years. However, the cutting continuity presents the version that appeared in the release print, which is quite different from the April 18 script. Here, Lars tells Jan that Glory has paid the house off but is not returning. The scene fades to the title, "With every boat Jan looked for Glory's return. The months ran into years— disappointment and longing aged his body and dimmed his mind before its time." The scene fades in with Jan waiting at the gangplank on the dock. Jan has aged significantly from the previous scene, indicating the passage of time. There are several shots of people coming off the boat and Jan's reaction to them. He finally walks up to August, Glory's childhood friend, and asks, "She'll come on tomorrow's boat. August — won't she?" [226]

Interestingly, the film was not an acquisition of the newly founded M-G-M, as was previously believed. Metro Pictures had obtained the rights to the story in 1922 under its original title, *The Emperor of Portugallia*, and in the studio reader's synopsis of the story, the following comment was noted: "Not picture material. Not enough action." [227]

The Blackbird, one of Chaney's two 1926 releases directed by Tod Browning, again allowed the actor to play a character who masquerades as another while hiding from the police. The character of Dan Tate, known as the Blackbird, is a coarse personality with little sympathy or concern for anyone but himself. Although he appears to have few redeeming qualities, he does show his feelings for others in his own way. For example, in a scene in the local music hall, he encounters a young white girl in heavy make-up walking out with an Oriental man. He blocks their way and makes it clear to the man that he is not wanted there. The Blackbird gives the girl a verbal lashing for being with a man of another race and threatens to tell her father. He orders her to go home and wash the make-up off, giving her a kick on the backside as she leaves. Although his actions are certainly crude, the paternal concern for the girl's welfare is obvious.

The Blackbird leads a double life, however, frequently disguising himself as his own nonexistent twin brother, a crippled Bishop. Once again, in the Blackbird's masquerade, Browning incorporates a variation of the old sideshow premise of fooling the suckers — a deception that allowed the actor and the director to illustrate the good and bad personality traits of the character. The kindness and compassion extended to the downtrodden by the Bishop emphasizes

A Thousand Faces

Chaney's theory that no matter how vile a character is, he still can possess some innate goodness. Although the Bishop is merely a disguise for the Blackbird, it is apparent that he has indeed helped the people who sought refuge in the mission.

Chaney portrays the Blackbird as a scheming but careful crook whose years of using the ruse of a crippled brother have bolstered his confidence. But his judgment becomes seriously clouded when a rival thief, West End Bertie (Owen Moore), threatens to steal the affections of Fifi (Renee Adoree), whom the Blackbird desires. The Blackbird's jealousy over the budding romance between Fifi and West End Bertie is triggered when Bertie joins him at a table in the Music Hall while awaiting Fifi's arrival. The Blackbird has left a wilted bouquet of flowers on Fifi's dressing room table, which she suspects came from Bertie. The class difference between the two criminals is apparent when she joins them at the table. The Blackbird remains seated, gesturing to an empty chair, while Bertie stands up and helps Fifi to her seat. The two are practically oblivious to the Blackbird, which slowly fans the flame of his jealousy. After she places a flower from her bouquet in Bertie's coat lapel, he looks disdainfully at the wilted bouquet and throws it into the floor cuspidor. Throughout all this action, the Blackbird's anger is building, yet he attempts to remain passive on the outside. To further irritate his foe, Bertie taunts him by buying Fifi a new bouquet of flowers. In an attempt at one-up-manship, the Blackbird takes a flower from the bouquet, leans over to his rival, and takes the wilted flower out of his lapel, replacing it with a fresh one.

The underlying tension between the two men is enhanced by Fifi's reaction and builds when Bertie suggests he take her to a nightclub. As they are about to leave, the Blackbird reminds her she hasn't finished the drink he ordered for her. Bertie provokes his adversary's anger by telling Fifi not to bother, as they will have champagne with dinner. In a medium close-up shot, the Blackbird sits alone at the table sulking over being bested by his rival. He places Fifi's drink in front of him and stares at it, while his anger builds within. Suddenly his rage boils over, and he swipes the glass off the table. The audience realizes that the Blackbird will turn his attention to destroying his rival at all costs.

Another common theme found in Browning's pictures is a character's regeneration through love — in this film, the character of West End Bertie. When Bertie renounces his criminal life for the love of Fifi, it pits him against the Blackbird and compels the Blackbird to act irrationally, in this case, framing Bertie for murder. As in all Chaney-Browning films, actions of this sort fail and cause the demise of the protagonist.

In the picture's climax, the police break down the door to the Bishop's room, knocking the Blackbird (disguised as the Bishop) to the ground and breaking his back. Chaney gives a gut-wrenching, extremely intense performance. He discloses his secret to his exwife: there is no brother, the Bishop and the Blackbird are one and the same, and therefore he cannot be examined by a doctor lest his true identity be revealed. She urges him to pretend to sleep while she tells the doctor he is all right, but when she turns around, she finds that he has died.

In the original draft of the script, the Mocking Bird (which was the original nickname of the Dan Tate character) does not die but accepts the ironic sentence imposed on him of remaining a cripple for the rest of his life. [228] His exwife, Polly (Doris Lloyd), offers to get him medical treatment, but he refuses, saying that the Mocking Bird is dead. He realizes that he has done some good as the Bishop and plans to continue that work. The Mocking Bird reaches out to Polly and she takes his hand. This sudden redemption of the Mocking Bird was hardly convincing, as screen writer Bela Sekely noted in his comments to Thalberg on October 13, 1925:

> The resulting regeneration of the Mocking Bird is a
> logical outgrowth of the story, but this is one
> instance where some improvement seems to be
> necessary in the script. The Mocking Bird-Bishop
> throughout the story has impressed us so strongly
> with his hypocrisy that it will need very persuasive
> reasons for his SPIRITUAL REGENERATION to be
> convincing to the audiences. As it is now we get an
> impression that it is his apparent physical
> impossibility to change back to the Mocking Bird
> rather than A CHANGE IN HIS SPIRITS that makes
> him resign himself to live in the future [in] only the
> one role of the Bishop. He seems to make,
> hypocritically, of necessity a virtue... It certainly
> needs a great shock, a REAL SHOCK to bring about a
> spiritual transformation in a man of so virile
> baseness as the Mocking Bird. [229]

In January 1926, M-G-M picked up the first option of Chaney's 1925 contract, boosting his weekly salary to $2,750. With the success of *The Unholy Three* and *The Blackbird*, the studio renegotiated his contract in April of that year, to include four renewal options and raising his salary to $3,000 a week. M-G-M's effort to renegotiate Chaney's contract demonstrates their realization of his value and box office appeal, not to mention making certain he would not be signed by a rival studio. Chaney's name guaranteed a solid showing at the box office.

As his appeal grew, many of his older films were rereleased to capitalize on his current success. One unscrupulous producer used Chaney's name to entice theatre owners, as Robert Lynch, general manager of M-G-M's Philadelphia distribution office, detailed in a letter to the company's New York office. He reported that during a local convention held by the Independent Film Exchange in Philadelphia, Joe Brandt, president of Columbia Pictures, indicated in a speech that he was very friendly with Louis B. Mayer. He further stated that Mayer had assured him that from time to time he would be in a position to loan out some of the studio's stars to Brandt's company. Lynch was later told by Jay Emanuel, a film broker for theaters in the Philadelphia area, that a salesman for Columbia Pictures hinted that the studio's upcoming production, *The Clown*, might feature Lon Chaney. It was a statement that Joe Brandt would neither confirm nor deny, and M-G-M quickly took steps to halt Columbia's misleading claims. [230]

Whereas *The Blackbird* is one of Chaney and Browning's best efforts, the same cannot be said for the existing print of *The Road to Mandalay*, their next endeavor. The movie performed well at the box office, even outgrossing *The Blackbird* by $68,000, but it did not receive as many favorable accolades as had its predecessor. It is difficult and rather unfair to critique this picture because the only surviving version is missing 25 minutes and has been enlarged from a 9.5mm print. [231] However, this print does give us an idea of the effectiveness of Chaney's blind-eye make-up and illustrates how, once again, Browning weaved his familiar themes into a picture. A studio reader's report did not paint a favorable impression of the original story:

> I do not think this is the type of story for Chaney; it
> is sordid enough certainly, but there isn't anything
> redeeming about it. [232]

Browning conceived the character of Singapore Joe as a man with a blind eye and scarred features, too ashamed to face his own daughter. The plot was enhanced from that point. In the original shooting script, Joe is first seen as a young sea captain whose wife died during childbirth. The young, handsome man, as seen in these scenes, is in direct contrast with Joe's later appearance, which not only illustrates his disintegration but also the passing of the years. The character of Singapore Joe was described by a studio reader as "an abhorrent thing, pockmarked and scarred. One eye is clouded and sinister. He is a wreck, disreputable and capable of anything." In the studio synopsis of April 2, 1926, the character of Father James was an old family friend who was once in love with Joe's wife but who entered the priesthood when he learned of her love for Joe. [233] In the final script, Father James had become Joe's brother, providing for more dramatic impact between the two characters. [234]

Chaney's make-up was relatively simple, yet extremely effective. Although the critics and the public marveled at his grotesque appearance, Lon felt the greater challenge was in appearing as the young Joe, minus the blind eye and scars. So striking was Chaney's blind-eye make-up that, as a boy, Marc Davis never forgot it. Davis, who later became a top animator for Walt Disney and one of the leading designers of many attractions at that company's theme parks, always wanted to incorporate Chaney's visage into a character. The opportunity presented itself when he was designing the famous *Pirates of the Caribbean* attraction for Disneyland. One of the pirates sports the famous scar and blind eye that Chaney created years earlier. [235]

As Singapore Joe, Chaney is the ruler of a Southeast Asian dive and its criminal population. He makes frequent trips to Mandalay to visit his daughter, who does not know that he is her father. She cannot stand the sight of this hideous man and expresses her feelings to Father James who has raised her since childbirth (unaware that the priest is Joe's brother). Joe plans to quit his shady dealings in two years, after he has accumulated enough money to support him and his daughter and allow him undergo plastic surgery to correct his disfigurements. The woman in this plot is Chaney's daughter (not a romantic interest), but his character is equally obsessive in his love for her. This concern becomes much more intense when Joe learns that his daughter is to marry the Admiral, one of his henchmen, who has given up his criminal ways for her. Browning takes an obsessive character (Joe), an alcoholic-criminal regenerated by love (the

Admiral), and a virtuous woman (Joe's daughter) and places them in a setting (Joe's dive) that leads to confrontation and the ultimate demand that the obsessive protagonist/antagonist character sacrifice himself for the sake of the one he loves. Chaney's performance in the surviving print is not as impressive as in his other roles, possibly because of the missing 25 minutes. This gap gives it an unbalanced presentation. What remains is a capable though not exacting performance. At times, it appears as if Lon is trying too hard to be believable, and some of his gestures come off as calculated rather than as natural extensions of the character. But there are other moments when he's completely believable, such as in the scene in the religious curio shop where his daughter works. He lingers in the store and strikes up a conversation with the girl so that he may jealously horde a few minutes with her, even though she is unaware of his true identity.

Based on the surviving print, Browning's attempt to capture the flavor of the Southeast Asia locale misses the mark. Although the scenes in Joe's dive are extremely colorful, they lack the forceful punch Browning was able to deliver in the music hall of *The Blackbird* or the dive in *West of Zanzibar*. Also, the lack of a strong female costar does not help the picture. This is apparent in the sequence in which she confronts Joe (who has shanghaied the Admiral before he could marry his daughter) and tells him she despises him. The absence of a strong actress opposite Chaney in this film, as in others, was an obstacle that occasionally hindered his performance. Because of this handicap, Chaney was shouldered with the burden of carrying the picture and ensuring its success. The climax of the film does not build the necessary tension needed to allow Chaney's character to sacrifice himself for his daughter. During a fight with the Admiral, Joe is stabbed by his daughter, but uses his remaining strength to fend off the despicable English Charlie Wing, who has immoral designs on her. The confrontation between the two men should be powerful, but it fails to reach a dramatic apex. Instead, the standoff is very slow and drawn-out, and lacks excitement. Joe manages to hold off his adversary long enough to allow his daughter and the Admiral to escape safely. This ending is similar to that in *West of Zanzibar*, but it does not convey that movie's emotional impact.

The fact that Chaney played many unusual characters, combined with his tremendous desire for personal privacy, has misled many writers over the years to paint Chaney as a tortured and morose human being and artist. In the years after Creighton's death, stories recounted by his alleged close associates began to surface. These accounts claimed that Creighton had often been beaten by his father for no reason, and even quoted him as saying that Lon could be unusually cruel, almost sadistic. Some critics have suggested that, in my biography, I chose to overlook Chaney's negative personality traits to present only a positive picture. Everything that could be factually documented regarding Chaney's personality, good or bad, was included in *Lon Chaney: The Man Behind the Thousand Faces*. I broached this sensitive subject with several members of the Chaney family, including Creighton's son, Lon Ralph Chaney. He branded these claims as "complete fiction." [236]

While it is true that Lon was a strict father who did not want Creighton to grow up with the attitude of a rich man's son, his sternness was never as excessive as these stories would have us believe. Lon Ralph Chaney was candidly open to this author about other unflattering aspects of his father's life, which leads one to surmise that the claims Creighton made may have been embellishments of the truth. Why would Lon Ralph Chaney be willing to discuss some negative aspects openly but conceal others? He also speculated that when Creighton was relating these incidents to co-workers, he was experiencing unfortunate upheavals in his own career and personal life. [237] Creighton sought escape from these problems in alcohol, a problem that unfortunately would haunt him for the rest of his life. [238] Lon Ralph Chaney felt that Creighton's telling these woeful tales provided him with a degree of sympathy and attention. Other Chaney relatives agreed that the stories were untrue, but unfortunately they continue to be a source of conjecture for those who relish malicious gossip about a film celebrity.

With his next picture, Lon Chaney not only tossed aside his make-up case but also avoided a twisted-protagonist role in favor of a truly heroic character. *Tell It to the Marines* proved that Chaney's audience appeal did not depend on layers of greasepaint and putty but rested squarely on his talent and charisma. Nowhere was this fact more apparent than in this picture, and the film went on to become M-G-M's second-highest grossing picture of 1926-27 and Chaney's leading box office hit while at the studio. [239]

In two early drafts of the scripts, dated February 20 and March 26, 1926, the lead character was a country boy by the name of Rod Maynard. [240] The role was written with an eye toward actor Charles Ray, who had proved to be popular in similar roles. [241] In these drafts of the screenplay, the role of Skeet Burns, the smart-mouthed recruit, was a secondary one, and the Sergeant O'Hara character was a supporting lead. In the conclusion of the January 20, 1926, script outline, Rod Maynard meets up with his hometown sweetheart after leaving the Marines. Realizing that he loves Nora (the naval nurse), he returns to the Marines. Rod takes the General up on his offer to enlist in Officer's Training school. He tells Nora that when he graduates he will return and marry her. The outline ended with Rod, the General, his son, Harry, and O'Hara linking arms and singing the Marine Corps Hymn to Nora and the audience. A more sentimental ending came in the March 1 script, featuring the title card: "Latest Model United States Sub-Marine." The scene would fade in on Rod (in his lieutenant uniform) and Nora giving a bath to their baby in the back yard of their home. O'Hara and Skeet (who is also a sergeant) are present and the gruff O'Hara bends down to the baby, pointing his finger. When the child playfully grabs at it, the sergeant's tough face breaks into a warm smile.

But by the April 29 script, the Rod Maynard character had been deleted altogether in favor of Skeet Burns (William Haines), and Sergeant O'Hara was given a leading role. E. Richard Schayer was credited with the screenplay, but Thalberg sought the input of another writer, Edward Kaufman, to interject comedy into the film. While Kaufman's suggestions did not make the final print, they do provide an interesting insight into how Thalberg sought the advice of several writers to produce a good picture. One of Kaufman's suggestions was to show Skeet having trouble with his hat after receiving his traditional Marine haircut. The hat sinks to his ears and he complains to Corporal Madden (Eddie Gribbon) that he wants a new hat, and he is either told or shown that all he'll get is newspaper with which he can stuff the sweat band. [242]

When the picture was completed, Thalberg asked screenwriter E. Richard Schayer to critique the film. Schayer noted several problems in his August 30 summary:

> What is missing throughout this part of the story is the element that I had in the first version—the sergeant's deep, but hopeless, love for the girl, and his determination to make a man out of Skeet Burns, as much for her sake as in the line of duty to the Marine Corps....

> The fight at the bridge should by all means reach melodramatic heights. As now played the arrival of the Chinese troops makes the whole situation fall flat. We have built up our tempo and the audience will expect to see this little group of Marines do something heroic. They don't. [243]

Schayer's final point is correct. The film was supposed to

illustrate the Marine tradition of fighting against and defeating the odds. Having the outnumbered group of Marines saved from annihilation by the Chinese Army was anticlimactic and didn't enhance the "First to Fight" motto of the Corps. As originally scripted and shot, the bandits retreat when they see the arriving Chinese military, and the Chinese officer of the troops shakes hands with the wounded O'Hara. In the final version of the film, the bandits retreat when they see incoming Marine airplanes, which drop bombs on the fleeing villains. Almost two months later, the climax still seemed to be a problem. Thalberg sought input from noted screenwriter Frances Marion (wife of the film's director, George Hill). Marion felt that having Skeet leave the service after his enlistment was up fell flat. She suggested that the death of O'Hara would provide a more dramatic impact, with him making the last request that Skeet carry on the tradition of the Corps. In her October 23 notes, Marion stated:

> Viewing this picture the second time with the
> retakes, I still think the climax misfires. Reel after
> reel of marvelous entertainment builds up to a
> complete transition in the character of the boy—
> then it flops. As it stands I cannot see it as a two-
> dollar picture; [244] if a climax is written into the
> picture and shot, it will hold them every minute....
> Up to the Shanghai sequence I still think it is one of
> the greatest pictures we have ever seen. [245]

Thalberg recalled the actors and crew to shoot additional retakes for the film, including added shots on the bridge with the bandits. [246] The scene with Skeet and Nora saying good-bye before he ships off to sea and the ending of the picture were also filmed at this time on the studio lot instead of the Marine Base in San Diego. Despite Frances Marion's opinion, Thalberg kept the scene in which Skeet comes to see O'Hara after finishing his enlistment and offers him a partnership in a ranch he and Nora (Eleanor Boardman) have bought. O'Hara declines; he and the Corps are meant for each other. After saying goodbye, he leaves to bawl out a new group of rookies. [247]

Before the cameras rolled, the film was involved in a dispute with Fox Film Corporation, which also wanted to use the Marines for their upcoming picture *What Price Glory?*. When Fox executives learned that M-G-M had already signed an agreement with the Corps, they attempted to void the contract, stating: "The contract made in behalf of the Marine Corps is illegal. No official of the Government can sign away the rights of the public for what is really governmental property to be used for profit." Fox planned to take their grievance to the Secretary of the Navy and even threatened to involve President Coolidge, if necessary. An aide to General John Lejuene, Commandant of the Corps, stated that M-G-M's contract with the Marines called only for the contribution of certain personnel for scenes in the picture and assistance with technical details. The Marines assured everyone that "the Corps would extend the same opportunities, facilities and assistance as they have in the past" to everyone. Fox did receive assistance from the Marines for their picture, along with the necessary personnel, and the matter was dropped. [248]

Tell It to the Marines is one of Chaney's finest pictures, and he gives an engaging performance. His portrayal of Sgt. O'Hara became the prototype for the tough-as-nails military officer with a heart of gold, a role other actors, including John Wayne, Randolph Scott, and Jack Webb, would later emulate. O'Hara is pure Marine; his life is the Corps. Yet Chaney allows this austere mentality to soften when he is in the presence of naval nurse Norma Dale. Suddenly his gruffness is replaced by a warm and friendly demeanor, bringing to mind a young boy experiencing his first crush. This emotional contrast induces not only sympathy, but also a sincere affection for Chaney's character. An example of this contrast is found in the scene where Norma approaches the sergeant on behalf of Skeet, O'Hara's rival for

Norma's affections. Happy to see her, O'Hara is warm and friendly until he hears her request. She asks O'Hara to release Skeet from the brig (he returned late to the barracks) and allow the young man to go with him on sea duty. O'Hara suddenly snaps back to the disciplined Marine, reminding Norma that the military is no kindergarten. Just as O'Hara is delivering this speech, Corporal Madden reports that he has released Skeet from the brig and told him to report for sea duty, as the sergeant had ordered. The sergeant sheepishly smiles; he was one step ahead of Norma, and now the gentler side of his personality has been accidentally revealed. Norma thanks O'Hara and gives him a kiss on the cheek before leaving. He is stunned for a moment but, smiling at his good fortune, he quickly hurries out to his squad.

In another scene, Chaney makes light of his own features after looking at a photo of Norma. He comes to the realization that he has little chance of winning her love. Looking into a mirror in his tent, he remarks to his bulldog, Sgt. Jiggs, that he has some nerve thinking about Norma with "a map like this." He laments that he certainly has the ugliest mug in the service, a remark that seems to hurt the dog's feelings. Chaney looks into the mirror once again and smiles back at the dog: "No, you've got this on me a little." His ability to poke fun at himself is one of O'Hara's more appealing qualities. Another equally attractive aspect of the character is his nobility. When Norma asks O'Hara whether she was right in terminating her relationship with Skeet, he is torn between his honor and the opportunity to win the girl for himself. As with many of Chaney's characters, O'Hara's nobility surpasses his personal desire for her. Because his code of honor is so strong, the audience cannot help but admire O'Hara, which builds compassion for the character at the end of the film when he watches the happily married Skeet and Norma walk off together.

Tell It to the Marines marked the first time the Marine Corps gave its complete cooperation to a motion picture production. The

A Thousand Faces

Marines were part of an elaborate celebration at the studio in late May 1926, when they presented a new American flag to Louis B. Mayer, prior to the start of production. Joseph Newman, who would later work as an assistant director for George Hill and go on to direct pictures at M-G-M, remembered the event:

> Something like this had never been done before. Every employee at the studio was allowed to leave their office and watch this event. It was a really big thing. [249]

In many respects the picture was a promotional tool for the Marine Corps, but it manages to live up to the definition of a "crowd pleaser." It is a competently made film by director George Hill, who recalled that Chaney "was a joy to work with. A director's delight." [250] The film was peppered with a strong supporting cast, although Carmel Myers' make-up as a native girl stretches us beyond the realm of believability! One of the best supporting performances was turned in by Eddie Gribbon as Corporal Madden. He supplies many laughs in several scenes, including getting one of the best lines (by means of a title card) in the picture. As the detachment of Marines stands guard while rescuing the Americans from Hangchow, a Chinese man runs into Madden. He grabs the man and verbally lashes out, before sending him on his way, with the parting comment, "That's for all the punk chop suey I got in Omaha!" [251]

The film not only did a great deal to advance Chaney's career, but also helped establish William Haines as one of the studio's most popular stars of the late 1920s. The photography added to the film's appeal, and cameraman Ira Morgan made extensive use of tracking shots, taking the audience along with the action of the picture. One of the most impressive sequences in the film takes place at sea aboard the battleship *USS California*. On the ship's deck, a squad of Marines has been lined up for inspection. In the background we see several other battleships making their way across the ocean. (All of them later fell victim to the Japanese attack on Pearl Harbor.) It is obvious to the viewer that this scene was actually filmed at sea and is not a rear-screen process shot, something that would later become routine with the advent of talking pictures.

Hazel Chaney said that *Tell It to the Marines* was one of Lon's favorite roles. She said he was extremely honored to be allowed to operate the breech of one of the ship's five-inch guns for a scene in the film. [252] Lon's handling of the breech appeared natural to his character, which was a compliment to his talent, making a complex task appear so effortless. Because his performance was so realistic, Chaney became the first actor to be granted an honorary membership in the United States Marine Corps.

To further exhibit Chaney's versatility, M-G-M chose *Mr. Wu* for his next picture. The movie was based on a 1914 stage play. Lon once again played two roles: the principal character, Mr. Wu, a mandarin educated in the West, and his elderly grandfather. A 1921 film version of this story featured Matheson Lang, who had played the role on stage, but it had not included the elderly grandfather. This part appears to have been concocted solely to display Chaney's unique talent and further enhance his reputation as "the Man of a Thousand Faces."

Chaney portrays the aged and venerable grandfather as a wise man of the Orient who realizes that his grandson must be educated in the ways of western civilization and culture. Once again, it is hard to believe that this frail and withered old Chinese man was played by a vibrant 43-year-old Caucasian. As Mr. Wu, the grandson who becomes a wealthy mandarin, Chaney is stern when dealing with business associates or servants, but his demeanor quickly changes when he is in the company of his daughter, Nang Ping, or his old mentor, Mr. Muir. There is an unmistakable bond between Wu and Muir that is illustrated by Wu's childlike prank of pulling the older man's coat lapels, a game that delights both of them. Wu's love for his daughter is obvious, almost bordering on excessive. He relishes his time with Nang Ping, even though she will soon marry.

This obsessional love for his daughter motivates Wu's thirst for revenge when she is seduced by an Englishman, making her unworthy to marry. According to Chinese custom, Wu must now take his daughter's life, although he promises Nang Ping not to harm her lover, Basil Gregory. Yet when he comes across a family emblem handmade by his daughter, Wu's grief overcomes him and he sets out to seek revenge. This is an emotionally charged scene for Chaney and for the progression of the story. When he finds the emblem in his daughter's room, he gently picks it up and suddenly realizes his child is gone. Chaney's whole body convulses and he begins to cry, slowly caressing the emblem. Blinking away his tears and composing himself, the anger builds within him. As he slowly straightens, his face turns harsh. Clapping his hands in a firm manner, he summons his servants and begins his quest for retribution.

Although it was one of Lon's highest grossing pictures while he was at M-G-M, *Mr. Wu* is very slow moving. [253] The sets and photography are exceptional, but the picture lacks strong direction. Chaney has a capable supporting cast, especially in Renee Adoree as his daughter and Louise Dresser as the mother of Basil Gregory. But Ralph Forbes, who plays Basil Gregory, lacks a strong leading-man presence and delivers a weak performance. A major problem with the picture lies in the script, which spends too much effort developing Nang Ping's romance and leaves little time to build the dramatic tension for Wu's revenge. The scene in which Nang Ping prepares to die at her father's hand is carried out poorly, thus losing the dramatic impact. As Wu walks to the altar, a large curtain parts to reveal Nang Ping at the top of the structure. Wu mounts the steps and takes a sword in hand as the curtain closes. The camera begins to move closer to the curtain before stopping to dissolve into the next scene. Had the camera followed Wu, watching him climb the steps and take the sword in hand, before the closing the curtain, it would have given the scene a stronger dramatic moment.

Mr. Wu was twenty-year-old Willard Sheldon's fifth picture as a script supervisor. He had started out at M-G-M in 1926, carrying camera cases for five dollars a day. Sheldon went on to work as a script supervisor and ultimately became an assistant director and unit manager before retiring in 1971. He recalled his experiences on the set of *Mr. Wu* and Lon's elaborate make-up:

> It took Lon six hours to complete his make-up as Grandfather Wu. During the course of production, I imagine he was able to cut it down a little, but it was at least 3 or 4 hours every day he worked in that make-up. Next to Cecil Holland [head of the studio's make-up department], I was the only one allowed in his dressing room during the filming, mainly because I was always there so early. I was there when he was putting on the make-up, after the tests. I wasn't there during the original make-up [tests]; nobody got in there but Cecil Holland.
>
> He later told me how he tested his make-up. They [studio executives and producer Harry Rapf] were worried about the grandfather make-up. They had no idea what to do. Lon worked on it by himself, and all Cecil ever did was to hand him things and maybe help him with a little line here and there. Finally he said to Harry Rapf, "I've got the make-up which I think will work but you can't see it—not yet. I've got to test it. I'll let you know." So what he did was he got some old clothes, some pajamas like the old Chinese used to wear, wrinkled it up so it was old looking and put it on. He took a laundry basket and filled it with all kinds of clothes, and left the studio early one morning. He got on a streetcar, any line—he didn't care which one, at the beginning of the line. I guess he had somebody drive him

there. He rode that car from the beginning to the end of the line, wherever it was, and from time to time he would change his seat and be in a different part of the car. He spent the whole day riding streetcars! When he was accepted as what he looked like, an old Chinese, he said fine, and that was that.

He talked very little when he was making himself up. He concentrated very heavily on what he was doing. Cecil didn't talk to him either. He just sat there, and if Lon needed something he handed it to him. I guess because I was so young and enthusiastic at the time, and because I was there so early in the morning [about 6 a.m.], he'd invite me in. I'd be walking by his dressing room and call hello and he'd say come in and I would sit there. His room was sparsely furnished, only a couch, a couple of chairs and a dressing table. He always made himself up. Definitely.

When he came in on the set as the old man [the Grandfather Wu character], quite a bit of fuss was made over him. When the crew talked to him they always addressed him as "Mr. Chaney," but in passing you would hear "Good morning, Lon" from the grips and electricians. But if you had some specific reason to go to him, you would address him as "Mr. Chaney."

Lon liked William Nigh [the director of the picture]. He never argued with Nigh. Everything was always very quiet, very well done. He and Nigh would discuss a scene, just the two of them, and maybe walk around a little bit [on the set], and maybe call the other people in. Then they would go right into rehearsal and shoot. Nigh wasn't the type of man who would shoot a scene forty times like some, maybe one or two takes at most. [254]

A Phantom Before Stardom at M-G-M

With the success of *Tell It To The Marines* and *Mr. Wu*, Chaney's popularity soared even higher. Despite the deformity of a character (either physically or mentally), Chaney was able to ignite sympathy in his audience, which ensured their return for his next picture. One critic suggested that Chaney's unpolished countenance, unlike those other leading male stars, provided the male population of his audience with a sense of hope: if Lon Chaney could get by with his looks, so could they. [255] Also, the fact that love always seemed to elude his characters must have struck a sympathetic chord among Chaney's fans. Lon evoked compassion for his characters, which in turn compelled his audience to embrace his performances. It didn't matter that the Phantom had released a chandelier upon an unsuspecting audience or that the Blackbird had killed an officer of the law. By the end of the picture, Chaney's character had redeemed himself and gained the sympathy of the audience. Lon once reflected to a reporter upon the philosophy found in some of his characters, claiming:

> It's in my pictures. I've tried to show that the
> lowliest people frequently have the highest ideals.
> In the lower depths when life hasn't been too
> pleasant for me I've always had that gentleness of
> feeling, that compassion of an underdog for a fellow
> sufferer. *The Hunchback* was an example of it. So
> was *The Unknown* and, in a different class of
> society, *Mr. Wu*. I try to bring that emotion to the
> screen. [256]

Certainly one of Chaney's most impressive characters is Alonzo in *The Unknown*. Most film historians readily agree that this is probably the best of the Chaney-Browning collaborations, and one of Lon's most outstanding performances. Featuring a tightly knit story, it is one of Browning's better films, and he moves the film along at a brisk pace that helps build tension for a dramatic climax. Most of

A Thousand Faces

Browning's films featuring Chaney were not of the horror genre, that is, a movie designed to horrify or one in which a monster plays the lead, such as in *Frankenstein* or *The Wolf Man*. Instead, Browning took a lifelike character, possibly displaying a physical or emotional deformity, and placed him in believable surroundings. From that point, Browning wove a tale that took the character to extremes, such as Alonzo's cutting his arms off so that he could marry a woman with a phobia of men's embraces. This is where the director's unique talent came into play, establishing lurid or macabre backgrounds for his tales. The possibility that such a character could exist made the story believable. For example, although it may be a little farfetched, it is within the realm of possibility that the Blackbird could have masqueraded as his crippled brother and never been detected. The same is true with the character of Alonzo in *The Unknown*. It is quite possible that a criminal, in order to commit crimes and remain anonymous to the police and everyone else around him, might pose as an armless knife thrower in a circus. Browning once pointed out what he thought made a mystery successful:

> The thing you have to be most careful of in a
> mystery story is not to let it verge on the comic. If a
> thing is too gruesome and too horrible, it gets
> beyond the limits of the average imagination and the
> audience laughs. It may sound incongruous, but
> mystery must be made plausible. [257]

The Unknown was set against the background of the familiar Browning terrain of a circus. As in most of his films, Browning sets the mood by establishing the one-ring Spanish circus featuring Alonzo's act. From Chaney's first reaction, it is clear he desires Nanon (Joan Crawford). [258] Browning again injects the fooling-the-suckers theme by not revealing that Chaney actually does have arms until twenty minutes into the picture. Thus, he plants in the mind of the

192

audience the belief that Alonzo is truly armless. Then when it is revealed that he is not, the viewer gets a jolting surprise. Browning magnifies the surprise by establishing that Alonzo has a double thumb, which also plays an integral part in the story's plot.

Alonzo is so obsessed with Nanon that he will do anything to have her. Knowing that she has a phobia about having men's arms around her, Alonzo urges the strongman, Malabar (Norman Kerry), to embrace her, thinking that this will drive a wedge between the strongman and Nanon. Of course, Alonzo's plan ultimately backfires, which compels him to seek revenge. In one sequence, Alonzo tells his companion Cojo (John George), the only person who knows Alonzo has arms and is a criminal, that he desperately wants Nanon. Cojo reminds him of Nanon's fear of men's arms and implies that she would never forgive Alonzo for lying to her. Alonzo, smiling dreamily, lost in his fantasy, says she would forgive him. When Cojo reminds him that Nanon saw her father killed by a man with a double thumb, Alonzo stares at his hands in horror, almost as if they were not part of his body. Agonizing over his problem, Alonzo rests his head on his upraised foot as if it were one of his hands. He lights a cigarette using his feet and is confused by Cojo's laughter until Cojo points out to Alonzo that he forgets he does have arms. Alonzo again stares at his arms (which had been resting on the sides of the chair) as if they were not part of his body, then seems to become aware of the solution to his entire problem. He will have his arms amputated and claim Nanon for himself.

This scene is extremely pivotal to the plot and is well played by Chaney. It is obvious that a double's feet were used in many scenes because Chaney sits in a large, oversized chair. The man who doubled him, Dismuki, appears in a few of the picture's long shots, notably a brief shot in which Alonzo and Cojo are seated at a table, drinking coffee. [259] But by incorporating the double's feet in such scenes as the one in which Alonzo waves his toes in front of the police officer, asking him if he wants to take his fingerprints, or when Alonzo sits at the table, rubbing his big toes together (much like twiddling one's thumbs) while lost in thought, the audience accepts the fact that Chaney could use his feet for these simple tasks. The idea that a double was used is no longer relevant.

The sole complaint regarding the picture's storyline is that Nanon overcomes her fear of embraces so quickly, instead of experiencing a gradual easing of her phobia. But to flesh out this point would have seriously harmed the pace of the picture and ruined the dramatic momentum for the exciting climax. When Alonzo learns that Nanon has fallen in love with Malabar and he has maimed himself for nothing, he plots revenge. In his new act, the strongman holds back two horses on treadmills pulling in opposite directions. Alonzo plans to engage the brake on one of the treadmills, in the hope of ripping Malabar's arm from his body. To heighten the suspense of this scene, Browning cuts to various shots of the horse's hoofs running on the treadmill, Nanon standing on a platform above the stage cracking a whip, and Alonzo's mounting excitement. We know Alonzo's intention and wait for him to carry it out, which also helps to build suspense. Alonzo engages the brake, and when Nanon attempts to stop the rearing horse, Alonzo pushes her out of the way — but he himself is struck down and stomped to death. The next scene shows Malabar and Nanon standing together in a garden, holding hands. In one of the earlier drafts of the script, additional reaction shots of the circus audience observing the action on stage were included, which could have added to the suspense of the scene. Also in this early version of the script, after Alonzo is crushed by the horse, the last shot was of the stage and the curtain quickly coming down, then a fade-out to the end titles. It is unclear whether the censors or the studio decided to install the last shot of the lovers together, giving the picture a happier ending. [260]

The Russian revolution found its way to Hollywood in several films, including De Mille's *The Volga Boatman* (1926) and Paramount's *The Last Command* (1928). This historic uprising served as a background for Lon's next picture, *Mockery*, in which he played Sergi, a slow-thinking Russian peasant. The storyline borrowed heavily from the *Beauty and the Beast* theme, with Sergi falling in love with a Russian countess whom he is helping to escort through Bolshevik-held territory. After Sergi suffers a severe beating at the hands of revolutionaries, the countess, Tatiana (Barbara Bedford), takes pity on him and finds him work as a servant at the residence where she is staying. He becomes infatuated with Tatiana, but his hopes of gaining her love are crushed when he sees her in a romantic embrace with Russian officer, Captain Dimitri (Ricardo Cortez). Listening to the influential speeches of Ivan (Charles Puffy), the household cook, Sergi slowly comes to believe that the Communist theory that all Russians are equal equates with his desire for Tatiana. When she is left alone at the residence, Sergi attempts to force his intentions upon her, but Tatiana fights off his advances and rebuffs him. Later, when her life is threatened by revolutionaries, he comes to her rescue, even though it is at the expense of his own life.

Sergi, a dull-brained hulk of a man, is mistrustful of all people. The horrible repercussions of the revolution have reinforced this feeling. Yet he is willing to help the countess reach her destination by posing as her husband, in exchange for food. The fact that a beautiful woman would even speak to him, let alone ask him to pose as her husband, plants the seed for his lustful desires. When they reach a cabin in the woods, it is obvious that Sergi cares for this woman, especially when he takes off her boots and bathes her feet. In this scene, Chaney conveys Sergi's childlike devotion to the woman who was kind to him, much the same way as he reacted to Esmeralda in *The Hunchback of Notre Dame*. Later, when he falls under the influence of the revolutionary rhetoric, Sergi becomes surly towards the upper class of the household. In one scene, Chaney displays splendid touches of comedy as he makes crude gestures towards Gaidaroff (Mack Swain), in effect telling him what he can do with his residence. This scene must have kept the censors busy because Lon turns his lower backside toward Swain and slaps it with one of his hands! In another scene, Sergi stands in a doorway, smiling smugly at the departing troops, including Captain Dimitri. His expression reveals that he has accepted the revolution's philosophy, and when he glances up at Tatiana waving to Dimitri, his look telegraphs that he will soon attempt to act on his desire for her. These two scenes help to illustrate the change in Chaney's character, and his performance is certainly believable; yet the scenario fails to build upon the character of Sergi and his interaction with Tatiana. Despite tremendous potential, the scenario does not produce the needed momentum to involve the audience and evoke the necessary sympathy for Sergi's character.

An example of this failure to develop a sympathetic scenario between Sergi and Tatiana occurs after he has attempted to force himself upon the countess. Dimitri has returned with his soldiers to round up some revolutionaries; Sergi is included in this group. When Dimitri asks Tatiana if the slow-thinking peasant has been loyal to her, she hesitates. Glancing at the scars on Sergi's chest — scars inflicted by a beating that saved her life — she acknowledges his loyalty and does not mention his attempt to attack her. Sergi cannot believe that she would lie on his behalf, and misinterprets her feelings as love. When Dimitri leaves, Sergi follows the countess around, pleading for forgiveness. Before this scene can develop into anything poignant, however, the revolutionaries attack the residence again. Sergi defends Tatiana with his own life, living long enough to see her reunited with Dimitri. Unfortunately, the scene, despite impressive lighting and camera work, fails to obtain any sincere sympathy for Lon's character.

The picture was originally called *The Harelip* and was then changed to *Terror*, before *Mockery* was settled on, prior to its release. The numerous title changes were consistent with the numerous versions written for the opening of the picture. In the March 10, 1927, synopsis, Sergi, because of his knowledge of the terrain, is forced to accompany a revolutionary and his wife. They are stopped by Russian soldiers, who find a document pertaining to the revolution in the anarchist's hat. The officer orders the trio shot, but Sergi pleads that he knew nothing and is thrown into prison. When the Countess Tatania is asked to smuggle a secret message to Russian headquarters, they have Sergi guide her through the territory. [261] A June 13 version finds Sergi in the forest, looking through dead soldiers' bags in the hope of finding food. The script then establishes Sergi hiding in a room of a small house. Two revolutionaries seek shelter in the house and, when Tatania passes by, they question her. Unsatisfied with her answers, they tie her in a chair next to a table with food. The Bolsheviks then wait outside for their leader. When the hungry Sergi sees the food, he attempts to take it without being noticed. Tatania pleads with him to free her, even saying she will be his slave. As he starts to untie her, the revolutionaries enter with their leader. They beat Sergi with a whip until Russian soldiers enter and kill the insurgents. Sergi faints from his beating, and Tatania relates her secret message, which is sewn into her apron. [262] This scene was later adapted as the opening of the picture, in which Sergi befriends Tatania and guides her through the woods. Resting in a cabin, they are accosted by revolutionaries and Sergi receives his beating, only to be rescued when Russian troops happen by.

Just a week before production began on the picture, writer Eddie Moran drafted a comedy bit that involved the stuffy Mr. and Mrs. Gaidaroff, played by Mack Swain and Emily Fitzroy. As the revolution rages outside the Gaidaroff mansion and residents begin to flee, the Gaidaroffs frantically pack their bags, the husband carrying his favorite painting. His wife insists on taking tons of clothes and shoes, while he comes out with only a few suits, still carrying his painting. As Gaidaroff goes to retrieve more items, he continues to hold onto his precious artwork. At one point, he bumps into his wife with the painting and she grabs it from him and smashes it over his head. As he stretches his arms out, asking what to do, he becomes another device for holding her clothes, hat boxes, and suitcases. He leaves the room with only his toothbrush in his vest pocket, looking abjectly at his smashed painting. As the couple exit their mansion they are run over by the escaping crowd. Mrs. Gaidaroff picks up her wrecked hat and begins to cry. The only thing not ruined is Mr. Gaidaroff's toothbrush, which brings a smile to his face. [263] Given the comedic talents of the two performers, this would have been a humorous scene. Unfortunately, this sequence was either never shot or, if it was, it never made it into the final print.

Film Spectator, the industry trade journal, released a survey in its August 20, 1927, issue that listed the rank and percentage of the motion picture audiences a specific star attracted. Only three stars, Charles Chaplin, Douglas Fairbanks and Harold Lloyd, drew 100%, while Valentino and John Barrymore came in with 96% and 93%, respectively. [264] Lon came in sixth with a percentage of 92%, well ahead of John Gilbert (86%), Greta Garbo (86%), Mary Pickford (81%) and Buster Keaton (74%). Most film historians are at a loss to explain Chaney's popularity. Welford Beaton, editor of the *Film Spectator*, was known for speaking his mind, and published his own assessment:

> Lon Chaney has great box-office value. He is not as
> handsome as Roman Novarro, and lacks the sex
> appeal of Jack Gilbert. His sole attraction is the
> quality of his acting. It bears out my contention that
> the public craves acting, or what it mistakes for it.
> The screen generally has learned nothing from

A Phantom Before Stardom at M-G-M

Chaney's popularity. It always is looking for more
pretty boys, and refuses to recognize the box-office
value of acting. [265]

As Chaney's popularity grew, M-G-M was busy devising new ways to promote their unique star. The publicity could range from simply claiming that it was M-G-M that made Chaney into "The Great Chaney," to devising elaborate stunts to coincide with the release of his films. Many films had a photoplay novel tie-in, which generally featured several pictures from the movie between the pages of the text. Usually a bookstore would prominently display the novel in its window, along with a window card announcing the film's engagement at the local theatre. Newspapers would run a contest for the best essay on what constituted Chaney's greatest role, with the winner receiving a pair of free tickets to his latest film. Newspapers would also run crossword puzzles featuring artwork based on Chaney's latest film and allowing the local theatre to get some free advertising.

For *He Who Gets Slapped*, the studio pressbook suggested having a clown stilt walker go around the city, wearing a sign announcing the movie. [266] To generate feminine interest in *London After Midnight*, a series of pictures of co-star Marceline Day, dressed in the latest fashions and, subtly mentioning the film's release, were displayed in the window of a woman's clothing boutique or on the fashion page of the local newspaper. In the *West of Zanzibar* pressbook, the studio promoted a "Lon Chaney slogan contest," in which the newspapers announced that M-G-M was looking for a better or more descriptive slogan to fit Chaney's accomplishments. Of course the contest winner's effort were never taken seriously, but they did get to keep the prize money they won (usually $10 or $15), and had their picture in the local paper. With the surging popularity of radio, movie studios turned to this relatively new media to promote their pictures. Chaney's only talking picture,

A Thousand Faces

The Unholy Three, was promoted by a radio broadcast (running either 15 or 30 minutes) in which the announcer read a synopsis of the plot with various musical interludes.

While most of these promotions were fairly mild, some other ideas lived up to the true definition of a "publicity stunt." *Tell It To The Marines* provided the willing theatre owner with a handful of interesting promotions. One involved someone dressed as a Marine being pulled down the street in a rickshaw, with the movie's title and theatre name lavishly displayed. Another idea was to place an ad for fifty bulldogs to appear in a newsreel. The willing dog owners would be told to show up at the theatre for an interview, where the dogs would be fitted with a lettered cloth blanket advertising the film. In some larger cities, M-G-M's newsreel department would actually photograph these events to later publicize the film in the weekly newsreels which ran throughout the world. The studio even suggested staging a fake fight to take place near the theatre between someone dressed as a sailor and a Marine military police officer. While this stunt probably did not help foster harmonious relations between the Navy and the Marines, it was sure to draw a crowd. As the on-lookers gathered, the "Marine" would interrupt the "sailor" with the quote, "Tell It To The Marines," and lead his prisoner off to the theatre. Certainly one of the most eye-catching stunts came from the pressbook of the silent version of *The Unholy Three*. It suggested having someone dressed as an old woman push a baby carriage down the street, with a midget dressed as a baby inside puffing on a cigar! As astonished pedestrians looked on, the midget would hold up a sign reading, "This is one of the tricks used by The Unholy Three." [267]

When it came to preparing the artwork for movie posters, most artists worked from photographs. But, on rare occasions, a star might sit for an artist. Such was the case Cardwell Higgins found himself in when Chaney posed for him:

A Phantom Before Stardom at M-G-M

> It must have been 1928 or 1929 at M-G-M. I had to
> work up images of Lon Chaney for a movie, [but] I
> can't remember which one.... On a couple of
> occasions Chaney came over [and] sat on the set as I
> sketched. He was a nice fellow, tan, with a craggy
> face. He looked like a carpenter or stage hand. You
> would have passed him on the street and never
> known he was a big star. Chaney wasn't particularly
> tall, and he had a wiry build. The first meeting he
> didn't say much. Later, he recognized me and felt
> comfortable I guess. We chatted and joked around.
> He rolled up his sleeves and relaxed. The studio
> gave me about thirty minutes with him each time.
> [268]

With the release of *The Jazz Singer* in October 1927, motion pictures took a dramatic leap forward into the dimension of sound. [269] Suddenly once-loyal patrons of silent pictures were mesmerized by dialogue. Producers and stars alike had concerns about this new element in motion pictures, but for different reasons. To the producers, it represented an enormous outlay of capital in order to connect the new sound systems to theaters and studios. Many producers, including Irving Thalberg, were confident that silent pictures could hold their own against the onslaught of the new dialogue films. One has to keep in mind that the fate of talking pictures was uncertain; they might catch on, or they might fade quickly from memory. Actors were equally perplexed because it was not known how their voices would record. The early recording devices were unreliable and tended to distort voices. Some performers who jumped into talking pictures in the beginning found their once-thriving careers in jeopardy because of these problems. Hollywood was besieged by stage actors and speech and diction coaches from New York and everywhere else in the world.

In the early days of sound films, dialogue was everything, superseding action or any kind of camera movement. For the silent film enthusiast today, this period is equally rewarding and frustrating.

A Thousand Faces

It is rewarding because silent pictures had gained a technical superiority to films made just five or six years earlier. The introduction of panchromatic film and incandescent lights gave movies a more lifelike appearance, obliterating the "whiteface" look and allowing the actors to appear more natural. Not only were silent films reaching their technical supremacy; the quality of the acting and the art of making movies, even the programmers, was approaching a pinnacle that lost its momentum in the early years of talking pictures. The frustration is that craftsmanship and quality filmmaking were cast aside for the new technology of seeing performers speak on the screen. The artistic quality of many of these early sound films lacks the panache of latter-day silent pictures. The prominence of dialogue in early talkies is akin to the numerous pictures made in the past two decades that have relied heavily on special effects to tell a story. One can't help but wonder what heights silent pictures would have attained had sound not intruded at that time.

Despite the encroachment of sound, Lon's next picture was the most financially successful film made under Tod Browning's direction. [270] *London After Midnight* is a much sought-after and eagerly anticipated lost silent film that has attained an almost cultlike status. Over the years, numerous rumors have surfaced regarding the existence of a print of this picture. Sadly, these rumors remain the wishful dream of many Chaney and Browning fans. A print of the picture has yet to surface. As the years progress, hopes of finding the film dissipate and unless a print was transferred to safety film stock from the deteriorating nitrate stock, the original will soon disintegrate. There is always a slim chance, giving life to the persistent rumor, that some film collector has a properly preserved print of the film in a private collection.

The storyline of *London After Midnight*, which was originally titled *The Hypnotist*, centers around a Scotland Yard detective who

202

uses a five-year-old crime to prove his theory that a criminal under hypnosis will reenact his offense. The inclusion of vampires in the story was probably influenced by the recent successful Broadway adaptation of Bram Stoker's *Dracula*. [271] Reviewers felt the first half of the film created an interesting atmosphere but that the story became muddled in the latter half. Critics stated that Lon's character, Inspector Burke, gave him little opportunity to create much of a unique character; however, they added that his portrayal of the vampire, who turns out to be Burke in disguise, added a sinister mood to the picture.

When creating a story for Chaney, Browning reportedly would come up with an idea for a character, and the plot would grow from there, usually as he worked out the screenplay with either Waldemar Young or Elliott Clawson. It is said that Browning came up with the storylines for *Road to Mandalay* and *The Unknown* in this way, acting out the plot, scene by scene, as the writer composed the scenario. [272]

Browning was one of the few complete or "auteur" directors of the twenties, according to Arnold Gillespie, an art director at M-G-M for more than forty years. [273] Gillespie recalled Browning's involvement in every detail of a film, from the script and casting the bit and extra players to wardrobe, sets, and editing. [274] One rather amusing incident happened during production of *London After Midnight*. Browning arrived at his usual half-hour before the crew call to find the dust-filled and cobweb-covered set totally spotless, the work of a new and obviously industrious janitor! It took two hours to return the set to its original decayed-looking appearance. But Gillespie felt that Browning was inwardly amused by the whole situation. [275]

For one Lon Chaney fan, Bob McChesney, seeing *London After Midnight* was a must, even at the risk of skipping school. He recalled that in early 1928, the film was accompanied by synchronized sound discs rather than the usual theatre organ. [276] It is entirely possible that the film may have been accompanied by synchronized sound discs as an experiment. Adding credence to this theory is the fact that *The Jazz Singer* was released in October 1927, and the other studios would have needed at least two or three months to obtain the necessary material to make sound discs and may have experimented with currently released pictures. Bob McChesney recalled that *London After Midnight* was so popular that it was shown at the Riviera Theatre in Rochester, New York two or three times that year. [277]

There's no doubt that Lon and Browning admired each other, although Chaney rarely spoke in public about his feelings for the director other than to say, "Tod Browning and I have worked so much together he's called the Chaney director. I like his work." [278] While this is his only public quote regarding Browning, Arnold Gillespie observed that

> his [Chaney's] rapport with Tod was seldom
> dented.... Tod's direction, as I remember, was
> generally accepted by him. But not always! Lon lived
> the character he was depicting and any out-of-
> character suggestions were vetoed, though
> amicably, by the master of character. He was very
> much his own man. [279]

Errol Taggart, who worked as Browning's assistant director and film editor, said that although Chaney respected Browning and his work, he was the type of actor who didn't need much direction. [280] After Lon's death, many writers claimed that Browning seemed to have lost some of his inspiration. When Browning had difficulty in communicating with an actor after Chaney's death, he reportedly remarked, "I wouldn't have this problem if Chaney was here." [281] Browning's relative ease and brisk pace in directing Chaney's pictures (usually under 30 days) was well known in the industry and in the fan magazines. Commenting on his work habits, Browning once stated:

> I am perhaps one of the few [directors who feel this way] but I never want to make a big spectacular production - or any kind of great picture. I like to make program films and to give enough of myself to them so that they are not just ordinary program films. I try to put something different into each. And in writing my own stories, I believe I am better able to do this than if I were to depend on somebody else's scenario. I am relentless and quick. The sooner I can get a movie out of my mind and megaphone, the better I like it. [282]

Browning's next picture, *The Big City*, marked Lon's first release of 1928 and found the duo returning to the familiar territory of the criminal underworld. The film, which is considered lost, involves two gangs of crooks trying to cheat each other. Ultimately, Chaney's character, Chuck Collins, renounces his criminal life because of the positive influence of Sunshine (Marceline Day), a naive young girl who works in the clothing shop that serves as a front for Collins's illegal activities. Browning's theme of regeneration through love plays an important part in the story, but unfortunately it didn't hold up this time. Critics felt the first half of the film was strong but that it later became "ponderous, slow moving and obvious." [283]

Despite the mixed reviews, the film was well received at the box office, although MPPDA censor notes indicate certain scenes or titles had to be deleted or changed before it could be approved. In Chicago, where Al Capone and gangsters were as common as paper clips, censors insisted that the film could not show any scenes in which a gun was used in a hold-up. Also removed were scenes of a hula dancer wriggling her hips and a scene in which the Arab (John

George) opens a knife with the accompanying title, "The cops can't hear a knife." [284]   New York demanded that the scene in which Sunshine wriggles her hips and asks, "Do you like it Big Boy?" be trimmed, as well as certain "indecent actions of Chuck's lips" (i.e., mouthing swear words). Australia was the toughest, rejecting the film outright in April 1928, on the grounds that it dealt "entirely with criminal life and methods." After cutting certain scenes and titles, the film was approved for distribution in September of that year. MPPDA censor notes concluded:

> Parts of the picture may cause protests. Scenes of
> the Harlem nightclub show rather close views of
> colored chorus doing an enthusiastic black bottom
> [a popular dance of the period]. Several sub-titles are
> rather suggestive. The average metropolitan
> audience is not likely to find any fault with this
> picture as it now stands. But in its general
> distribution it is likely to cause some criticism. [285]

The brisk filming schedule of a Chaney-Browning picture is astounding when one considers that a typical motion picture today takes upward of three months to complete. While making *The Big City*, Browning fell five days behind during the second week of production, yet by the end of the prescribed thirty days, he had caught up and finished on schedule. [286]   Browning's company worked an average of eight to ten hours a day, which makes his schedule even more impressive when compared with the twelve to fourteen hour days (sometimes even longer) needed for current productions.

In 1928 and 1929, Lon Chaney would confound studio executives and the editors of industry trade journals with his increasing popularity in silent films, despite the disquieting presence of sound.

WESTERN UNION
TELEGRAM

WESTERN UNION

Receiver's No.

Check

Time Filed

NEWCOMB CARLTON, PRESIDENT   GEORGE W. E. ATKINS, FIRST VICE-PRESIDENT

Send the following message, subject to the terms
on back hereof, which are hereby agreed to

Nov. 22nd   1923

To BOBBS - MERRILL Co.

Street and No. (or Telephone Number) 18 UNIVERSITY SQUARE

Place INDIANAPOLIS IND.

Please wire me at seventy one fifty two Sunset Boulevard Los Angeles California whether or not the worlds motion picture rights to Leroux's The Phantom of the Opera is available and if so best what price and terms

LON CHANEY

7152 Sunset Blvd

SENDER'S ADDRESS
FOR ANSWER

578574

SENDER'S TELE-
PHONE NUMBER

This telegram indicates Chaney was instrumental in bringing *Phantom of the Opera* to the screen. (Courtesy of the Alfred Grasso Family Collection)

Lon and Dorothy Mackaill in the poorly-received *The Next Corner* (1924).

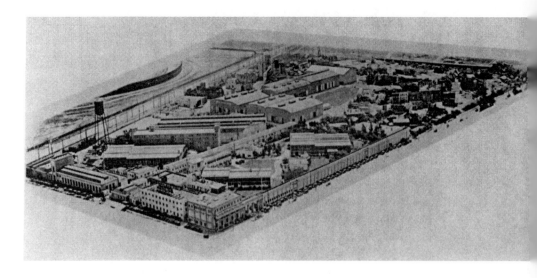

Metro-Goldwyn-Mayer Studios shortly after the 1924 merger.

Lon as the defeated scientist, Paul Beaumont in *He Who Gets Slapped* (1924).

This picture shows a deleted scene from *He Who Gets Slapped*, in which Chaney's character joins the circus as a clown. Left to right: Clyde Cook, Ford Sterling, Lon, and Harvey Clark.

Lon Chaney and George Austin in *The Monster* (1925).

Irving Thalberg, Lon, and Harry Earles during production of *The Unholy Three* (1925).

Unholy Three and its director: Lon, Harry Earles, Tod Browning, and Victor McLaglen.

e deleted scene where Tweedledee (Harry Earles) chokes the Arlington child (Violet Crane) during e Christmas Eve robbery.

This is probably the closest Lon and director Rupert Julian ever got to each other during filming of *Phantom of the Opera* (1925).

One of the many trucks bringing lumber to build the first steel and concrete stage in Hollywood. Note the banner on the side of the truck. Universal didn't miss an opportunity to publicize their up-coming project!

Workers pose in front of the partially-completed stage. Note the set from *The Hunchback of Notre Dame* on the top of the hill in the background.

The scrapped ending where Ledoux (Arthur Edmund Carewe) finds the Phantom lying dead at his organ.

An ad proclaiming the San Francisco engagement of the picture, *Phantom of the Opera*. It was anything but successful.

...ning *Tower of Lies* (1925) in the local mountains of Los Angeles. The round white object above Chaney's ...d was used to diffuse the sunlight. The man to the right, holding what appears to be a large frame, is ...ually holding a reflector board. These boards were made of white cloth or canvas and were used on ...ation to reflect light on the actors' faces.

...n, Tod Browning, Renee Adoree, and Owen Moore on the set of *The Blackbird* (1926). Actress Polly ...ran can be seen at the bar, between Browning and Adoree.

Herald for the picture. These heralds were handed out to the patrons upon their arrival or exit, and announced the upcoming picture.

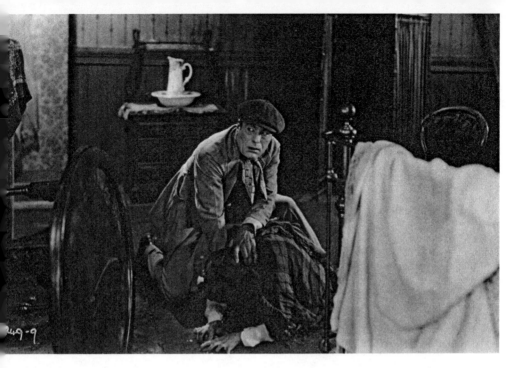

er Browning establishes the mood of the picture with numerous characters of the Limehouse
trict, the scene featured Lon struggling with a man. The robbery goes awry when the Blackbird
ls the victim. No doubt, the censors would have objected vehemently to this sequence, resulting in
deletion.

Little Miss Muffet
Sat in a buffet
Eating dill pickles and pies
Along came a spider
And sat down beside her,
'Twas Lon Chaney in a disguise.

s Lon's popularity grew, cartoonists found ways to illustrate his unique talent. This appeared in one
f the many fan magazines of the late 1920s. (Courtesy of the Lamar D. Tabb Collection)

Chaney and Tod Browning on the set of *The Road to Mandalay* (1926).

Cut from the final release print, the film opened with a young and handsome Joe (Chaney) being comforted by his older brother (Henry B. Walthall), after his wife's death during childbirth.

Chaney's salary at this time was $3,250 a week. This check was obviously an adjustment.

on rests during a break in filming on location at the United States Marine Corps Recruit Depot in San Diego, California. Left to right: Thomas Butler (hand to face), Eleanor Boardman (under parasol), General Smedley D. Butler, Lon, and actor Maurice Kains (in glasses). *Tell it to the Marines* (1927)

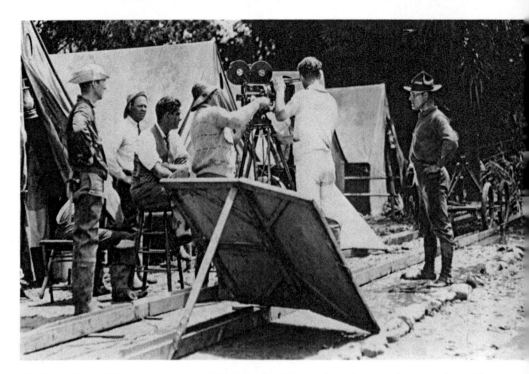

Filming the Tondo Island sequences on M-G-M's backlot. The track on the ground was used to guide the camera dolly (far right). Left to right: assistant director and long-time friend of Chaney, M.K. Wilson (wearing rain hat and white shirt and tie), director George Hill (seated on stool), cameraman Ira Morgan (behind camera), and Lon.

Attempting to give Sgt. O'Hara (Lon) the slip from the train station, "Skeet" Burns (William Haines) is caught. This scene was cut from the final print.

During breaks on location at Iverson Ranch, Lon would sing songs from his musical comedy days. Set musician and long-time friend Jack Feinberg (left) accompanies him.

Originally shot, the bandits are repelled when the Chinese military arrive to help the out-numbere[d] Marines. Cpl. Madden (Eddie Gribbon, center) and "Skeet" Burns (William Haines, left) can be seen helpin[g] a wounded Sgt. O'Hara (Lon, blood streaming from head and clutching shoulder). This scene was deleted i[n] favor of one in which the Marines fight off the bandits with the help of Marine fighter planes.

An unidentified theatre in America prior to a matinee. No doubt, most of these boys (and probabl[y] some girls!) are among the legion of Lon's admirers. A poster for *Mr. Wu* can be briefly glimpse[d] along the wall, next to the marquee.

ude King (left), Ludwig Lawrence (M-G-M's manager of French office; left, standing), Lon (in make-
for early scenes as Grandfather Wu), director William Nigh (right, standing), and Arthur Loew
G-M's general manager, seated) on the set of *Mr. Wu* (1927).

n discusses a scene with director Benjamin Christensen on the set of *Mockery* (1927). Actor
rles Puffy (right) looks on.

While many believe *London After Midnight* was a horror film, it was actually promoted as a mystery thriller, as evidenced in this herald.

Director Benjamin Christensen, cameraman Merritt Gerstad, and Lon. Note the difference between the make-up and Lon's actual skintone on his arms.

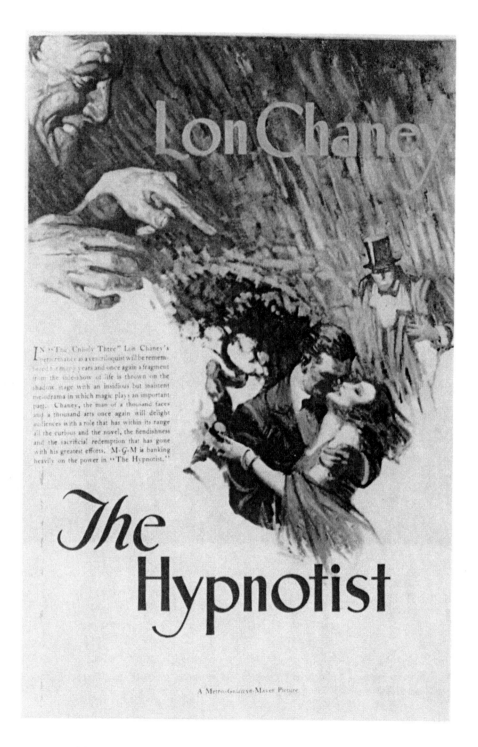

An ad from M-G-M's exhibitors book for the 1927-28 season, when *London After Midnight* was originally called *The Hypnotist*.

Notice how the ad claims no one shall be admitted during the last 15 minutes of the picture. This was done to build up the audience's curiosity for the film.

Tod Browning, Lon, and scenarist Waldemar Young on the set of *The Big City* (1928).

The Actor's Actor

(1928 - 1930)

Lon and Hazel attend the première of a picture at Grauman's Chinese Theatre with their close friends, William and Mabel Dunphy.

Theatre exhibitors voted Lon Chaney the most popular male star at the box office in 1928 and 1929. The fact that he was given this honor in 1929, when a large percentage of films were either all talking or part talking, is an indication of Chaney's star power and appeal at a time when silent pictures were quickly becoming extinct. Lon's popularity was something of a phenomenon. He lacked the polished good looks which appealed to female movie fans, and most of his characters were not the type one would equate with a huge box office draw. What Chaney had was a distinct talent and magnetic charisma that enveloped moviegoers and critics alike. It was this uniqueness that made him stand out from the crowd of ordinary performers. The tragic yet heroic characters he portrayed not only elicited sympathy from his fans, but also reminded them of the strict moral code maintained by their families during this period of jazz babies. There was something about Chaney's characters, no matter how tough or grotesque they appeared, that imbued his audiences with a certain sense of loyalty; and even though he didn't win the girl's heart, the audience wanted to see how Lon would handle the outcome. No doubt his films probably helped to ease the pain of many a boy's broken heart; young men who could easily relate to Chaney's character losing the girl he loves. Interestingly, at least one of his fans, Patricia Ward from Tulsa, Oklahoma, wrote the following to one of the fan magazines:

A Thousand Faces

> Why not change the tables regarding Lon Chaney
> and have him win the girl in the picture? Surely
> among all the story writers you could find one who
> could write such a play for our Lon Chaney. His
> stories are too much alike.... If you could just sit in
> the many different audiences and hear the remarks,
> such as "I surely hope he wins the girl—he
> deserves to," I feel sure you would give him fair
> play. [287]

Another female Chaney fan, Mettie E. Bailey, had quite the opposing opinion, stating, "A play with a romantic ending for Lon Chaney would be a deplorable thing, from my point of view. Why change an unequaled character actor into an ordinary lover?" [288] Despite the repetitious plots of unrequited love, Chaney's fans remained loyal. Whether in a role with extensive make-up or playing it "straight," Chaney's talent is what brought his numerous fans back to the box office again and again. This talent was not lost on many of his admirers, including one George Devon, who voiced his opinion in the letters section of *Photoplay* magazine:

> There have been so many quips current concerning
> Lon Chaney-the "don't-step-on-the-spider kind"—the
> flip references to the "man of a thousand faces,"
> that there is a tendency to think of him merely as a
> master of the make-up box, and of the weird
> terrifying features which putty and distortion can
> create. The main thing about him is being
> overlooked;—that, aside from being top of his class
> in visualizing his character, he is an artist. Chaney
> can put life and sympathy and understanding
> behind even the most gruesome features. [289]

Once again the outspoken editor of *Film Spectator* dissected Chaney's popularity. This commentary was published during the time when most of Hollywood's stars were daring to speak before a microphone — that is — most stars except Chaney.

At a luncheon table the other day some executives
discussed Lon Chaney's box-office standing. They
tried to account for it. It was agreed that he lacks
the good looks of Buddy Rogers, the allure of Dick
Barthelmess, the insinuating grace of Adolph
Menjou, the vitality of George Bancroft, the general
impressiveness of Emil Jannings and the matchless
profile of Jack Barrymore. Notwithstanding these
drawbacks, his pictures are tremendous money
makers. There were five executives in the group,
and five weighty and conclusive reasons were given
for Lon's popularity. None of the pronouncements
contained any reference to Chaney's acting ability,
yet it is this ability, and nothing else, that has made
him such a strong box-office magnet. All of his
pictures are not good, but all of his performances
are. There never has been a time since the Greeks
developed stage technique that audiences have not
wanted acting. They get it in only a few motion
pictures, and among these few are numbered those
in which Chaney has the leading parts. Lon Chaney
is lucky in that he is one of the few really good
actors in Hollywood who have passed the stage of
adolescence and still are being given opportunities
to act on the screen. [290]

Another explanation for Chaney's success is the efforts of
Irving Thalberg. His shrewd moves placed the actor in the right
films, and he used the studio's tremendous publicity machine to
publicize Chaney's talents. Thalberg carefully watched the material
the studio chose for all of its stars, which explains their subsequent
popularity at the box office. Unlike other celebrities, Lon Chaney
did not behave like a typical movie star. He refused to grant many
interviews and rarely signed autographs or attended movie
premières. Some of this can be attributed to his reticent attitude, but
a good deal of it was Chaney's shrewd business sense. The public
wanted Chaney, and if he carefully apportioned his appearances

A Thousand Faces

and interviews, he would be in greater demand; hence, his films would be even more successful. In the 1925 M-G-M studio tour, he appears with his back to the camera as it pans across the long row of stars. At just the right moment, Lon quickly turns to face the camera (sporting eyeglasses), just long enough for the audience to get a glimpse of him. He said that that brief appearance garnered him more publicity than if he had appeared in a close-up. [291] Many stars endorsed products or allowed their likenesses to appear in conjunction with commercial products, although not to the degree of today's celebrities; but Lon flatly refused to jump on that bandwagon. He once was asked by M-G-M's publicity department to fill out a questionnaire, which included an inquiry as to what kind of breakfast he ate. He replied, "What of it? I can just hear them saying 'Eat Lon Chaney's favorite cereal and look like the Hunchback of Notre Dame.'" [292]

Despite his success and the wealth that came with it, Lon refused to become caught up with the material trappings of stardom. Unlike most stars, who lived in palatial estates, the Chaneys lived in a modest English Tudor home in Beverly Hills. Whereas most stars employed a large number of servants, there were only two in the Chaney household: Viola, the housekeeper, and John Jeske, the family chauffeur and one of Lon's closest companions. Lon and Hazel never traveled to Europe, preferring to stay within the United States. For the most part, their trips took them to Hazel's hometown of San Francisco, to Lon's hometown of Colorado Springs, or to see other relatives, such as Lon's cousin Hugh Harbert in Seattle, Washington. One area Lon frequently visited was the eastern Sierra Nevada, where he would camp and fish for weeks on end and where he eventually built a cabin.

Lon's reluctance to appear at movie premières, sign autographs or grant interviews, not to mention playing offbeat characters, has provided fodder over the years for writers who have attempted to

234

paint a picture of him as a morose and tortured artist. Nothing could have been further from the truth. Lon Chaney was considered a warm and friendly man by those who knew him, but he was not outwardly sociable. He once was quoted as saying, "I do my own work and mind my own business." [293] Willard Sheldon recalls that Lon never discussed his personal feelings about any other performer or director, even remaining silent on the political issues of the day. [294] His reclusive attitude aside, he was known to be very generous to studio personnel with both his time and money. He never forgot the studio guards, gardeners, and janitors, nor the office workers at Christmas. [295] He was very well-liked by studio employees and extra players, who were not afraid to greet him on a first-name basis. He was their champion. No other star in Hollywood would stand up to the studio powers as Chaney did. On the set of a Lon Chaney film, there were always plenty of benches so that the extras would have places to sit, and he would quit work at five o'clock (unless working nights) so that he and the crew could enjoy evenings at home with their families. [296] Between scenes, he would sit by himself or wander around the stage watching other companies working, and occasionally he conversed with crew members. [297] Actress Penny Singleton, who is best remembered for her work in the *Blondie* films, recalled her first meeting with Chaney:

> I had been working on one of the stages, and during a break I went outside to sit on a bench. There was this man sitting on the bench who I thought was a crew member. I started a conversation with him and he related to me that he worked in pictures, but I never got his name. The next day I passed him on the lot and we exchanged greetings. A few days later, a studio publicist took me onto the stage where Lon Chaney was making a picture. That's when I learned that the man on the bench was Lon Chaney! [298]

A Thousand Faces

Lon was always extremely helpful to younger actors and would often offer words of encouragement to a struggling newcomer. He became very uncomfortable and somewhat gruff when offered profuse thanks for his generosity, which was his way of covering his sentimental feelings. One veteran actor who sought Chaney's advice was actor Harry Carey. His son, Harry Carey, Jr., a well-known actor in his own right, recalled the incident:

> My dad had finished *Trader Horn* and when the studio looked at it, they realized they didn't have enough of a story. So they wanted my dad to come back and do additional scenes at the same salary. Chaney told him he should take advantage of the situation and ask for more money, since they couldn't very well replace him. But, my dad didn't take his advice and decided to settle for his original salary. [299]

Lon Chaney's generosity even extended to five-year-old Malcom Sabiston, who was appearing in the *Big Boy* Educational Comedy series:

> My family lived across the street from his [Chaney's] father and step-mother, and most of the kids in the neighborhood stayed away from them because they were deaf. Back then we weren't aware of this affliction and I was too young to pay much attention, so I wasn't afraid of them. I used to visit her [Cora Chaney] a lot and she'd bake me cookies. At some point later when I was working, Lon came over to the studio. I don't know whether he came over to see me personally or not, but the only reason I can think of why he bothered to visit was because I was kind to his step-mother.
>
> He'd put me on his lap and spoke very softly to me. He was very gentle, and talk about a man of a

236

thousand faces! He could make faces without make-up! He'd be talking with me and all of a sudden he'd make this face and I'd laugh. Then he'd do more and I'd keep laughing. The day he came to visit I had a scene where I was supposed to pull a hat over the eyes of the wise-guy kid and wink at this girl I liked. The only problem was, I couldn't wink! Everyone, including director Charles Lamont, tried to coach me with no success. Then Lon pulled me aside and told me to close both eyes and then slowly open one. Because of his help, they were able to get the shot. [300]

For all his kindness, Chaney could be equally unforgiving, as author and scenarist William Dudley Pelley found out. His writing was taking a back seat to his attending various Hollywood social functions and, at the same time, Pelley was expressing publicly his growing anti-Semitic feelings. Lon was quick to make his opinions known. This became abundantly clear to Pelley one day when he found himself stranded in Beverly Hills without any cash. He walked over to Lon's home in hopes of getting enough money to take the trolley back to Hollywood. Lon was alone at the house, finishing a cold roast with a loaf of Italian bread and a glass of wine. They exchanged greetings as Lon finished his meal, then glanced at his watch and remarked that he had an appointment. Pelley was hurt when Lon told him frankly, "It'd be a danged good thing, Bill, if you sorta got wise to yourself." After that exchange, Pelley never bothered Chaney for the trolley fare, feeling that he'd rather walk all the way to San Francisco than ask him for a helping hand. "Somehow he was not the Lon whom I had known. His address was perfunctory," he later wrote. [301] Analyzing the reasons behind Chaney's brusque attitude, Pelley claimed that

I knew Lon was piqued for a handful of reasons. I had failed to click with the Jew crowd because I

> would not let them bulldoze me at Metro-Goldwyn-
> Mayer's where he had a contract at three thousand
> a week. He was likewise piqued that I played with
> the Hollywood screen crowd—forgetting that the
> situation with my work was different than his, that I
> had to do it to stand in with directors. Finally, he
> had previously had some tiff with Eddie Eckels. He
> was rugged and direct, this fellow Chaney, even if
> he did put birdies back in nests. If you failed to
> measure up, he contrived to let you know. [302]

Shortly after this incident, Pelley had his next-to-last meeting with Lon on the M-G-M lot. Pelley told Lon he had given up the social life of Hollywood to settle down and simply write. "Chaney grinned broadly. He reached his hand across and squeezed my leg above the knee. 'Smart fella' was his comment. He was the old Chaney whom I had known the previous six years," the writer remembered. [303]

Aside from his work, Chaney's family was most important to him. According to Alfred Grasso, one of Lon's joys was to pick out Christmas gifts for each relative personally and hand them out himself. The holiday season was a big event for the Chaneys, with Hazel and Lon's relatives gathered at their home for dinner. [304] Hazel recalled how grateful Lon was for his success and the rewards it had brought:

> He was not earning enough to own an automobile
> [in the early days], so when Universal moved from
> Hollywood to Universal City, he used to take the
> street car to Cahuenga Boulevard and from there
> beg rides with the directors or others driving out to
> the studio. There were no buses running to
> Universal City at the time. Later on in years, when
> he was earning enough money to own a Lincoln

car, he would often drive past the little house
where we had lived when we were first married
and say, "Do you remember how we lived here and
wish we had cars like other people? God sure has
been good to me." [305]

Challenging roles that run the spectrum of human emotions are an actor's passion; Hamlet, Cyrano de Bergerac and Willie Lohman are a few that come to mind. A clown who masks his own personal unhappiness while making others laugh is another that can provide an actor the opportunity to carry out an emotional whirlwind performance. This is the role Chaney enthusiastically played in *Laugh, Clown, Laugh.* It had been a popular play on Broadway years earlier, with Lionel Barrymore playing the clown who endured a hopeless love. M-G-M had been aware of the play as early as 1925, when a studio reader's report noted:

It has everything that would go to make a successful
picture for Mr. Lon Chaney, if sufficient time
elapses between the release of *He Who Gets
Slapped* and this picture, so the public would not
be struck with the similarity of the pictures. They
are similar, but to my mind this play is better than
He Who Gets Slapped. [306]

In this film, Chaney plays Tito, a carefree clown who, with his partner Simon (Bernard Seigel), travels the Italian countryside performing in small villages. During their travels, Tito finds a little girl who was abandoned by her family. Despite the objections of his partner, Tito adopts the girl and raises her as his own child. When Simonetta (Loretta Young) grows into adulthood, Tito realizes that his parental affection for the girl has blossomed into a romantic love. His hopeless desire culminates while seeking medical treatment for his uncontrollable melancholy. In this scene, Chaney displays remarkable emotional power in attempting to suppress his despondency while describing his dilemma. Even though this is a silent picture, Chaney's emotional display transcends the silence as he finally bursts into tears. The doctor points to a poster outside his office advertising Flick the Clown and urges Tito to go see the harlequin, for he surely will lift his spirits. Tito shakes his head solemnly, stating, "I am Flick." Lon's somber expression helps to make this moment more dramatic and also emphasizes a poignant scene later in the film. In that scene, believing Simonetta's lover, Luigi (Nils Asther), has stepped aside so that he may claim the girl as his own, Tito is extraordinarily happy while performing in front of the audience.

Bounding off the stage, he is crushed to find Simonetta and Luigi in a romantic embrace. Chaney's entire body appears to collapse from within, suggesting his character's emotional devastation. The crowd gives Tito a standing ovation, but he is completely oblivious to their cheers. Simon quickly realizes the situation and tries to convince Tito that he must take a bow. But the pain of his loss is too much for him to bear and the clown refuses, until Simon reminds him that Flick belongs to the audience and they must have their fun, regardless of Tito's feelings. Pushed onto the stage, Tito makes a dramatic transformation into the lovable clown. Simon watches his partner while standing in the wings. "Laugh, Clown, Laugh" he says, "even though your heart is breaking." Tito continues clowning, but when the curtain closes, he collapses into Simon's arms. Lon plays this emotionally charged moment with just the right amount of pathos, avoiding the obvious risk of overplaying the scene and hitting just the right dramatic chord.

Unfortunately, in existing prints of *Laugh, Clown, Laugh*, one reel is missing and several scenes appear to be incomplete. Despite the irregular tempo caused by the missing footage, the film remains satisfying and involving and Lon provides a moving performance as the tragic Tito. However, Loretta Young fails to supply Chaney with strong support in her role as Simonetta. This could have been because of her strained relationship with director Herbert Brenon. Miss Young became the object of director Herbert Brenon's tirades, causing her a tremendous amount of anxiety and ultimately affecting her performance. Interestingly, Brenon would not lash out at Miss Young when Lon was present. One day Chaney happened to walk onto the set and witnessed Brenon berating the young actress in front of the crew. From that point on, even when his presence wasn't required, Lon remained on the stage, and Brenon's outbursts against Miss Young ceased. [307] The director was not very popular with the film crew either, as Willard Sheldon recalled:

> I did not particularly care for Brenon. He was not a nice man. He was rough and gruff and would hardly talk to anybody. He'd talk to Jimmy [cameraman James Wong Howe] and Lon, and that was about it. It was hard to say if Lon liked Brenon. I never saw an argument between them. They'd come in and rehearse, occasionally doing a scene many, many times, which would annoy Lon.

> We'd usually have a 9 o'clock shooting call and Brenon would give them [the cameraman and assistant director] the set-up. And while they were lighting the set, he'd go over the scenes with the actors. Then it was break off time. Everybody had to leave the stage. There would be a couple of worklights on the set and he would go through the action on every scene he had in that particular set-up—without the actors, just himself. Ray Lissner [the assistant director] use to see that the stage was completely empty, but on two or three occasions I climbed the ladder and got up on the catwalk [above the set] and just sat and watched him. I'd probably been fired if he caught me.

A Thousand Faces

> Lon did most of his own stunts for the "slide for life"
> act. There was a stunt man on the set, but he didn't
> do much. He and Jimmy [Wong Howe] were very
> good friends. When he wasn't working, Lon was
> standing around the camera a lot, watching. [308]

Both the critics and public responded positively to the picture, making it Lon's second highest grossing M-G-M film. [309] This popularity was enhanced by the release of the title theme song, which became one of 1928's popular hits. *Laugh, Clown, Laugh* encountered few problems with the censors at the MPPDA until it came to New York. There, the title "You can fish in the gutter for harlots with pearls, but you can't buy Simonetta" was ordered cut. Also deleted were any shots showing Luigi kissing Simonetta in a sensuous manner. The censors claimed the cuts were necessary because such scenes "will tend to corrupt morals." The MPPDA noted in their summary:

> Although the story is in no way very new, it benefits
> by a certain originality of treatment and sincerity in
> the acting. The direction is smooth and imaginative,
> the camera work splendid. The picture seemed to
> take well with the audience, there being quite a bit
> of applause at its conclusion. [310]

The studio filmed an alternative happy ending to the film, as they had done with *The Crowd*. The happy ending allowed theatre owners to choose which version they wanted to present. The alternative ending begins after Tito deliberately falls from his wire act, and Simon calls for a doctor. As Simon holds the fallen clown, Tito tells him that he fell because he didn't want to ruin Simonetta's happiness with his tears. Some children have managed to sneak into the theatre, and when they see Tito lying on the floor, they think he is only pretending to be hurt and so they begin to laugh. When

Simonetta and Luigi enter the theatre, Tito explains that he didn't want her happiness sacrificed on his account. As they help Tito into a chair, she tells him they could never be happy if he died. Tito then assures everyone he'll be fine, and that his happiness will come from watching Simonetta and Luigi marry. Simon replies, "That's the spirit! Laugh, Clown, Laugh!" Tito then smiles at the young couple, who begin to laugh. Tito joins in the laughter. The camera moves in for a tight close-up of the clown laughing and fades out. [311] This was certainly a more uplifting ending than the somber conclusion found in the existing print, in which Tito dies in Simon's arms after his fall.

Since the beginning of motion pictures, criminals have occupied a prominent place in film stories. Whether a picture was comedic or dramatic, the criminal served as the antagonist who imposed his evil will until he met his demise in the final reel. The public seemed to be fascinated with the real and mythical accounts of the gangland activities of such infamous criminals as Al Capone. Hollywood was quick to capitalize on this fascination by making numerous films on the subject, including Josef von Sternberg's *Underworld* (1928). [312] Because of *Underworld*'s success, Hollywood producers began to develop more gangster-themed pictures, and M-G-M was no different. A year earlier, the studio had presented *Twelve Miles Out*, featuring their leading romantic star John Gilbert in a drama about rum-runners and Prohibition agents.

When Gilbert's film proved popular at the box office, Thalberg wanted to star Chaney in a gangster story, this time, with the actor appearing, on the side of law and order. The only problem was a clause in Chaney's contract stating that he would make no more than four pictures per contract year. Lon had recently finished his fourth film under the current option of his 1926 contract. M-G-M was so eager to cash in on the current furor of gangster films, however, that they brokered a special deal with Lon that allowed him to waive the clause in his contract and make a fifth picture. In exchange for waiving the clause, Lon received a $25,000 bonus, in addition to his regular weekly salary of $3,500. [313]

Despite a missing reel and a few scenes that exhibit signs of nitrate decomposition, *While the City Sleeps* is one of Chaney's finest pictures. He gives a flawless performance as Dan, a detective of the old school who will stop at nothing to get his man. [314] His devotion to duty has only one distraction: Myrtle (Anita Page), a naive flapper whom Dan loves. Like most of Chaney's characters, Dan's love for the girl is one-sided, and the twenty-plus years' age difference between the two characters is very obvious. But Lon's earnest performance of his character pursuing Myrtle carries the audience into a willing suspension of belief for this part of the storyline. Dan's tenderness toward Myrtle is evident when he tells her the police have an idea where Skeeter (Wheeler Oakman), the gangster who tried to kill her, is hiding.

Since the attempt on her life, Myrtle has been staying at Dan's place, and she has brought a warm and orderly quality to his bachelor apartment. As she places a flower in his coat lapel, Dan is lost in his thoughts. Myrtle remarks that he has been wonderful to her and she kisses him on the cheek. This gesture gives Dan the courage to ask for her hand in marriage. She is torn between her love for her boyfriend, Marty (Carroll Nye), and her gratitude to Dan for saving her life. While Dan looks on hopefully, Myrtle's back is to him, allowing the audience to see that her emotions are divided. She reluctantly agrees to accept his proposal. Beaming with happiness, Dan gently and quickly kisses her. Myrtle forces a smile, telegraphing to the audience the idea that Dan's happiness will be short-lived.

On the job, Dan is a complete professional. He is not above forcing a confession from a known gangster by using his fists, nor is he afraid to intimidate a young man with threats of prison to keep him from associating with gangsters. Yet for all his tenacity, Dan complains daily of how police work isn't what it used to be and threatens to quit, a statement to which his fellow officers give little credence. Chaney once said that life is like that, the things you are most derogatory about are the things you like the best. [315] His complaints aside, Dan remains loyal to his profession. Knowing that Skeeter and his gang are responsible for a murder and robbery at a jewelry store, he doggedly follows their trail. When Dan shows up at the funeral parlor Skeeter uses as a front for his illegal ventures, the gangster places one of his men in a closet with orders to kill the detective should he try to arrest them. Dan walks in on the group nonchalantly, appearing to suspect nothing out of the ordinary. As he speaks to Skeeter, Dan attempts to open the coffin in which the criminals have hastily stashed their weapons. Skeeter steers Dan away from the coffin by introducing him to his partner, and the detective calmly walks over to him, keeping his eye on the group, and seemingly unaware of the gunman in the closet behind him. But with a quick gesture, Dan pulls a high-backed chair in front of him for cover and draws his pistol. He orders the man in the closet to surrender his weapon and uses the telephone to call for reinforcements, all the while holding the group of seven men at bay.

Lon's portrayal of a detective at work is thoroughly convincing, from giving a quick frisk to a suspect to examining a door for fingerprints. It is obvious this was a part the actor thoroughly enjoyed. The role even allowed him to inject light comedy into his performance, particularly in the scene in which Dan visits Myrtle's home. He admonishes her because of her skimpy "flapper" wardrobe, pointing to a childhood photo and remarking, "You wore more clothes when you were twelve." She scoffs at his comment, telling him he is too old fashioned, and gets a current magazine to prove her point. Sitting next to Dan, she shows him some of the latest styles. He, in turn, finds pictures of some more conservative clothes. As Myrtle looks at his choices, she leans back in his arms and within a few moments Dan finds himself lost in a dream, enjoying the closeness of the girl he loves. Just as quickly, he remembers himself, wipes his face with his hands and pounds the arm of the chair as he fights his desire. He slowly pushes the unsuspecting Myrtle away, remarking that he has to leave. When she innocently wraps her arms around his neck, it is all he can do to push her away and control himself.

The film was released as a silent picture with a synchronized musical score and accompanying sound effects for theaters equipped with the new sound systems. Many studios were injecting silent films with partial dialogue sequences, and M-G-M was no different. A dialogue scene was written for the conclusion of *While the City Sleeps*, when Dan reunites Marty and Myrtle in his apartment and sends them off to the marriage license bureau, just as Mrs. McGinnis (Polly Moran), his landlady, enters. The landlady is happy to learn of the couple's impending marriage because she has eyes for Dan, herself. Dan puts his arm around her shoulder. She remarks that he has such a soothing way, just like her late husband — Mrs. McGinnis's signature line throughout the movie — but Dan interrupts her and finishes her sentence before walking out as the film ends. [316]

The studio may have hoped to inject this dialogue sequence into the film, but Chaney undoubtedly would have refused. His contract did not specify that he would make talking pictures (something Lon would point out to the studio a year later when they were working on dialogue scenes for *The Bugle Sounds*). [317] Another reason he may have resisted appearing in this talking sequence was that he did not want to jeopardize his box office appeal. Many actors felt sound pictures were only a passing fad, and the equipment used to record sound at this time was imperfect.

It is interesting that there were two versions released of *While the City Sleeps*: one silent and the other accompanied by synchronized music and sound effects. In the silent version, the picture opens with numerous shots of New York City, and cuts to a parade of police officers on foot and on horseback. It then refers to the title, "And there is another kind of police...unknown to the public they protect, but hated and feared by The Underworld....the Plain Clothes Men." The picture then cuts to a close shot of a man's feet as he moves down a sidewalk before the camera pans up to reveal him as Dan Coghlan. As he starts to cross the street, Dan is almost hit by a truck. When the driver makes a rude comment, Dan flashes his badge and the driver quickly apologizes. The scene then fades to Dan breaking up a fight between a husband and wife and giving a warning to an Italian fruit peddler. As he takes an apple from the peddler's cart, Dan observes some children scattering a Chinese man's laundry basket. He chases after them, and the scene once again fades to a shot of Dan's feet as he runs down the street, then dissolves to Dan—still with the feet—slowly walking up some steps into the police headquarters hallway. There he finds a custodian placing a new name on the plaque of fallen officers. [318]

In the sound version, the opening remains the same up through the title referring to the Plain Clothes Men. The scenes of Dan confronting the truck driver, the fighting couple, the fruit peddler, and the Chinese laundry scamps are deleted. Instead, the film cuts to a large room of detectives gathering in front of a stage with bright lights that, we learn from a title card, is the "Shadow Box," where officers can observe suspects without being seen. As various suspects, including Skeeter, are questioned, the scene dissolves to Dan interrogating Skeeter in a private room. Dan is about to force the answer out of the criminal when he is interrupted by the chief of detectives, who has to release Skeeter for lack of evidence. As Dan bemoans the untimely arrival of his boss, the scene dissolves to a title card that reads: "Day in and out....they never stop. It takes a lot of heart to be a plain clothes man...and a lot of feet, too." From there the scene picks up with Dan's entrance into police headquarters, and watching the new name being added to the plaque. [319] In the silent version, the "Shadow Box" scene takes place after Dan arrests Skeeter and his gang at the funeral parlor.

The surviving print of *While the City Sleeps* is the sound version, which is missing reel six, which contained the sequence of Dan going to the criminals' hideout to find Skeeter. While his gang keeps Dan occupied, Skeeter makes a hasty escape and attempts to kill Myrtle. However, when the gangster shows up at her front door, she recognizes his voice and seeks refuge in Dan's apartment, much to the disapproval of Dan's landlady, Mrs. McGinnis. When Dan learns of Skeeter's murder attempt, he calls for extra officers to stand guard outside his apartment. Mrs. McGinnis is disturbed that the girl is staying in the same apartment with Dan, but he assures her he will be sleeping on the couch. After she leaves, Dan glances outside his window and sees an officer standing guard. He looks at his front door and slowly opens it. Finding Mrs. McGinnis eavesdropping, he briskly orders her away. A title card indicates a week has passed while the dragnet for Skeeter continues, and the scene fades in on Dan's apartment. The existing print then picks up the action, showing that Myrtle has brought a semblance of order to the apartment. Dan watches her affectionately as she attends to household chores. As she places some flowers in a vase, Dan approaches her with the intention of proposing marriage.

While the City Sleeps was shot on a brisk 28-day schedule and encountered very few problems during production. While Lon claimed he never worried about the scripts the studio handed him, an interesting note is found in the film's daily production report for May 1. The set call for that day was 12:30 p.m., but the company was delayed for twenty minutes because Lon and director Jack Conway were "talking over the story in Conway's office." [320] This notation not only appears to contradict Lon's statement, but also illustrates his willingness to become actively involved in solving script problems.

The film interjects many moments of light comedy, particularly in the scenes with Polly Moran as Dan's Irish landlady, which help the pacing of the picture. While the lightheartedness between her and Chaney is not of the belly-laugh variety, it does provide much-needed humor and comic relief. It's interesting to speculate what kind of a team these two performers might have made had they been featured in the type of material given to Wallace Beery and Marie Dressler a few years later.

The fingerprinting of suspects, use of the "shadow box," machine guns, and tear gas bombs all provided audiences with an insight into police work, similar to what Jack Webb would present years later in his "Dragnet" and "Adam-12" television series. One of the more unusual techniques used by detectives to get information is illustrated when Skeeter and his gang are at the funeral parlor discussing their plot to kill Myrtle's boyfriend. As they leave to carry out their plan, one of the gangsters puts a small reserved tag on a coffin, remarking that it's for the boy's future use. A few seconds later, Dan opens the coffin and climbs out!

Jack Conway, who was one of Chaney's better directors, makes effective use of the camera by allowing it to flow and move with the action, further helping the tempo of the picture. Chaney was given solid support from the rest of the cast, including his female co-star, Anita Page, but it is Lon's performance that dominates this film and obviously both the public and critics agreed. It was his fourth-highest grossing M-G-M picture and proved that Chaney's popularity was not based upon unique make-ups or disfigured bodies. [321]

After the completion of *While the City Sleeps*, Lon and his wife left for a ten-day vacation in New York City. During their visit, the Chaneys caught several Broadway shows and visited with Mayor Jimmy Walker. Lon spent one day as a typical tourist, taking along his 16mm Filmo camera to photograph the various sights, including Wall Street, old Trinity Church, and the New York skyline from the

A Thousand Faces

Manhattan Bridge. When Lon arrived at City Hall to meet Mayor Walker, a large crowd assembled outside as word spread of his appearance. When he left the building, the crowd was remarkably restrained, unlike the usual New York crowd that would try to make personal contact with a celebrity Only a few bold newsboys attempted to be familiar with the actor. As his car pulled away, they led a cheer and Lon stood up in his car and filmed the crowd. [322]

Lon Chaney was probably the most famous amateur photographer of his time. Fan magazines have documented how Lon took full advantage of his position to photograph celebrities who visited the famous M-G-M studios. Amateur home movies were just beginning to catch on; but, unlike the average amateur photographer, Lon had the distinct advantage of being able to have his film developed and printed at the studio, which enabled him to achieve fade-outs and other professional touches not readily available to the public. Lon amassed a considerable amount of footage, not only of visiting dignitaries but also of wildlife shot on his many camping expeditions. He once boasted that "the best thing I do is thread my camera on horseback." [323]

Lon and Hazel made a one-night stop in his hometown of Colorado Springs before returning to Los Angeles. In typical fashion, he refused to pose for photographers at the train station, but they defiantly snapped shots of the reclusive star anyway. Lon returned to work almost immediately upon his return. An interoffice memo addressed to Thalberg indicated that the studio wanted to begin a new production by late May, noting, "I understand that Browning is practically ready to start." [324] Because of the special agreement with Lon for *While the City Sleeps*, M-G-M was obliged to delay the start of *West of Zanzibar* until June 25. [325] It was Chaney's ninth picture with Tod Browning and, with the exception of *The Unknown*, probably their best film. Unlike their previous collaborations, *West of Zanzibar* was not based on an idea or story by Browning but from the stage play *Kongo*. But like the former characters Browning had created for him, Chaney portrays an individual who is driven by unfortunate circumstances to seek revenge upon those who have wronged him.

Phroso is a magician and a loving husband who adores his wife, Anna (Jacqueline Daly). But these admirable qualities merely set the stage for the character's emotional downfall, for he soon learns that his wife has abandoned him for her lover, Crane (Lionel Barrymore). Phroso cannot accept his wife's rejection. Even after suffering a horrendous fall at the hands of Crane, he pleads for her return. The accident leaves Phroso crippled, and a year later, when he receives word of Anna's return, he hurries to meet her, pulling himself along the street on a wheeled platform. As he crawls into the church where Anna has gone, he finds her lying dead on the floor in front of a statue of the Madonna. Not far from his wife's body sits a baby girl. As Phroso slowly approaches Anna's body, his expression is merciful and he gently takes her hand, saying he never followed her because he thought she loved Crane. Glancing at the religious statue and then at the baby girl, his demeanor slowly changes to revulsion as he swears revenge upon the man who ruined his life.

Phroso's hatred for Crane and for the girl he believes to be Crane's daughter stirs his thirst for revenge. He follows his enemy to Africa, but not before arranging to have the girl, Maizie (Mary Nolan), raised in one of the lowest dives in Zanzibar. When Maizie reaches the age of eighteen, Phroso's plan for revenge is put into effect. He uses his old magic tricks to fool the local natives so that they will carry out his commands. The natives' strange custom of cremating either a wife or first-born daughter along with a deceased man becomes part of Phroso's monstrous plan of revenge. When Crane is summoned to his compound, Phroso takes vicious delight in displaying Maizie to him. She has become a physical and mental wreck. Phroso's evil exhilaration grows as he tells how Maizie was brought up, and finally reveals that the girl is Crane's child by Anna. Crane is dumbstruck, collapsing into a chair and burying his face in his hands. His body convulses in spasms and, because his face is hidden, Phroso believes he is crying. Suddenly, Crane looks up; he is hysterically laughing. Phroso's maniacal expression slowly fades as he watches his adversary's composure change, and Chaney's face registers the slow realization that his plan has failed. As Crane explains that Anna left him when she learned he had caused Phroso's paralysis, Chaney's expression changes from disbelief to acceptance and finally to a tear-filled plea for help from God. Realizing that he is responsible for ruining his own daughter's life, tears well up in his eyes as he tries to suppress his outburst. His emotions build and he desperately claws at his throat, ultimately emitting a tragic wail. The impact of this scene and Chaney's performance is further heightened by a reaction shot of Babe (Kalla Pasha), one of Phroso's henchmen, who walks onto the set and freezes when he sees Phroso crying.

When we first see Phroso as a cripple, he pulls himself along on a wheeled platform with his useless legs doubled up underneath him. Crawling into the church, he pulls himself along much like a lizard, placing his hands in front of him in a slow, deliberate way, dragging his body and legs behind him like a tail. When we see him in Africa, sitting in a wheelchair, his tattered costume and slumped posture enhance the effect of his paralysis. His pants are torn at the cuffs, which gives his lower legs a thinner appearance, as if the muscles have deteriorated. His shoes are scuffed and worn on one side. Chaney does not sit erect in the wheelchair but slouches, his body like that of many wheelchair-bound paraplegics, a lazy S, his lower half apparently completely nonfunctional. Plotting his revenge, Phroso seems void of any sense of compassion, yet Chaney injects a sliver of humanity into this wreck. As the natives carry out his orders, he tenderly holds a chimpanzee in his arms, much as a father would lovingly embrace his child. By using these gestures, Chaney illustrates his philosophy that no matter how vile a personality, everyone has some innate goodness. It also helps the audience accept the scene later when he learns Maizie's true identity and holds her in his arms after she has fainted, gently stroking her hair. This scene would have rung false had Chaney not displayed some earlier humanity in his character.

Browning employs his fooling-the-suckers theme to its most compelling degree in this picture. *West of Zanzibar* opens the film with the title "Ashes to Ashes! Dust to Dust!", and the viewer is greeted with the sight of an upright coffin. As Chaney (wearing a top hat and with his back to camera) removes the upper portion of the box and steps out of frame, we see a skeleton. Returning, Chaney reacts to the skeleton by doing a double-take and slowly turns toward the camera. The camera dissolves to a wider shot, and we see that he is a magician in the middle of a stage performance. [326] The skeleton in the coffin plays an important part in the storyline; it changes into Chaney's beautiful wife during the act by means of a revolving backside in the coffin. Browning shows this transformation in a medium shot. The revolving backside will be used later in the film as part of Maizie's escape.

West of Zanzibar has two weaknesses: the lack of a strong female co-star and the ending, dramatizing Phroso's death. The former problem is one that can be found in several of the Chaney-Browning films. While Mary Nolan's performance is not as weak as Lois Moran's in *The Road to Mandalay*, she is merely adequate. The character of Maizie is never fully developed. Thus, she serves only as a prop in the scenario's revenge plot and ensuing climax, and as a catalyst for the regeneration (and a subsequent romantic interest for) the character of Doc, another of Phroso's henchmen. The ending, in which Phroso falls prey to the natives, appears to have been hastily executed. Throughout the African scenes, Chaney has held the natives mesmerized by his magic, and they have followed his orders out of fear that he might use his mystical powers against them. But one of the natives overhears Doc discussing Phroso's plan for their escape with Maizie, and we assume that he informs the tribal chief. After Phroso places Maizie into the coffin with the reversible backside, he goes through several tribal-like arm gestures. Browning makes a conspicuous showing of Chaney's hands resting under the medallion that he wears around his neck. As the tribal chief watches Chaney, Browning cuts to a close-up of the medallion and then back to the chief's reaction. When Lon reveals the skeleton in the coffin, the tribal chief says he does not believe him and the natives close in on Chaney. The film dissolves to the natives dancing around the huge fire where they cremate their dead. The tribal chief, sitting next to the fire, uses a stick to pull the medallion from the burning coals, indicating Phroso's demise.

Unfortunately, the significance of the medallion is not explained prior to the finale, although we do see the medallion around Chaney's neck throughout the jungle sequences. There is nothing in the surviving print or cutting continuity to suggest that a scene was concocted to establish the tribal chief's acceptance that Phroso's powers may have come from the medallion. Despite these discrepancies, though, *West of Zanzibar* is a solid picture, with the ending (despite its flaws) rivaling that of *The Unknown* in power.

Interestingly, one would not surmise *West of Zanzibar* would be a powerful movie when comparing the final product to the pallid May 17th, 1928 draft. This version did not contain the shot of Phroso falling from the second-story balcony while arguing with Crane. In this script, Anna (Phroso's wife) embraces Crane and the scene dissolves to an act performing on the stage. The next shot shows a rather excited stage manager rushing from the wings onto the stage asking if there is a doctor in the house. An audience member stands up and goes backstage with the stage manager. The crowd separates, and we see Chaney lying in a crumpled heap on the floor. One stage employee explains the situation to the doctor and points to the broken rail of the balcony indicating Phroso's fall. This version lacks the dramatic impact of the existing sequence, where we see Chaney's character fall over the railing and land on the floor below. The ending, which is somewhat reminiscent of the conclusion of *The Road To Mandalay*, lacks a dramatic finish. According to the May 17 script, Phroso kills Crane and has the natives hang the body by his feet with a goat's skull tied around his neck. This ritual is performed to set an example of what happens to thieves. Phroso's compatriots become suspicious about his total change in behavior towards Maizie (after he learns she is his child), believing he desires the girl for himself and plans to leave them behind. As they load a canoe with supplies to make a hasty exit, Maizie, who is in a dream-like state believing the murdered Crane to be her father, goes into Phroso's room where he's sleeping. She stabs him once fatally. He yells out that Crane was not her father and her real father (whose identity he does not reveal) loves her. Doc (Warner Baxter) enters the room and the two lovers flee while Phroso crawls after them yelling, somewhat hysterically, that her father loves her. We then see Chaney's character looking out of a window from his post, watching the canoe disappear into the darkness as he dies. [327]

While the funeral pyre sequence is not featured in the May 17 draft, it does contain a rather sadistic scene when Maizie arrives at Phroso's compound. Doc is completely drunk, overcome with booze and hashish, according to a title card. Phroso orders two natives to restrain Doc while he makes small cuts on his upper body and legs. When he is finished, he orders the natives to take Doc out into the swamp and "let the leeches suck out the poison in him." [328] No doubt this sequence would have had the censors in an uproar, and this scene, along with others, was deleted in the final script. One sequence in both the May 17 and June 7 drafts features a unique shot illustrating the travels of Chaney's character in his attempt to find

A Thousand Faces

Crane. The camera, acting as Phroso's eyes, showed various faces of French, Italian, Turkish, Arabic, and, finally, African people pass by (the background in this shot was indistinguishable), indicating the various countries through which he passed on his search. When the Africans walk past the camera, the scene dissolved to the dive where Phroso comes in on his cart pleading for money. He is taunted by two men, Babe and Tiny, who throw him through the saloon's window. This brutal act upsets the patrons of the bar, and Doc pleads for pity on behalf of Chaney's character. The scene ends with money being thrown into a hat, and dissolves to Phroso, Doc, Babe, and Tiny counting the collected coins. This scene, along with the one with Chaney appearing as the "human duck," were actually filmed, but deleted from the final print.

The latter scene must have been a powerful sequence, but, no doubt, would have had the censors ordering the scene cut. After Chaney and his compatriots pull off the ruse in the saloon and count their illicit profits, the film cuts to the dive in Zanzibar. It is here that we learn that Chaney's character has left Anna's child in the custody of the local madame. As Chaney smiles at the progress of his plan, the shot dissolves to numerous scenes of various carnival acts in Zanzibar. We come across Doc acting as the spieler for the "human duck." People peer into the pit (the camera cannot "see" into the pit at this point) and begin to laugh at the antics they observe. One of the people watching is Crane. The camera then establishes Chaney's character in the duck suit, laughing hysterically and quacking. The more Phroso realizes that Crane doesn't recognize him, the crazier he becomes. When Doc is apprised of his antics, he increases his spiel, telling the patrons to "see it while its lasts — the duck's gone crazy!" [329]

With the saloon and "human duck" sequences deleted, Joseph Farnham, M-G-M's leading title writer, solved the problem of bridging the scenes where Chaney finds his wife in the church to his arrival in the African jungle. As Chaney and Lionel Barrymore argue in the dressing room, Barrymore claims he's taking Anna with him to Africa. When Chaney finds his wife's body in the church and vows revenge, the scene dissolves to a title card reading, "Eighteen years later — West of Zanzibar." We then see Chaney (with his shaved head) in his African compound.

While the May 17 script had a flat conclusion for the film, the June 7 script also failed to work out a satisfactory climax. The last scene in this draft ends with Phroso saying goodbye to his daughter as the native drums beat louder. The final page of the script indicates action that would be developed in a subsequent draft:

> There will be twenty additional scenes in which, in
> his efforts to save the girl, Chaney sacrifices his life
> and is burned upon the funeral pyre with the body
> of Johnson, and following which, the girl, Moore
> and Kalla Pasha are seen gliding over the lagoon in a
> boat filled with provisions. 330

Throughout this draft, as well as the May 17 script, the characters are referred to by the actor's last names. Lon is simply referred to as Chaney, not Phroso. The role of Doc was written with Owen Moore in mind, and the character is identified by that actor's last name in the script, as are the roles for actors Kalla Pasha (Babe) and Constantine Romanoff. 331

If *West of Zanzibar* were produced today, the filmmakers would probably ship the entire cast and crew to Africa or some similar exotic locale. But in 1928, the entire picture never left the confines of the Culver City complex. The exterior of Chaney's jungle compound was constructed around the studio water tank, which was designed to resemble a jungle lagoon. The tank was located on Lot Two, across the street from the main studio lot. 332 The jungle set had numerous steam pipes running through it to keep the many

A Thousand Faces

tropical plants from wilting in the hot, dry, California sun. Because of the steam pipes, incandescent lights, and hot summer temperatures, Lon's long-time friend and studio publicist, Clarence Locan, dubbed the set, "Emoting in a Turkish Bath," for an article in the September 1928 issue of *Hollywood Magazine*.

The emotional impact Lon Chaney brought to his roles has not been overlooked by current filmmakers. One director, Stanley Kubrick, used the example of Chaney's vivid performances to make his point to an actor on the set of *Full Metal Jacket* (1987). Vincent D'Onofrio played the troubled Marine recruit in the picture, who ultimately goes over the brink and kills both his drill instructor and himself. Throughout the thirteen months they worked on the picture, Vincent said, Kubrick never gave the actors any direction regarding their performances (which evidently is an idiosyncracy exclusive to Kubrick). At the end of his next-to-last-day on the picture, Vincent and Kubrick were walking together toward their respective cars. Kubrick asked the actor if he knew which scene they would be filming the next day. Vincent told him it was the scene in which his character kills the drill instructor and himself. The director nodded and continued toward his car, stopping midway, he turned toward Vincent. "Make it big. Make it Lon Chaney big." Kubrick said before driving away. [333]

As 1928 drew to a close, Lon Chaney's popularity was firmly entrenched at the box office, and he prepared to make his tenth and what would be his final movie with Tod Browning. *Where East Is East* is the duo's most unsubstantial picture, with the director's formulaic plots appearing to have lost much of their steam. Although the idea of having Chaney appear as a wild animal trapper could have offered numerous possibilities, the final scenario, adapted and written by two otherwise excellent writers, is poorly structured. [334] Lon portrays Tiger Haynes, who was deserted years earlier by his wife, leaving him alone to raise their daughter, Toyo (Lupe Velez).

258

The strong bond between father and daughter has led some film historians to suggest the relationship may have had overtones of incest (a ludicrous statement in this author's opinion), and they hint that the mother's relationship with the woman she travels with is either bisexual or lesbian in nature.

When Tiger learns that Toyo has fallen in love, his reaction is that of any protective father opposed to his daughter's marriage. Part of his resentment stems from the emotional scars left by his own unhappy marriage, for his wife, Mme. de Silva (Estelle Taylor), had frequently cheated on him before ultimately leaving. When Tiger and Bobby (Lloyd Hughes), Toyo's fiancé, go downriver to ship animals to Bobby's father (a circus owner), the young man and Mme. de Silva meet. She quickly seduces him. Tiger orders her to stay away from the boy, which only escalates Mme. de Silva's desire to conquer Bobby, especially after she learns he is planning to marry her daughter. Tiger is a devoted father. His hatred for his ex-wife is obvious, but because of Toyo, he restrains himself from voicing his feelings. Knowing this, Mme. de Silva taunts him when she returns to Tiger's home, and attempts to make amends by helping Toyo plan for her wedding. Tiger says nothing in fear of risking his daughter's happiness—but Toyo accidentally overhears the true reason for her mother's return. Filled with anguish over his daughter's suffering, Tiger releases a gorilla, which attacks his ex-wife.

Chaney's performance does not come up to his usual standards. He appears simply to walk through his role, which, in any event, is not a typical one for a Tod Browning production. Chaney's characters in a Browning film always had dominant emotional power, but Tiger Haynes expresses little of that quality. Because his daughter's happiness is essential, Lon's character is reduced to being a powerless spectator, giving sullen or dejected looks, reacting rather than taking charge. His usual bravura performance is sorely lacking in this picture, particularly compared with his work in *West of*

A Thousand Faces

Zanzibar. Tiger's anger fails to register on Chaney's face, although numerous reaction shots are meant to convey his rage. Unfortunately it doesn't work.

Many other scenes lack the drama needed to propel the story. When Bobby rescues Toyo from a tiger, the episode fails to build suspense. Bobby intervenes before Toyo is even aware of the impending danger. Tiger takes a chair from Bobby, which the young man has been using to hold off the animal, and while Bobby gets Toyo safely away, Tiger manages to coerce the animal back into its cage. After Toyo learns the true reason for her mother's return, Tiger embraces his daughter to comfort her. This could have been a tender moment between father and daughter, building on her unhappiness and realization that she may lose Bobby to her mother. And it would have provided the breaking point for Tiger, compelling him to release the gorilla. Instead, when Toyo tells Bobby she hopes he'll be happy, Browning cuts to reaction shots of the unhappy Tiger and a smug Mme. de Silva, who returns to her room to wait for Bobby.

When the gorilla, which supposedly was treated badly by Tiger's ex-wife, attacks her, her cries for help arouse Bobby and Toyo. But before the young man can act, Tiger goes to the room himself. Thus the gorilla becomes the *deus ex machina* that brings an end to Mme. de Silva's threat and causes Tiger to die unnecessarily as a hero. Unfortunately, the gorilla is rather an improbable device for Mme. de Silva's end. (For one thing, it's quite obvious it is an actor in a costume, which takes away any believability.) Had Browning used a tiger instead, the dramatic impact would have been stronger. The entire sequence is poorly shot and Chaney's intervention as a hero not only fails, but also makes no sense. Had Toyo gone to her mother's room first, placing her own life in jeopardy, Tiger's actions would have been justified. As it is, he manages to live long enough to see his daughter happily married, but the entire conclusion fails to gain any real sympathy for Chaney's character.

Both Lupe Velez as Toyo and Estelle Taylor provide strong support and, in some respects, upstage Chaney. His character is certainly the weakest and most poorly delineated in this Browning picture. Tiger lacks substance. And Chaney had to deal with two actresses known to display fits of temperament. Asked by a writer how he was getting along with Lupe Velez, Lon replied that she was behaving herself. The writer pressed the subject, asking whether she was on time or showing up late. Lon brusquely replied:

> Say, I'm not temperamental, and I won't tolerate temperament in other people. I'm always on time; if the leading woman isn't on the set I just walk off and take off my make-up. Lupe and I are getting along all right; she's a great little actress. [335]

Although the daily production reports do not indicate whether or not he walked off the set if Lupe Velez were tardy, Lon did hold up production himself one day. On January 11, the production report noted that filming was delayed for forty minutes because Lon was having trouble with his make-up. [336] The scars he created by means of collodion could cause problems. When collodion is applied to the skin, it puckers and draws the flesh together, drying almost immediately. A bottle of collodion starts to slowly evaporate as soon as it is opened and prolonged exposure to the air causes the chemical to lose its potency. When this weakened collodion is applied, it fails to achieve the desired effect. Applying additional coats of the ineffective material or diluting it with acetone only makes the situation worse. The only remedy is to remove the make-up and start anew with a fresh bottle of collodion. The cause of Chaney's problem is not stated in the production report, but it is likely that this is what transpired.

It's unfortunate that the last picture Lon Chaney and Tod Browning made, despite its fairly positive reviews and a good turnout

A Thousand Faces

at the box office, is less than adequate. Despite the accepted belief that the Chaney-Browning pictures were huge money-makers, only three of Chaney's top ten profit-earning M-G-M films were directed by Browning. [337] Many film historians have wondered what caused Browning to produce such a poor movie. Browning biographer David J. Skal suggests that one reason might be related to Browning falling off the sobriety wagon after the death of his mother. [338] He also speculates that whereas Chaney and Browning may have enjoyed a solid professional relationship, the two men did not appear to have a personal friendship away from the camera. Joseph Newman has said he was told by Browning's assistant director and editor, Errol Taggart, that the two men "were not bosom friends." [339] It's entirely possible that Browning's departure from sobriety could have pushed the relationship to a point where Chaney might have refused to work with the director again.

In 1929, as more and more films were being released in either part-talking or all-talking form, Chaney still steadfastly refused to speak in pictures. During the first year after the introduction of talkies, studio executives were dubious of the success and endurance of sound pictures. [340] But despite the uncertainty, Lon prepared to make what would become his last silent picture, *Thunder*.

Thunder dramatized the life of a veteran train engineer whose entire life is dominated by the railroad. Nothing matters to "Grumpy" Anderson except bringing his train in on time. His stubborn, single-minded outlook eventually affects his relationship with his son, who also works for the railroad, and their quarrel results in Grumpy's causing a train wreck. Because of his many years of service Grumpy is not fired, but is relegated to the machine shop, where he oversees the repair of his old engine. This is a touching moment in the movie: Grumpy is working on a drill press as his wrecked engine is hauled into the shop. The engine's bell rings as it is being moved and Grumpy stops at the familiar sound. The bell rings

262

again, and this time he realizes it's not his imagination. He quickly begins supervising the placement of his old friend, tenderly running his hands over the large wheels and smiling like a proud father.

Thunder opens with an enormous blizzard sweeping across the Midwest, playing havoc with the train schedules. There are numerous scenes of trains plowing through large snowdrifts, as well as several shots of the Chicago terminal. [341] These sequences are exciting and definitely set the mood of the picture, but procuring them was far from easy. Numerous telegrams between Jerry Mayer, the film's unit manager and brother of studio head Louis B. Mayer, and studio production manager J. J. Cohn reveal a desperate search for snow because the Chicago area was experiencing an early spring. On February 22, 1929, Jerry Mayer, who was staying in Chicago, wired Cohn that "as far east as North Platte there is no snow." [342] Cohn replied the following day that "Omaha had snow extending as far as Denver. It could be the heaviest of the season." Cohn dispatched two camera crews, one headed by Charles Levin and the other by Charles Marshall, to obtain footage of trains plowing through snow and scenes of wintry railroad yards. Levin's unit was ordered by Cohn to detrain in Cheyenne, Wyoming, and wait for instructions; Marshall was in Salt Lake City with the same orders: "Be ready to move on short notice." On February 24, Cohn wired Mayer in Manitowoc, Wisconsin, that it was "snowing in Denver. There is 2 1/2 feet in yards at Minneapolis. Investigate these as possibilities." [343]

Two days later, Cohn requested photographs showing all angles of the locomotive and tender and to indicate which sections would have to be built at the studio for interior stage work. Meanwhile, Charles Marshall was sent to Omaha to photograph train yards covered with snow. Marshall wired Cohn on February 27:

> Shot today but don't feel getting much worth while.
> Snow going fast today. None on trains, ground only.
> Bright sun today so even less snow tomorrow. [344]

A Thousand Faces

Cohn replied that if Marshall heard of any train yards covered with snow within a three-or four-hundred-mile radius, he was to go photograph them, otherwise he should return to the studio. Jerry Mayer requested that Cohn wire a description of Chaney's make-up so that they could make up a double to shoot some footage of Chaney's character driving the train. [345] Alfred Grasso said that Lon objected to using doubles except in circumstances in which he could be physically hurt. Although a double was used for certain wide shots, in many scenes Lon drove the locomotive himself. To make his character as believable as possible, Lon obtained his engineer's certificate and became an honorary member of the Brotherhood of Locomotive Engineers during production. [346]

Filming commenced in Green Bay, Wisconsin, on February 27 for fifteen days, shooting in and around the train yards of the Chicago-Northwestern Railroad. Lon arrived on Sunday, March 3, and began work the following day. The company left for Chicago on March 14 for additional location work in that city's famed railroad terminals. [347] On March 20, the company completed its location work and started the three-day trip back to Los Angeles, returning to work at the Culver City plant on March 25. Additional location work was shot in the rail yards of the Santa Fe train station in downtown Los Angeles as well as on a spur track of the Southern Pacific Railroad in a suburb southwest of M-G-M studios. [348] On April 18, the production report noted that Lon was having trouble with his make-up, so director William Nigh decided to shoot another scene, one in which Chaney did not appear, which caused a forty-five minute delay. Two days later, the company was once again forced to film a scene minus Lon while he tried on a new wig. [349] But make-up and hair were not the only problems plaguing this picture, for the morning of April 22 also proved to be less than productive when the interior scenes of the engine cab were being filmed. During rehearsal, the glass window in the cab was broken; it took fifteen minutes to replace. Meanwhile, when the special effects were tested, it was found that the compressed air and steam did not work properly. By 11:25 a.m. the oil line on the furnace was discovered to be stopped up. Another twenty minutes went by as this problem was corrected; then the fire box would not work. The company was sent to lunch at 11:45 while technicians made repairs. The first shot of the day was taken at 1:15 that afternoon. The picture was now six days behind schedule. [350]

Chaney caught a cold while filming in the frigid temperatures of Green Bay and Chicago, and it quickly developed into walking pneumonia; but he continued to work even after returning to Los Angeles. Because of Lon's illness, the production was shut down entirely on April 25 and remained idle for seventeen days until he returned to work on May 13. But it was obvious that Lon's strength was depleted. The production report noted, "Mr. Chaney here this AM, but claims not able to work until after lunch. Only a few scenes to shoot without him." [351] (Ironically, the scene with Chaney required him to be in a hospital bed.) Six days later, production was again shut down because "Mr. Chaney refused to work today." No doubt the previous sixteen-and-a-half-hour work day, which included night filming in San Bernardino, proved to be a strain on Chaney's health. On May 20, Lon was an hour late, and he was similarly tardy the following two days. Production was finally completed on May 23, but two additional days of retakes were required, on May 28 and June 3. [352]

Working on what would be his last picture with Chaney, Willard Sheldon remembered *Thunder* as

> a great picture to work on. I didn't go back with
> them to Green Bay. I had prepped the film and was
> set to go, when they pulled me off of it. William
> Nigh, the director, raised hell, but Louis B. Mayer
> had a nephew who worked at the studio and he had

relatives near the location. So he was sent in my place and I came back on the picture when they returned. It was a very rough location to work [referring to the bad weather]. When they returned, Lon kept working while he was sick. I didn't realize how ill he was, and when he finally came back [from being absent while sick], I never asked how he was and he didn't say. Everyone was glad to see him, but he looked rather pale when he returned. After his return, I never saw him wanting to rest. If he did, he never showed it. When I worked with him before, he always had a lot of energy.

Lon drove the train for the scenes we shot in Inglewood. What he might have done on location I don't know, but I doubt very much [that Lon would have driven the train himself] because railroad rules were very strict. All the flood scenes were shot on Lot Two and we used a lot of miniatures for that scene and for the derailment sequence. We had real trains laid on the ground by a crane out in San Bernardino to film the aftermath of the derailment.

Nigh let me direct some of the insert shots on the picture, which took two days. Normally a director will let the assistant director or, in my case, the script supervisor handle these chores. Insert shots usually comprised shots of letters or hand inserts, things like that. But Nigh deliberately skipped things and I was directing scenes with some of the principals, such as over the shoulder shots. Every so often he would open the door to the stage and peek in to see how I was doing. He tried real hard to get me on as his assistant director, but it never worked.

We had Jimmy [James] Murray in the picture playing the second lead. The studio was grooming him for stardom, but unfortunately he had a very bad drinking problem. One day, when we were out in Inglewood using the Southern Pacific track, Jerry Mayer brought out some executives from the

railroad to watch the filming. Nigh knew about this
in advance and had decided to keep Murray in the
train cab until they arrived. That way he couldn't
start drinking. He wasn't allowed to come down for
anything, and Nigh even had a box lunch brought to
him. Well, the executives arrived and Nigh called
Jimmy down to meet them. He stepped off the train
and fell flat on his face. Out like a light. We later
learned that someone had been sneaking him bottles
of booze, because we found the empties stashed
under the coal in the tender. It's really a shame what
happened to him, because he was such a nice
guy. [353]

Before its release in July 1929, *Thunder* underwent some
changes to appease the MPPDA censors. The words "helluva,"
"damn," and "hell" were ordered cut as well as the title "Any bum
can be a quitter." The latter would be eliminated by every censor in
England, Canada, and Australia because in those countries, the term
"bum" alludes to "ass." In his summary of the picture, Jason Joy of
the MPPDA, noted,

It tells a story which I predict will be enthusiastically
accepted by the average motion picture fan. In fact,
I think it will be a very attractive box office picture.
There is no dialogue in it; however, there is a good
deal of very effective synchronization, particularly
the sounds having to do with railroads, etc. [354]

Joy's predictions regarding the film's box office success were
correct. *Thunder* became Lon's fifth-highest grossing M-G-M picture.
Unfortunately, it is also one of Chaney's lost pictures. During the
movie's run, executives at the H. D. Lee Mercantile Company made
an interesting proposition for a promotional tie-in with the picture.
When they learned that Lon had borrowed a pair of Lee garments
from a railroad worker (which he replaced with a new pair) to use

as part of his wardrobe, they wanted to use a picture of Chaney in his costume in their advertising. The studio publicity department debated whether or not it was necessary to obtain Chaney's permission in accordance with his contract. But when the legal department was asked their opinion, they quickly vetoed the idea, advising them to do nothing without procuring Chaney's permission ahead of time, adding that if they went ahead without securing the actor's approval, it would put them "in a very bad position." [355]

Whether he liked it or not, Lon Chaney would soon face a crossroads in his career. By the summer of 1929, talking pictures appeared to be a permanent fixture in Hollywood, and numerous stars were facing the dilemma of how their voices would record. Lon's recalcitrant attitude to speak made news, and many of the fan magazines reported on his steadfast refusal:

> Lon Chaney's thousand faces are all still silent, in spite of the menace of the microphone. His next picture for M-G-M will be called "Sergeant Bull," a romantic English war story.... And Lon won't talk. And that's flat. As if any Chaney picture could be flat! [356]

Sergeant Bull was originally planned as a silent film, much like *The Bugle Sounds*, but it was quickly being adapted into a talkie. Yet Lon refused to speak. His unwillingness to make his debut in a sound picture was twofold: first, he felt that recording techniques had not yet been properly developed; second, his contract did not contain a clause regarding his appearance in a sound picture. Whether these reasons were a delaying tactic to see how the medium progressed or a ploy to negotiate a new contract remains unknown. M-G-M had ordered dialogue written for *The Bugle Sounds*, which the studio had announced as a Chaney picture. The studio assigned Laurence

Stallings to write dialogue for the film, a fact that Lon did not miss. He questioned studio manager M. E. Greenwood about Stallings' writing dialogue when there was nothing in his contract that called for him to make a sound picture. Greenwood lied to Chaney, saying that as far as he knew, the writer was working only on the continuity. [357] Even a fan magazine reported Lon's refusal to speak in the picture, noting,

> Lon Chaney is not yet ready to talk on the screen.
> M-G-M wanted him to speak in "The Bugle Sounds,"
> but Lon refused. While the star ponders, plans for
> his next film stand still. [358]

The Bugle Sounds had been in preproduction dating back to 1927. The picture never materialized, although the title was used in the 1941 picture starring Wallace Beery. [359] According to the MPPDA censor notes, the picture faced several obstacles, the most serious being the French government. In a letter to Jason Joy on December 23, 1927, F. L. Herron, head of the MPPDA's foreign department, cautioned:

> I note that Metro is going to make a story of the
> French Foreign Legion called *The Bugle Sounds*.
> They had better watch their step on this, as of
> course the French have never allowed *Beau Geste*
> to be released in France and have raised an awful
> row about it every place else. [360]

The picture was put on hold until a workable script could be produced. Herron relayed his continuing concerns to Joy regarding the subject matter in a February 13, 1929, letter. Although M-G-M said they had obtained the approval of and cooperation from the French government, Herron was worried. He urged Joy to remain in close contact with the studio, noting, "It is playing with dynamite to deal with this subject at all." [361] A few weeks later, Herron received word from Jason Joy that a real story had yet to be fashioned from the material, and production would be postponed for another month or two. [362] Five months later, a script was close to approval, and on July 10, Herron wrote to Joy that

> *Bugle Sounds* much improved but treatment of
> barroom scenes should be watched. They have done
> a splendid job on rewriting *Bugle Sounds*. I think
> they have taken out quite a little red meat which I
> am sorry to see eliminated, but presumed it had to
> be done. The only real trouble that I can see a
> possibility of is the drinking contest between the
> two sergeants. I think this should be handled very
> carefully.... I am interested in knowing who are to
> play the parts of the two sergeants. That will really
> be the deciding point as to whether the finished
> product will be attacked or not. [363]

The Bugle Sounds was slated to be directed by George Hill. The story treatment of the March 14, 1929, synopsis had Chaney teamed with Wallace Beery. The two were to play rival sergeants, McDonald and Groot. In the March 14 version, Chaney plays the introverted, easy-going McDonald, who eventually becomes a sergeant. The synopsis also detailed the climax of the film, in which the legionnaires are caught in a firefight with natives. Because of McDonald's heckling, Groot makes a mistake that results in his detail being completely wiped out, save for himself. When McDonald is ordered to select a detachment of volunteers to destroy an enemy cannon, he chooses Groot to accompany his group. Chaney's character valiantly dies while covering Beery's advance, allowing him to capture the native leader and the cannon. [364]

By the August 12, 1929, script draft, Groot would be played by Chaney and McDonald by Beery. Here it is Groot who dies the hero, disabling the cannon and killing the native leader. [365] McDonald unpins his *Medaille Militaire* and asks the major to place it on the body of Groot. As a volley is fired in honor of their fallen comrade, McDonald begins to cry. The end of the picture finds the legionnaires lining up for another duty, and as the column passes the graves of their fallen brothers, including Sergeant Groot, they salute as they are ordered "eyes right." The June 8, 1929, issue of the trade paper *Hollywood Filmograph* announced that M-G-M claimed much of the picture would be filmed on location in Africa. By July 20, cinematographer Ira Morgan (who lensed *Tell It To The Marines*) had been assigned to the production with assistant director Fred Messenger. [366]

Hollywood Filmograph had a section in the paper titled "Bulletin Board," which recorded the status of various studio productions (i.e., preparing, shooting, etc.). This column listed *The Bugle Sounds* as "preparing," but Lon's name was not mentioned as the star until the August 3 edition. A week later an article claimed that the film would start production in one or two weeks, but there was no mention of Chaney playing the leading role. The article concluded with the notations that director George Hill had already shot some scenes in Northern Africa. [367] In the "Flicker Flashes" column of that same issue, Wallace Berry and Ernest Torrance were mentioned as playing McDonald and Groot in the movie. *The Bugle Sounds* was scheduled to commence filming by August 27, 1929, with the new cast, which also included Karl Dane, Ivan Lebedeff, and Robert Montgomery. But the start of production never happened. However, the "Bulletin Board" section of *Hollywood Filmograph* continued to list the picture as preparing until October 26, 1929, when it quietly disappeared.

Despite his refusal to make a talking picture, Lon Chaney's popularity in the waning days of silent pictures did not go unnoticed in the newspapers:

A Thousand Faces

> The passing of Clara Bow and Lon Chaney from the
> front line of motion picture stars was the prediction
> most freely voiced by a considerable number of
> critics during the closing months of the past year
> [1929].... Chaney's death warrant was written out
> on the grounds that he had refused to go talkie. His
> continuation as a silent star in the face of a
> unanimous wave toward sound was considered too
> great a handicap for any star to overcome...
>
> Both predictions may come true in 1930, but
> certainly there is no indication of an anti-Bow or
> anti-Chaney trend in the nationwide survey of the
> "best box office stars" just completed by the
> Exhibitors' Herald-World...[who] discovered, as it
> did in 1928, that Clara Bow leads the feminine
> money winners at the box office, while Lon Chaney
> is still the exhibitors' pride and joy among male
> contenders. [368]

Universal announced that they were preparing a sequel to
Phantom of the Opera, entitled *Return of the Phantom*, which had
supposedly been penned by Gaston Leroux shortly before his death
in 1927. Actually, nothing had been written except the title, which
Universal quickly copyrighted. [369] The studio had hoped to obtain
Chaney for the sequel, but when M-G-M refused to loan out their star,
Universal shot some additional scenes with dialogue featuring Mary
Philbin and Norman Kerry and rereleased *Phantom of the Opera* as a
part-talking picture. [370] In all the advertising for the film, however,
the studio carried the disclaimer, "Lon Chaney's Portrayal of the
Phantom is Silent." [371]

Following the dismal release of Tod Browning's *The Thirteenth
Chair* (1929), the director left M-G-M and returned to Universal. The
reason for his departure, after Browning had turned out several
successful pictures, remains speculative. The March 15, 1930, issue
of *Hollywood Filmograph* announced that Browning had signed a

new contract with Universal, stating "At the termination of his M-G-M contract he went to Europe for a rest and upon his return he signed with Universal again." The article said Browning would direct *The Yellow Sin*, but there is no mention of his helming *Dracula*. [372] Some have suggested that after *Where East Is East*, and the poor direction of *The Thirteenth Chair*, Thalberg may have simply released him, feeling he was incapable of directing sound pictures. Browning's drinking may have been another reason for his departure. Another theory holds that Chaney was not happy with *Where East Is East* and may have stated that he didn't care to work with Browning again. [373] Another explanation, offered by David J. Skal, concerns the announcement that Browning was assigned to direct *The Sea Bat*, which was to star Chaney. [374] At this time, Browning's 1926 contract with the studio was nearing its expiration, and when Chaney's contract was suspended due to his poor health, the director found himself in limbo. [375] Because his contract was about run out and it appeared unlikely that he would receive an interim assignment, and because Chaney's recovery and return to work were uncertain, he may have felt forced to leave M-G-M. Giving further credence to this theory is the fact that Browning was paid $50,000 for three unproduced pictures when he returned to M-G-M to direct *Freaks* a year and a half later. [376] Skal speculates that two of the unproduced pictures may have been *The Sea Bat* and *Dracula*, because the studio was negotiating for the latter's film rights at the time. [377] Lon was listed as the star of *The Sea Bat* as far back as the May 11, 1930 issue of *Hollywood Filmograph*, which described the film as "a tropic tale of voodoo." But, by the June 15 issue the film was no longer listed on the Bulletin Board schedule. [378]

The truth behind Browning's departure from M-G-M will probably remain a mystery. After he left the studio and set up shop at Universal, most film historians have blindly assumed that Chaney would follow his director to appear in *Dracula* for Universal. In fact, the first choice for the role was actor Conrad Veidt, but his thick German accent put an end to his career in American sound pictures for many years. [379]   Chaney was the studio's second choice, even though the reality was that Universal's chances of obtaining his services were extremely slim. Contrary to claims by some writers, Chaney's contract with M-G-M was not about to expire, and there is no evidence to suggest that the studio would not have picked up the final option on one of their most lucrative and popular stars. [380] It is also doubtful that M-G-M, which had tried to buy the rights to *Dracula*, would have loaned Chaney out to a competitor, especially Universal. In order to obtain Chaney for the role, M-G-M would have demanded a hefty fee from Universal on top of Chaney's $3,750 weekly salary. Also complicating matters was the fact that M-G-M would have been legally bound to consider the loan-out as one of the four pictures made during Chaney's contract year. In that regard alone, the studio would have lost a considerable amount of money, given Chaney's large box office popularity, and let Universal reap the benefits.

While *Thunder* was proving to be a success at the box office, Chaney's health was ebbing. The pneumonia had diminished his strength and he began to develop a persistent cough. On July 25, 1929, M-G-M suspended his contract and salary until he was healthy enough to return to work. [381]   Fan magazines carried the news that Hollywood's favorite character star was ailing and his return to the silver sceen was in question. *Photoplay* reported, "*The Bugle Sounds* was to have been his [Lon Chaney's] vehicle, but his illness and his refusal to face the microphone caused the film to be given to other players. Now *Brother Officers* is to be done with an all-star cast, [Fred] Niblo directing. It is still doubtful when Chaney will return to work." [382]

Despite the actor's illness, Universal pressed the matter of obtaining Lon's services for *Dracula*. A June 23, 1929, letter from the offices of Loeb, Walker and Loeb, M-G-M's legal representatives, to Carl Laemmle, Jr., stated:

> We are enclosing herewith three copies of the proposed agreement with Lon Chaney. Will you be good enough to give special attention to the examination of this contract in order to ascertain whether or not it fully complies with the understanding between yourselves and Mr. Chaney....
>
> You will, of course, notice that the within contract is somewhat larger than the contract which Chaney had for *The Phantom*; but in view of the fact that some difficulties were encountered in the production of that picture, we have deemed it advisable to include in the within contract all possible precautions.
>
> While we do not know whether or not you desire to carry insurance on Chaney during this period of production we have included a clause allowing you to do so, and requiring Chaney to submit to the usual examination for that purpose. Mr. Stern [Walter Stern, Universal studio's business manager] did not specify if Chaney has, in fact, agreed to a dual role. [383]

The reference to the difficulties encountered during production of *Phantom of the Opera*, probably alluded to Chaney's having to return for additional retakes on the picture while *The Unholy Three* (the silent version) was in production. A notation was scrawled on the bottom of this letter, "Jr. emphatic—keep Stern away from Chaney." No doubt Universal and M-G-M were aware of Chaney's inability to continue working at this juncture, but Carl Laemmle, Jr., was so insistent on obtaining the actor's services that he was willing to place Chaney under a personal contract instead of typical studio covenant. [384] This would have allowed Laemmle, Jr., to ignore any clause requiring Chaney to be examined for insurance purposes, as suggested in the June 23 letter. A month later, Universal's legal counsel, Sigfried Hartman, wired Edwin Loeb:

> Discussed situation fully with Metzger [Universal executive]. This morning he telephoned Junior emphatically advising against making Chaney contract personally. Agree that regardless legal aspects, highly objectionable from standpoint business ethics. Told Junior so last night. [385]

On August 23, 1929, M-G-M had drafted a letter to Chaney notifying him that his contract had been suspended as of July 25. The first letter was ordered canceled, and a new one drafted which contained an explicit sentence that no doubt referred to Carl Laemmle, Jr.'s, desire to sign Chaney:

> It is, of course, understood that during the term of such suspension you shall not have the right to render any services for any person, firm or corporation whatsoever. [386]

Whether M-G-M was ever really serious in loaning Chaney out to a rival studio may never be known. It's possible that the letters and negotiations were merely M-G-M's attempt to pressure Chaney into signing a contract to make talking pictures for the studio. On the other hand, the contract talks with Universal may have been Chaney's ploy to obtain a new contract from M-G-M, with its attendant higher salary. Whatever the case, Universal's chances of signing Chaney for *Dracula* had reached a dead end, but the studio proceeded with the purchase of the rights to the novel, rather than see it go to a rival company. [387]

By the end of November 1929, Chaney's attorney had begun the process of conferring with Louis B. Mayer about the details of a new contract, one under which Chaney would make talking pictures. After a spirited round of negotiations in which the studio threatened to keep making silent pictures with Chaney, a new contract was signed on January 23, 1930. After Chaney passed his voice test, Thalberg began looking for the right project for the debut of one of the studio's leading moneymakers.

Sound versions of *The Bugle Sounds* and *Cheri-Bibi* were considered, but Thalberg settled on a sound remake of *The Unholy Three* for Lon's talking picture debut. An original dialogue treatment by Samuel Shipman and John B. Hymer was drafted on February 1, 1930. [388] This film was probably chosen because, aside from its obvious ability to display Chaney's vocal talents, it would be easier to develop the dialogue. The writers merely had to enhance the material from the script of the silent film. Additional writers were assigned to the project, including Robert Hopkins and Mr. and Mrs. Willard Mack, but only J. C. Nugent and Elliott Nugent received the scenario credit when production commenced on March 26, 1930. [389]

The Unholy Three is almost a scene-for-scene remake of the silent version, except for the final courtroom scene and the ending. Many film historians and Chaney-admirers prefer the silent version for its dramatic content. And, as it turns out, the talking version's most notable flaw is the sound itself. In the silent version, the audience is willingly transported into the realm of disbelief, but the addition of sound makes everything "real," and the film's mystery becomes less effective. In other words, certain events that seemed plausible in the silent movie are dubious in the sound version. An example is the inclusion of the gorilla in the plot. The need for the gorilla to serve as the *deus ex machina*, to kill the giant and the midget, is rather contrived. In the silent version, the gorilla was actually a chimp placed in scaled-down sets; the natural movements of the animal allowed the audience to accept the rather implausible events of the plot. Yet in the sound version, a man dressed in an ape suit impersonates the gorilla and the effect is strained. [390] The incredibility that an old woman who runs a bird store would have a gorilla in her establishment is the first of many questions that come to mind. Why doesn't the police detective make a remark or, as in the silent version, register a reaction. After the gorilla kills Hercules (Ivan Linow) in the cabin, what happens to the animal? The talkie, that much closer to reality because of its soundtrack, undercuts itself with such itches-that-can't-be-scratched questions.

This especially is true when Echo (Chaney) orders Hercules and Tweedledee (Harry Earles) to wait for him in the kitchen while he keeps an eye on Rosie (Lila Lee) and Hector (Elliott Nugent), who are trimming the Christmas tree. The giant and the midget become quarrelsome; Hercules picks up Tweedledee and takes him out to the truck, intending to commit a robbery without Echo's supervision. As they start the truck, it appears as if only Echo (in his disguise as Mrs. O'Grady) can hear the rather loud engine. Why doesn't Hector react to the argument between Hercules and Tweedledee in the kitchen? In the silent version, we could imagine that the giant and the midget are whispering, and the idea of truck's engine turning over is not as intrusive as the actual sound.

Despite these minor infractions, the sound version of *The Unholy Three* is a well-made picture. The supporting cast performs proficiently, with the exception of Elliott Nugent (whose Hector is a dull, ineffectual young man, making it hard to believe that a woman such as Rosie could care for him). Also, Nugent looks too well groomed and sophisticated for the character. Matt Moore, who had played the role in the silent version, was far more believable as the milquetoast Hector. The audience could not only accept that he could be duped by this gang but could hope he'd win Rosie's affections. Lila Lee performs well as Rosie, but lacks the worldly streetwise attitude Mae Busch had brought to the role in the original film. Some supporting players are obvious in their enunciation of the dialogue — a common defect in the early years of sound pictures.

Chaney's performance is well-executed and he appears remarkably natural in his first speaking role. It was readily apparent that his voice recorded well and that his future in talking pictures would be endless. [391] The film offered Lon the opportunity to quickly switch from his normal voice to that of Mrs. O'Grady and illustrated how adaptable he would have been in talkies. In this version, Chaney's Echo takes on a more assertive edge. His relationship with the midget and giant has hostile overtones, and his voice becomes harsh when he addresses his cronies, and even occasionally Rosie. Yet when he performs for the sideshow audience, Echo is warm and engaging, allowing Chaney to present a multi-dimensional performance. When he belittles Hercules and Tweedledee for committing murder during a burglary, Echo is not as remorseful as in the silent version.

In the sound version, Chaney's approach is more or less to scold the two, which brings an entirely different emphasis to the scene. For the most part, Chaney's gestures fit the character well, and only occasionally do they appear a trifle overdone. When the trio and Rosie hide in the mountain cabin after framing Hector, Echo displays an inner anger because his conscience is troubling him. After he slaps Rosie, he is even more upset with himself for taking his anger out on the one he loves. But when she tells him she'd even accept the slap if he would just free Hector, his guilt becomes the catalyst for Echo to go to the courthouse.

While sitting in the courtroom, Echo tosses a note at the feet of the defense attorney that says that Mrs. O'Grady will show up to testify for Hector. This sequence is much more believable than the silent version, in which Echo manages to sneak a notepad from the defense attorney's table, scribble a note, and toss it back to the

A Thousand Faces

defense attorney without anyone sitting nearby noticing. In the sound version, both Hector and his attorney absent-mindedly play with the letter before reading it, but the running summation by the prosecuting attorney interferes with the audience's concentration, causing the tension to be lost. Again, this is an example of the dialogue intruding on the action of the picture. On the other hand, when the prosecuting attorney questions whether there truly is a Mrs. O'Grady, Echo throws his voice, saying, "Oh, yes, there is, your Honor!" In this case, sound served as a gimmick for the scene, something that couldn't have been accomplished as effectively in the silent version.

In the March 27, 1930, script, Echo, in disguise, is exposed by the prosecuting attorney during intense questioning. Echo complains of a headache and reaches involuntarily to his head. This gesture slightly disarranges his wig, enabling the prosecutor to notice the natural hair underneath. In a quick gesture, the attorney rips off the wig to reveal the masquerade. [392] But in the existing version of this scene, Echo's voice slips back to its natural tone under the intense questioning. This not only showcases Chaney's vocal talents but is also much more believable. In the abovementioned draft, Echo is sent to prison and Rosie promises to wait for him. Meanwhile, Hector has received a letter from Rosie in which she explains that she can never see him again. A few years later, Echo is released from prison and returns to the sideshow, performing his ventriloquist act. Rosie arrives and tells him she is willing to fulfill her part of the bargain, but Echo rebuffs her offer and tells her to go find Hector. The script concluded with Rosie finding Hector working in an architect's office, whereupon the lovers were reunited.

Jack Latham recalled the time he snuck onto the stage where Chaney was filming this scene, when he workied as an office boy at M-G-M:

> Lon was sitting alone on the box [the small stage of
> the side show], and [director] Jack Conway came up
> to him and briefly discussed the shot before the
> cameras started rolling. It was very touching where
> he says good-bye to Lila Lee. She was a good foil for
> Chaney and they played well off of each other. It
> was a very, very moving scene and I think they [the
> studio] should have left it in. It had a tremendous
> impact.
>
> Unlike many other actors, Chaney never had trouble
> with tears. He could cry on the spot, and in this
> scene the tears were pouring out of him. He was
> amazing. [393]

The sequence between Rosie and Echo at the sideshow, as well
as Rosie's reunion with Hector, were filmed but were subsequently
replaced with the stronger and more poignant ending in which Rosie
and Hector bid goodbye to Echo as he takes the train to prison. This
sequence is well-played, with Lon's character displaying sensitivity,
vulnerability, and a sense of heroism. Hector thanks Echo for saving
him, and gives him a carton of cigarettes before saying good-bye. (In
retrospect, this is an ironic twist, to have Chaney accept as a gift
what was ultimately responsible for his death!) When Rosie reminds
Echo that she will be waiting for him, Echo is surprised, as he had
not expected her to remain faithful to her bargain. But he realizes
that in spite of her promise, she really loves Hector. He gently tells
her he cannot let her wait: "When a girl waits for a fella that long,
he's got to marry her. And I don't want another ball and chain." [394]
To lighten the sentiment, Echo throws his voice so that Rosie thinks
the police officer has made some comment. She cannot control her
joy and says she doesn't know whether to laugh or cry. Echo reminds
her, "That's all there is to life — just a little laugh, a little tear." When
Chaney speaks this line, there is tremendous meaning behind what

A Thousand Faces

he says, elucidating his ability to play a delicate scene without broad gestures or flamboyant make-up.

The Unholy Three was well received both by critics and the public. Yet when it had been announced that Lon would make his talking picture debut, some fans were divided about his speaking on screen. One fan's letter stated:

> I am personally in favor of the Silent Drama.
> Although an actor is able to change his make-up, his
> dress and his mannerisms, he is never able to
> change his voice. Lon Chaney may be "The Man of a
> Thousand Faces," but with movietone he is merely a
> man of one voice. [395]

But another fan took exception to those comments and added her thoughts in a letter to *Photoplay*:

> If he [Lon Chaney] had only one voice, that would
> not make him lose his appeal. He could speak with
> an accent, lisp, or in a sing-song way. He could even
> have other men (and perhaps women) voice-double
> for him.... He would be the man of more than one
> voice.
>
> But before he tries any of those, I sincerely hope he
> speaks via the talkies with his natural voice. Lon
> Chaney is my favorite actor and it would be the thrill
> of thrills to hear his voice. I'm for talkies—especially
> when they bring me his voice—WHEN.
>
> Give us more and more of Lon Chaney—the actor of
> actors. [396]

Before the release of *The Unholy Three*, many stories circulated stating that Chaney wouldn't speak in any role or that he might use a voice double (although the technique for dubbing had yet to be perfected). To assure his fans that the voice they heard was indeed his own (and also for publicity purposes), Chaney signed a notarized affidavit that his voice, and the four others he used in the picture, were actually his own, and that he was in no way doubled at any time. [397] The film enjoyed a successful sneak preview at the Belmont Theatre in Los Angeles, and Lon's appearance at the screening was noted in the *Hollywood Filmograph*:

> After the show, like the kid idolators, we streaked
> after Lon (who had been let out of a side enterance)
> to get his reaction on the film.

> That it was perfectly satisfactory was easily
> evidenced as Chaney, crawling into the front seat of
> his sedan, expanded his features into a ten-minutes-
> after-ten smile of delight. Gee — how the gang
> cheered him! [398]

Lon Chaney's future in talking pictures was certain, and M-G-M planned several projects for him, including *Cheri-Bibi* and *The Bugle Sounds*. Sadly, however, this would be the actor's final performance.

During production, he struggled to get through each day's work, and on June 21, he was diagnosed as incapacitated and his contract suspended until he was able to return to work. [399] One can't help but wonder why M-G-M would sign the actor to such a lucrative contract if they knew he were terminally ill. It is possible that Lon and his doctors concealed the true nature of his illness. More likely, the studio decided to gamble on Lon, hoping he would be able to make a few talking pictures (thus allowing them to reap some financial benefit) before his death. Lon and Hazel ventured to New York City in late June with hope of finding a cure for his cancer. He stayed at Memorial Hospital, which was one of the leading medical institutions for the treatment of cancer at that time. There, he was examined by Dr. Burton J. Lee, and for the next two weeks, he

A Thousand Faces

underwent several radium treatments. Mary Bourne, who was a lab technician at Memorial Hospital during Lon's sojourn, had some revealing recollections:

> Chaney's arrival to the hospital was done in great secrecy. He came in under an assumed name to protect his privacy, though we were all notified he was coming. I recall the excitement among the staff; we had all seen his movies and there was quite a great deal of competition as to what nurse would go in and see him. There was a note at the nurse's desk for the head nurse to tell all those necessary; but we were told to act accordingly, which meant to be professional and not bother asking him questions about his movies.
>
> I know the nurses used to get a laugh out of the fact that they were calling him by an assumed name, which I can't remember. When they did say "Good morning, Mr. _____," and he'd look at them with a smirk, or would make some kind of a slight gesture that he knew that they knew. And perhaps he himself thought it was a little foolish.
>
> Back then no one ever mentioned the word cancer. It was considered dirty or taboo. They often referred to it as tumors and allied diseases. I remember that he was treated by a Dr. Quick, who was an ear, nose and throat specialist. He had a private hospital, which Chaney might have gone to for surgery. I'm rather sure he had surgery and would assume he had radium treatments. Of course both of these things could have been done at Dr. Quick's private hospital. Most patients who had radium treatments eventually died.
>
> I would go to his room every morning, usually between eight and nine o'clock, and draw blood. He had a private room located at the end of the hall. His room was quite scarce. As for flowers and the

like, there was nothing. You must remember no one
was supposed to know he was there. He'd either
say, "Good morning," "How are you?" and
sometimes, "Get the hell out," because obviously
when I came, it wasn't going to be enjoyable. He
had a deep, sharp voice. I remember they followed
his blood very closely. They always asked that his
room number, which was 172, be done first and the
results sent to Quick's office before 10 a.m.
Something rather odd about him was that he didn't
wear the usual hospital attire. He always wore a T-
shirt. I just thought it was awkward, as if he was
planning on just staying for the day, whereas in
reality he was there for a few weeks. When I usually
came into his room, he was in bed, but one time he
was sitting by the window smoking a cigarette. He
smoked quite often. When I walked in he remarked,
"That time again" or "Here we go again," something
to the effect that he was getting a little uptight with
hospitals and having his blood drawn. He was a
great one for puzzles and the like. Not that I can say
I ever saw him doing any puzzles, but they were
next to his bed with a pen.

His leaving the hospital was as quiet as his arrival.
He was just gone one day when I came to work and
I can't remember if I recalled his leaving or not. I
remember having a vague idea he wasn't doing too
well. I know he didn't look too well. He was rather
grey in color and was always in bed. He appeared to
be a very small man, not that I'm a large woman by
any means, but he always hit me as small and, I hate
to say it—-frail. I wouldn't say he looked sick, but he
looked under the weather, like he wasn't feeling
well. [400]

At the time of Lon's illness, radium was the only accepted
treatment for those suffering from cancer. Exposing a person's body
to doses of radium, no matter how minimal they were, probably did
as much to hasten the patient's death as the cancer itself did.

A Thousand Faces

There has been much speculation as to how Lon's cancer began. One account claimed it originated while Lon was filming the snow scenes for *Thunder*, when a piece of artificial snow (which was supposedly made from gypsum and asbestos) became lodged in his throat. Adela Rogers St. Johns, in a magazine article about Chaney that appeared the year after his death, stated that Lon had had his tonsils removed in September 1929 and began work on *Thunder* shortly thereafter. [401] According to her, during the filming of the storm sequences, the artificial snowflake lodged in the unhealed portion of Lon's throat, which ultimately caused his cancer. However, *Thunder* was released in July 1929, five months before Lon had his tonsils removed.

In reality, the snowflake story was a concoction of the M-G-M publicity department, made up to minimize the severity of Chaney's illness. Also, in an attempt to keep the ever-curious press at bay, the studio released a statement declaring Chaney had gone to the Mayo Brothers Hospital, not Memorial Hospital. [402] Even the staff at Memorial Hospital had been given the snowflake story as the reason for Chaney's visit. [403] It is preposterous, however, to believe that an artificial snowflake, even one made of known carcinogens, could have caused Chaney's illness in the seven months between the filming of these sequences and his diagnosis of lung cancer! Overlooked (especially at that time) is the fact that Lon was for many years a heavy cigarette smoker and this no doubt is what caused his cancer.

The studio was a willing accomplice to these rumors, even pointing out that Lon had burst a blood vessel in his throat during the filming of *The Unholy Three,* while imitating a parrot. [404] This incident, according to coworker Harry Earles, never happened. [405] The story appeared in several newspapers at the time of Chaney's death and was probably released to the press to circumvent the fact that Lon had suffered yet another throat hemorrhage (a common occurrence for those suffering from lung cancer) which kept him off production for two days. [406]

Another rumor, one that one family member suggests may be true, is that Lon's death from a hemorrhage of the throat was the result of a doctor's accidentally nicking an artery while treating his throat, which caused the actor to bleed to death. [407] Unfortunately there is no way to substantiate this claim, so it joins yet another misleading story that surfaced about eighteen years ago. A writer of filmscript books asserted that Chaney had been a morphine addict! (When I questioned the writer's sources, he recanted his claim.) Even Chaney's grandson, Lon Ralph Chaney, branded this statement as ludicrous. [408] While it is probable that in the last few months of his life Chaney may have been given morphine to ease his pain, this certainly doesn't qualify him as being an addict. [409]

After returning from New York, the Chaneys took up residence at the Beverly-Wilshire Hotel while awaiting the completion of the final touches to their new home on Whittier Drive in Beverly Hills. Lon personally selected the furniture for the house he dreamed about but which, sadly, he would never occupy. [410] In late July, Lon and Hazel went to their new cabin outside Big Pine, California, in the eastern Sierra Nevadas, but the combination of the high altitude and recurring hemorrhages cut their visit short. On August 20, Lon entered St. Vincent's Hospital after suffering the first of three serious hemorrhages. Shortly after his arrival, he was diagnosed with a serious case of anemia. He was close to death when the newspapers detailed the seriousness of his illness on August 22. After this announcement, the switchboard at M-G-M studios was so overwhelmed by phone calls from fans across the country offering to donate blood for their hero that the studio was forced to hire extra operators to answer all the calls. [411]

In an effort to conserve his strength during his final days at the hospital, Lon used sign language to speak to his wife and son. [412] No doubt the numerous treatments he was receiving not only irritated his throat but also depleted his energy to such a degree that talking became difficult. Hazel Chaney said she had learned sign language from Lon's father, of whom she was very fond because he had so many of the same characteristics that Lon displayed. These lessons proved valuable because she was able to act as an interpreter between Lon and the doctors and nurses. [413] On Sunday, August 24, the hospital issued a statement to the effect that Chaney had passed the crisis and, if there were no complications, his condition was expected to improve. The following day he slipped into a coma, and on August 26, 1930, at 12:55 a.m., Lon Chaney died from a hemorrhage of the throat. He was 47 years old.

Newspapers carried the shocking announcement that one of Hollywood's most popular stars was dead. Co-workers and fans alike were dumbstruck by the unexpected news. "The people [M-G-M studio employees] I talked with couldn't believe it," Willard Sheldon recalled. [414] Joseph Newman, an assistant director at the studio, agreed. "None of us knew he was terminally ill. It was a great shock to all of us. There was a sad feeling all over the lot." [415] On the day of his funeral, all of the studios observed a moment of silence. Several theatres, many of which were showing his talking picture at the time of his death, held memorial services in Chaney's honor.

Eulogies were printed in several newspapers and fan magazines honoring Chaney's memory. One of the most eloquent appeared in *Screen Book Magazine*:

> "The Man of a Thousand Faces" has turned them all
> toward the Unknown. Lon Chaney has hit the
> longest trail. The trail which, soon or late, must be
> traveled alike by star and extra—alone. But there is
> no death for those who live in beloved memories,
> Lon Chaney attains immortality. Although the long
> farewell is spoken, the parting is not absolute. For

Lon lives, too, in the shadowland of celluloid which holds for posterity the power of his dynamic personality, the strength of his resonant, vibrant voice.

No man in pictures—nor woman, either—has won the wide space in the popular heart which Chaney could call his own. For years millions thronged to the lure of his name. A name which was spoken and known in lands where presidents and princes and potentates meant nothing. It was not so much that pictures made him famous, as it was that he, in his inimitable artistry, advanced the far-flung banners of filmdom....

Chaney was one of the two or three truly great artists, and the screen may never know of a greater, more accomplished pantomimist. There never was an actor whose every gesture carried more feeling, more eloquence than Chaney. He will be missed...not only by the producers to whom he represented a gigantic box-office attraction, but to the millions who have seen him on the screen and who took him into their hearts. [416]

After Lon Chaney was laid to rest and the tributes had faded from view, Creighton Chaney said, "Hollywood forgot my dad." [417]

But to say that Chaney is forgotten is inaccurate. In the years since his death, especially from the 1930s through the early years of television in the 1950s, Chaney, along with his contemporaries from the Silent Era, was often featured in short subjects dealing with cinema's early days. Of course, these clips usually featured Lon in *The Hunchback of Notre Dame* and *Phantom of the Opera*, which helped foster the misconception of him as a "horror actor." Thanks to the 1957 film biography and even to the monster magazines, Chaney's memory, albeit stereotyped as a performer in horror films, has not diminished. Weber's Bread even used Chaney in one of

A Thousand Faces

their advertising campaigns in the early 1970s, featuring Lon in a pose from *Phantom of the Opera* with the accompanying tag line, "When Lon Chaney was making faces, Weber's was making bread."

Today, a new generation is discovering the masterful artistry of this unique actor. In 1994, Lon Chaney was the subject of three film festivals that drew large audiences at the Film Forum in New York City, the Roxie Theatre in San Francisco, and the International Mystery Film Festival in Cattolica, Italy. That same year saw the dedication of a United States postage stamp series featuring ten silent screen stars, which included a questionable rendition of Chaney by famous artist Al Hershfeld. *The Hunchback of Notre Dame* was presented in March 1995, with a full orchestral accompaniment at the Copley Symphony Hall in San Diego, and all 2,200 seats sold out. The demand to see this frequently-screened picture led to a second showing the same evening, and despite the late hour, it played to a large and appreciative audience. At The Silent Movie Theatre in Hollywood, Lon Chaney continues to be a popular draw. Whereas once only those who had originally seen Chaney's pictures were the common patrons, now a younger group of admirers makes up a large percentage of the audience.

As long as his unique talent is able to reach out and magically touch a viewer, Lon Chaney will never be forgotten.

ew photo from *Laugh, Clown, Laugh* (1928). Left to right, kneeling in front row: Willard Sheldon hird from left), cameraman James Wong Howe (sixth from left). Standing: Cissy Fitzgerald (third om left), Lon, director Herbert Brenon, and Bernard Seigel (in clown make-up behind Brenon). Courtesy of Willard Sheldon)

_on shakes hands with director Herbert Brenon on the theatre set of *Laugh, Clown, Laugh* as ameraman James Wong Howe watches.

This scene is missing from the existing print. In it, Tito (Lon) and Simonette (Loretta Young, left) meet his former partner, Simon (Bernard Seigel), who has been reduced to performing on the streets. The two men get back together and become a successful team.

A scene from the deleted happy ending of *Laugh, Clown, Laugh*. Bernard Seigel, Lon, Loretta Young, and Nils Asther are seen.

ıpular songs tied to movie releases are nothing new. Here are two copies of sheet music from two ıaney films. The song *Laugh, Clown, Laugh* was one of 1928's biggest hits, although there is no :ord that *Ching, Ching, Chinaman* shared a similar spotlight in 1922.

:his scene is missing from the existing print of *While the City Sleeps*, where Dan (Lon) requests that ı officer be stationed outside his apartment to protect Myrtle, as his landlady (Polly Moran) ıvesdrops.

These three photos show scenes from the opening of the silent version of *While The City Sleeps* (1928).

. Roy Harlacher (left) of the Los Angeles Police Department points out the proper way to handle a
police shotgun to Lon, as director Jack Conway (right) watches.

on attracts a crowd as he inspects his car at the Los Angeles train station upon his arrival from New
ork City.

Lon shows his 16 mm Filmo camera to the Prince of Sweden (center) and the Prince of Denmark (left) during their visit to the M-G-M studio.

Lon photographs William Haines (front row, third from left) with several Marines while on location at the Marine base. Sgt. H.H. Hopple (next to Lon) speaks to director George Hill and actor Eddie Gribbon (right).

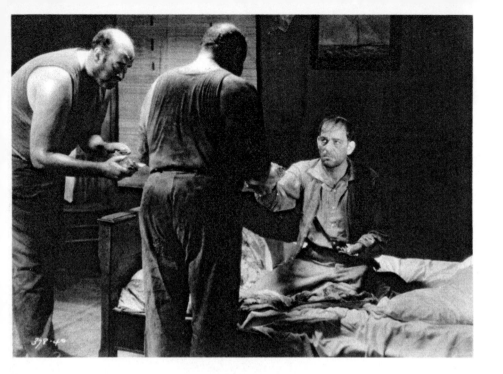

t from the final print of the picture,this scene shows Phroso (Lon) splitting the profits from his gging and being thrown out of a bar with Tiny (Roscoe Ward, left) and Babe (Kalla Pasha, center).

azel Chaney said that Lon burned the roof of his mouth while learning how to eat fire for scenes in *est of Zanzibar* (1928).

The Human Duck scene was also cut from the final pint. Doc (Warner Baxter) acts as the barker to draw the curious, as Babe (Kalla Pasha, sitting on stool) acts indifferent.

on's popularity wasn't only the subject of that well-known joke, but also extended to a song (*Lon Chaney's Gonna Get You If You Don't Watch Out!*), as well as many comic strips of the period, as an be seen above.

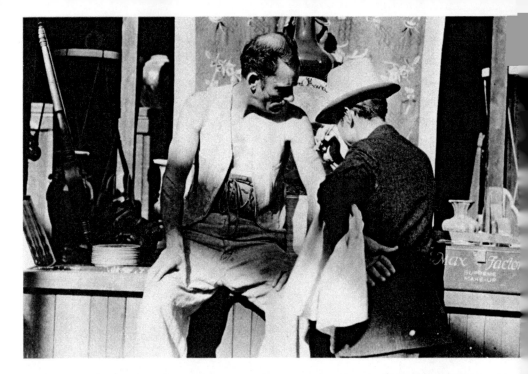

Lon is given a helping hand by an unknown make-up artist on the set of *Where East is East* (1929).
order to paint some scars on his own upper arm, it was necessary for Chaney to have some help.

Tod Browning (center) watches Lon and Lupe Velez. *Where East is East* was the last picture the tw
men would make together.

Novelization of movies was quite popular in the 1920's, released in either hardbound or paperback. Here are some paperback versions based on some of Chaney's pictures.

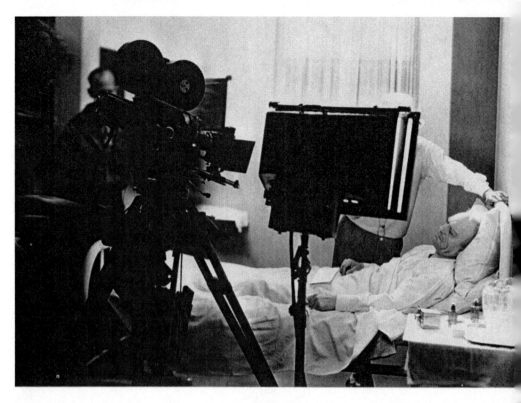

This scene from *Thunder* (1929) was shot the day Lon returned to work after being out sick for ▮ days.

Director William Nigh (second from left) and Lon (center) on location in Green Bay, Wisconsin.

INTER-OFFICE COMMUNICATION

METRO-GOLDWYN-MAYER STUDIOS

To ____ Mr. Thalberg _____

Subject ____ LON CHANEY _____

From ____ M. E. Greenwood ____ Date ____ Oct. 1st, 1929.

On account of incapacity, Lon's contract has been suspended since July 25, 1929. We have the right to extend for the time of his incapacity.

Lon saw me Saturday morning and said that he had notified you that he was still sick and not ready to work; and that he was leaving on a trip to be gone for possibly six weeks.

If the above coincides with his notice to you, will you please initial this memorandum so that there may be no question whatsoever about the term of his incapacity?

M.E. GREENWOOD

He Told me 4 weeks

This inter-office memo refers to Lon's continuing absence from work. It was about this time that he was diagnosed with lung cancer. Note Thalberg's writing and initial at the bottom.

Lon looks warily at the microphone that director Jack Conway (left) points to as Lila Lee (right) looks on. *The Unholy Three* (1930)

494-23

The end sequency of *The Unholy Three* that was discarded. In this scene, Rosie (Lila Lee, left) makes good on her promise to Echo (Lon) by returning to him. Realizing she really loves Hector, Echo releases the girl from her bargain. The scene was replaced with Echo saying good-bye at the train and reuniting Rosie and Hector.

s herald for *The Unholy Three* trumpets Chaney's talking debut.

Promotional ad. *The Bugle Sounds* was announced as one of Lon's upcoming talking pictures after the release of *The Unholy Three*.

INTER-OFFICE COMMUNICATION
All Department

To _____

Subject _____

Mr. Mayer   August 27-30
From _____ Date _____

> To honor the memory of our beloved friend, Lon Chaney,
> whose untimely passing has been a severe blow to us all,
> this studio will observe a period of silence tomorrow,
> Thursday, at three o'clock.
>
> At this time the remains are to be lowered to their final
> resting place and in respect to our departed co-worker
> everyone at the studio is requested to maintain complete
> silence at his post, between signals of the siren.
>
>   LOUIS B. MAYER

This inter-office memo was sent to every department notifying them of the moment of silence to be observed for Chaney.

Lon's casket is carried out from the chapel of the Cunningham and O'Connor Funeral Home on August 28, 1930. Lieutenant-Commander H. S. Dyer (left, hat over heart) leads the procession. Lon's pallbearers are as follows — On the left side of casket: Clinton Lyle (partially obscured), Claude Parker, and R. L. Hinckley On the right: Phil Epstein, John Jeske, and William Dunphy.

Chaney's death sparked many tributes, including this touching editorial cartoon. The small lion cub named Leo referred to the trademark lion that introduced each M-G-M picture. (Courtesy of Lamar D. Tabb Collection)

HIS LAST MASK

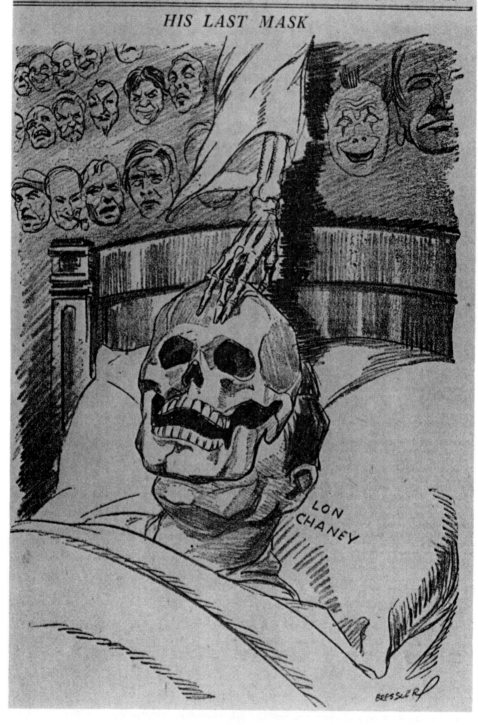

Another editorial cartoon, albeit a little morbid, honoring Chaney's talent. (Courtesy of Lamar D. Tabb Collection)

Chaney's Life on Film:
Man of a Thousand Faces

(1957)

An early conception of the artwork for the movie poster. Even though Lon Chaney was a silent screen actor, the artist must have forgotton. Notice the microphone and boom in the conception of the *Hunchback* at the lower left.

Hollywood has always found biographical films of notable personalities to be lucrative, and the industry first turned its attention to one of its own in 1946 with *The Jolson Story*. By the end of the 1950s, twelve film biographies had been produced, the subjects ranging from serial queen Pearl White to Buster Keaton, Will Rogers, and Eddie Cantor. Most of these movies were either moderately or highly successful at the box office.

Ralph Wheelwright, who had worked in M-G-M's publicity department in the late 1920s, had written a story based on Lon Chaney's life. While working with James Cagney on *These Wilder Years* (1956), Wheelwright mentioned his treatment to the actor. Cagney expressed interest in the project, and agent Lester Salkow put together a deal with Universal-International to produce the picture with Cagney as its star. [418] On May 3, 1956, *Variety* announced that Robert Arthur would produce the picture and had assigned R. Wright Campbell to write the screenplay. Ivan Goff and Ben Roberts, who had penned other screenplays for Cagney, were later brought in to polish the script. [419] Joseph Pevney was chosen to direct the movie, which was scheduled to go into production in early November 1956.

With Cagney signed at a salary of $75,000 plus a percentage of the profits, [420] attention turned to the casting of the co-starring, supporting, and bit roles. To obtain the use of Irving Thalberg's name in the picture, the studio agreed to give Thalberg's widow, actress

A Thousand Faces

Norma Shearer, the final say in casting the role of Thalberg. One day at the Beverly Hills Hotel, she spotted a young man, Robert J. Evans, who bore a strong resemblance to her late husband, and she insisted he be given the role. [421] Universal was forced to acquiesce to Shearer's demands, despite the fact that Evans had little professional training. In his autobiography, Evans recalls how Shearer coached him to look and sound exactly like Thalberg. [422] In her obsessiveness, she even dictated that he wear no make-up, lest he look like a "pretty boy actor." Evans was told by the studio that in spite of Norma's wishes, he'd have to sit in the make-up chair because otherwise, since Cagney was so heavily made up, their skin tones wouldn't match on camera. When Shearer saw the footage, she was enraged that Evans had not followed her strict orders. But director Joseph Pevney was able to explain the situation, calming her anger. [423] (In the early 1970s, Robert J. Evans acquired the position he had played in *Man of a Thousand Faces* when he was placed in charge of production for Paramount Pictures.) Silent screen comedians Hank Mann and Snub Pollard were signed to appear in the scene in which Cagney finds work as an extra in a slapstick comedy. [424] Clarence Kolb, who with his partner, Max Dill, had hired a relatively unknown Lon Chaney in 1912, agreed to give the producers clearance to use his old stage routines and to supply technical advice for $2,500. [425] Actor Troy Donahue, who at that time was a contract player at Universal, played an assistant director in several of the scenes in which Cagney, as Chaney, finds work as an extra on the early Universal Studios lot.

Cagney went through a variety of make-up tests in preparation for the re-creation of several famous character faces that would be used in the film. While making motion pictures had changed quite a lot since Chaney's time, make-up had yet to graduate to the technical levels of recent years. The days of cotton and collodion were passé, but foam rubber appliances had yet to advance from the full-face mask to individual pieces. In order to re-create Chaney's make-up for *The Hunchback of Notre Dame* and *Phantom of the Opera*, Bud Westmore (who had replaced Jack Pierce as head of Universal's make-up department in 1948) made foam rubber pieces that covered the entire face, save for the areas around the mouth and eyes. (Today, individual pieces—cheeks, neck, eyelids, foreheads, and so on—are made and applied separately. This gives a more realistic appearance to the appliance and allows the actor to speak freely.) Cagney's make-up as the Phantom was an entire mask glued onto his face. While it left the mouth area open, his speech nevertheless was limited in this make-up. Also, because Cagney had several scenes of dialogue while in his Quasimodo make-up (which bears no resemblance to Chaney's), the entire piece had to end just above the upper lip, for a full-face appliance would have been too restrictive. One advantage the full-face appliances had over the individual pieces of today, however, was the shorter amount of time needed for their application. It took roughly an hour and a half to apply these two well-known make-ups to Cagney's countenance. [426] Even in scenes in which he appears "as is," Cagney wore a foam rubber piece on the tip of his nose to make it appear longer and more similar to Chaney's nose. The make-up budget for the picture amounted to $28,500, which was extremely high for that time, although by today's standards, this budget could conservatively be quadrupled. [427]

Filming commenced at nine o'clock on the morning of November 7, 1956. Appropriately, the first day's filming took place on Stage 28, the Phantom stage, where Chaney had filmed *Phantom of the Opera* thirty-two years earlier. [428] Cagney's dance number with the dressmaker's dummy was the first scene to be shot. The recreation of the unmasking scene for *Phantom of the Opera* was also shot on the Phantom Stage, using the original chandelier that had appeared in the Chaney picture. The entire picture was filmed on the Universal lot, with the exception of one sequence which was shot at a house in nearby Toluca Lake, California, which served as Chaney's Hollywood home. [429] The scene at Chaney's cabin, was filmed on the studio's back lot in an area called Pollard Lake. In 1977, when the lake area was designated as the home of the now-popular *Jaws* attraction for the studio tour, the cabin was moved to an isolated hill behind what was then the transportation department. It was finally torn down ten years later.

The picture was shot on a brisk thirty-five day schedule, and completed principal photography on December 27, 1956. [430] What is truly amazing is that the average work day never lasted longer than ten and a half hours, including time for lunch! To those who work in the industry today, that is nothing short of a miracle. (Currently, an average work day on a motion picture or a television show can vary between twelve and eighteen hours, and most pictures require between two and three months to complete principal photography.) On January 9 and 10, 1957, the company was recalled to shoot additional scenes that involved Irving Thalberg's arrival on the Phantom stage and his subsequent memorial speech. The following day, the scenes featuring Chaney as a young boy, coming home after getting into a fight, were shot on the New England Street section of the studio's back lot as well as on Stages 6 and 7. The company then returned to the Phantom stage, where they shot additional scenes of Cagney dancing with the dress dummy. Ironically, the picture started and completed photography on the very stage where Chaney made one of his most famous pictures for Universal. [431] The final negative footage count for the picture was 136,935 feet. As of August 15, 1957, the budget was $1,267,000, and the final estimate (which included studio overhead and publicity) was $1,317,000. [432]

The picture had its first preview at the Broadway Theatre in Santa Ana, California, approximately 40 miles south of Los Angeles, on May 25, 1957. The preview proved to be a success for Universal. Two additional previews were held in southern California, one on

Chaney's Life on Film: Man of a Thousand Faces

May 29 at the D'Anza Theatre in Riverside and the other on June 7 at the Fox West Coast Theatre in Long Beach. [433] Both echoed the reaction at the first preview, and the audience's comments indicated that Universal had a hit on its hands. [434] Audience members, asked which scenes they liked best, made the following comments on the questionnaire cards:

> No scene stands out in particular. They were so beautifully integrated.

> Scenes depicting characters he made famous.

> The one of the Hunchback and where Lon leaves his son at foster home.

> Last fishing scene [where Chaney and his son are reunited].

> Which petal of the rose is loveliest? [435]

Asked what they didn't like about the picture, most people responded that the re-creation of the whipping scene for *The Hunchback of Notre Dame* was too gruesome. Others faulted Robert J. Evans' portrayal of Thalberg as too stiff. Asked what they would say to their friends about this picture, the preview audiences gave very positive replies:

> Very moving picture.

> Very good picture! Don't miss it!

> Cagney is great.

> The picture is fabulous. You should go see it right away.

A Thousand Faces

One interesting question, which was written by a member of the preview audiences was, "Who was Lon Chaney, Jr.?" [436]

Like any picture, *Man of a Thousand Faces* had scenes that, for one reason or another, were cut before its release. Unlike some films, the deleted scenes were of minimal importance to the story; yet some of them would have helped to enhance the character of Chaney. The following descriptions will give the reader a general idea of the nature of some of the deleted scenes:

> Cleva (Dorothy Malone) is wheeled in the delivery room while Lon and Clarence Locan (Jim Backus) are assured by a nurse that she is in good hands. [437]
>
> After learning Lon had her fired from her singing job, Cleva runs back into the taxi from the theatre (where she and Lon had gone to pick up Creighton) and orders the driver to go. Lon exits the theatre with his son in his arms, watching the taxi leave.
>
> In the film, just before making her suicide attempt, Cleva enters the theatre and starts down the hallway toward Chaney's dressing room. A missing sequence features Cleva entering Lon's dressing room and caressing her sleeping son with tears coming down her cheeks.
>
> After getting some encouragement from Gert (Marjorie Rambeau) regarding extra work, Lon watches the various assistant directors call for certain types. In the film, the scene dissolves to Chaney getting hit in his face with a pie. A deleted scene had Lon watching the events in the extras' bullpen; after the extras have been chosen, he overhears someone talk about going to grab a sandwich. Lon reaches into his pockets but stops halfway indicating that he's broke. The scene then dissolves to a saloon, where we see Chaney dancing to the music from a player-piano. (It is one of those

saloons where a beer for a nickel came with a free sandwich.) As Lon continues dancing, Gert and the fourth assistant director (Troy Donahue) enter. Gert watches Lon and pantomimes something to the assistant director. When Lon finishes his dance number, he takes one of the free sandwiches. Gert approaches him and tells him to be in the bullpen after lunch. The film then cuts to Lon getting hit in the face with the pie, and Lon's career in motion pictures has begun.

In re-creation of the whipping on the pillory from *The Hunchback of Notre Dame* was a brief, deleted scene in which Lon stops and talks to Gert, who working as one of the extras, while an assistant director gives directions to the crowd before the cameras roll. [438]

In his autobiography, James Cagney relates a story that the producers wanted to use but, because Creighton was alive at the time, could not. As the story goes, Creighton was searching for Cleva after his father's death. He approached a house where the young man believed his mother to be working. A woman answered the door, and Creighton inquired about Cleva Chaney. The woman replied that no one by that name resided there, but, just then, another voice from inside the house called, "Who is it, Cleva?" [439]

For director Joseph Pevney, *Man of a Thousand Faces* was one of three pictures he made for Universal in 1956. Before turning to film directing in the early 1950's, Pevney was a well-known stage and screen actor. His directorial credits range from such feature films as *Tammy and the Bachelor*, *The Midnight Story*, and *Away All Boats* to "The Munsters", "Star Trek," and the "Adam-12" television series. Pevney, who was not originally interested in making the Chaney biography, recalled:

A Thousand Faces

Robert Arthur had asked me to direct the Chaney
film and I told him I had wanted to make this other
picture, *Tammy and the Bachelor*. The Chaney
film was a heavy drama and I really wanted to make
this nice little film. He finally said that if I would
direct *Man of a Thousand Faces*, he would get me
Tammy and the Bachelor, and that's what
happened. I never had any personal contact with
the Chaney family and none of them ever came to
visit the set. I worked with [screenwriters] Ivan
Goff and Ben Roberts to help the beginning and
ending of the scenes move smoothly. Jimmy
[Cagney] liked their work, and they could pound
out material really fast. I had wanted the whole film
to show more of Chaney the actor, but the script
tended to play up the problems with Chaney's
domestic life.

Jimmy was a wonderful actor to direct. The thing I
remember most was his interest in the dance
numbers. I think one of the reasons he took the role
is because he knew Chaney had danced on the
stage, and this would give him the opportunity to
do some dance numbers. He spent a lot of time
rehearsing so they [the dancing sequences] looked
right. I can't tell you how many times we shot those
two dance numbers until Jimmy was satisfied. He
was almost like a child in his desire to dance in a
scene. At the end of some scenes, he would break
into a dance step and asked me to keep the camera
rolling. I don't think he realized what a great actor
he really was. To him it was more of a job and he
never got excited over it.

Bud Westmore and Jack Kevan [of the make-up
department] didn't have enough time to prepare
the make-up. They didn't have the luxury of time
Chaney had in his day. When Jimmy was in a
certain make-up, we had to film everything right
then and there. When it came to the various make-

ups, Jimmy made enormous contributions as to what would be easier for him to wear. He ran Chaney's *Phantom of the Opera* several times, trying to get his gestures correct. I sent him several stills of Chaney and he looked them over, but he wasn't deeply concerned about the acting. I remember he didn't think the scenes with Chaney in the extras' bullpen was very important, but to me it was an essential part of the picture.

Jimmy recommended Dorothy Malone for the role of Cleva after he saw her performance in *Written on the Wind*. I thought she was a little to old for the part, but she turned out great. She turned Cleva into a real bitch. We had to cut the scene of her going into the dressing room to see her son before she attempts suicide. If we had left it in the picture, it made her role too sympathetic, and she was really the villain of the picture. The other scenes were cut mainly because the picture was running too long and the studio was getting nervous that a long-running picture would affect ticket sales. Jimmy also recommended Roger Smith for the older part of Creighton. I had another actor in mind, but we decided to give Jimmy what he wanted. When it came to the role of Thalberg, we didn't have anyone in mind because Norma Shearer walked in and said she wanted this guy [Robert J. Evans] for the part. She had the final word in casting the part, and I just wish she had cast someone with a little more experience. I spent a lot of time with Evans working on his scenes. Thalberg wasn't as important to the story as Norma thought. The part could have been called anything, but [Robert] Arthur wanted to use the name Thalberg, so we had to deal with Norma.

I spoke with Hank Mann and Snub Pollard before we shot the scene where Chaney appears as an extra in a slapstick comedy. They offered some advice about the old days, but we didn't really have

A Thousand Faces

a technical advisor for the scenes of "old Hollywood." We had quite a few extras on the set who said they had worked on *The Hunchback of Notre Dame* or *Phantom of the Opera* with Chaney. I know the art department had spoken with people who had worked on some of Chaney's films and they were given some ideas.

I found our sign language technical advisor, Marion Ramsey, in the director's building at the studio. She was working as the secretary for some of directors on the lot, including myself. When I learned that her parents were deaf and she knew sign language, I hired her to teach the actors. We were searching for a kid to play Creighton at age four. Finally, this guy in the studio's film library suggested his kid [Dennis Rush] and we took a look at him. He was great! That scene where Jimmy says good-bye to him at the foster school broke me up. I was crying like a baby behind the camera during that scene.

The ending of the picture simply finished with Chaney dying in bed, and his family standing there. I wasn't very happy with that idea, so I had the camera dolly out of the room and slowly pan across, taking in all the various sketches of Chaney's face that adorned the wall. It gave the picture a strong ending and allowed the musical score to reach a higher crescendo for the finale.

We ran Chaney's *The Hunchback of Notre Dame* and *Phantom of the Opera* for everyone in the film. It helped give people an idea what we were trying to accomplish. When we shot the recreation of *The Hunchback of Notre Dame*, I wanted it to be very important. I had requested a large number of extras, and the morning we shot it on the back lot, I had only 75 extras! Well, I couldn't shoot this big scene with only 75 people. I mean, I have this big square and I wanted to fill it up just like the Chaney picture had done. So I went to the unit manager and said,

"Look, I can't shoot this scene without more
extras." He asked me how many I wanted, and I
replied 300 or 500. Well he almost had a heart
attack! I think he was expecting me to say 10 or
20. But 300 or 500 was a lot of people and
Universal was extremely tight with a buck. So he
said I'd get more tomorrow and to make due with
what I had for the day. So I would bunch these
people up in one section and then when we moved
the camera, I would move 'em around so you
couldn't recognize anyone and bunch them up in
another area. The next day the studio gave me an
additional 100 extras! [440]

Man of a Thousand Faces offically premièred at the RKO Palace
Theatre in New York City on August 13, 1957. James Cagney,
Dorothy Malone, Jane Greer, and Robert J. Evans attended the much
heralded event. Two days later, the film premièred at the Paramount
Theatre on Hollywood Boulevard. [441] At the same time, the London
première took place at the Odeon Theatre in Leicester Square, with
several English performers in attendance, including Boris Karloff. [442]
The movie did exceptionally well at the box office, taking in $14,000
in its first two days. [443] During its seven-week run at the RKO Palace
and the Paramount, the film earned $213,600. Audience response
was very positive, and one Universal employee noted when exiting
the Paramount Theatre:

I think the teeners (and everyone else) showed
unusual respect for the picture all the way
through....All the mature and elderly people I saw
were weeping at [the] finish, which, I guess,
precluded any applause (8:30 show) although the
picture did get quite a hand at the earlier show
(before the house filled up). Outside, it was
interesting to see the one-sheet [movie poster] with
the make-up stills and explanatory captions got all
the attention. [444]

A Thousand Faces

Most critics praised the picture, although several pointed out that it tended to focus on Chaney's domestic problems rather than his talent. Many reviewers thought that Cagney's performance, as well as that of Celia Lovsky (who played Chaney's mother, Emma) were worthy of Academy Award nominations. The studio discussed the possibility of using these glowing reviews to subtly push Cagney and Celia Lovsky for nominations, but the only nomination the picture did receive was for best original screenplay. [445] *Man of a Thousand Faces* was selected by the Department of Health, Education and Welfare to be captioned for the deaf. The film earned more than $2.4 million for Universal, making it one of the studio's biggest hits of 1957.

This author is often asked how close this picture comes to capturing its subject matter. My reply is a mixture of appreciation and frustration. On the one hand, because it introduced me to Lon Chaney, *Man of a Thousand Faces* always will have a place in my heart. On the other hand, the more I learn about Lon Chaney, the more frustrated I become with this picture. It glosses over many facts and tends to paint Lon Chaney as a morose and unhappy man, whereas his personality, as I have learned over the years, was just the opposite.

Many film biographies, notably *The Buster Keaton Story,* seem to plagiarize their main character and, despite the facts, create whatever story suits the time. In that respect, *Man of a Thousand Faces* follows the facts much more closely than some, although it hardly gives one a true portrait of Chaney. The most glaringly inaccurate scenes include Cleva's (Dorothy Malone) not knowing that Lon's parents were deaf; Lon's being forced by the court to place his son in a foster school; Creighton's (Roger Smith) learning the truth about his mother before Lon died; and Lon's passing on his make-up case to his son. Of course, these scenes provided a considerable amount of drama and, accompanied by Frank Skinner's touching musical score, they kept many viewers reaching for their Kleenex boxes.

Overall, the picture is a success, despite the dramatization of many incidents. Although James Cagney does not resemble Chaney, he gives a credible performance. In recreating several of Chaney's performances, Cagney does not try to imitate the actor gesture for gesture but gives the essence of Chaney's performances. And despite the limitations of the script, Cagney manages to inject a few light moments into the role to show that Chaney was not a brooding and unhappy performer. For instance, when Locan (Jim Backus) brings Chaney's parents to his cabin, he waves a script at Lon. In mock fright, Cagney drops their bags and lets out a yell. "Oh no! This is vacation. Not allowed to read. My wife won't let me." In another scene, as Cagney takes a phone call on the studio stage, he walks past one of the set musicians and playfully kicks him on the backside, eliciting a *ba-rump-pump* from the musician's cello. The supporting cast delivers strong performances, with the exception of Robert J. Evans as Thalberg, who is dull, stiff, and uncharismatic. Dorothy Malone delivers a powerful performance as Cleva. Her work is so good, that she quickly creates sympathy for Cagney's Chaney.

The one scene, in this author's opinion, that captures Chaney's persona and talent with greasepaint, as well as the flavor of the early days of filmmaking, is the one in which he shows up one morning in the extras' bullpen with make-up case in hand. Reading the list of available parts, Chaney spots "Four Lascars, two with scars." He promptly sits on a bench and opens his make-up case. Within moments, he dexterously begins to alter his features into those of an East Indian sailor with a pronounced scar, as a group of extras huddle to watch the transformation. When the assistant directors assemble the extras, Chaney makes his way through the crowd, sporting an eye patch and a scarf on his head. Naturally, the assistant director spots him. "And you. I want that scar!" As Chaney closes up his make-up case, another assistant director comes over to get his name. Recognizing Chaney's name from a previous day's work, he asks, "What are you trying to do? Be a one-man crew on this ship?" To which Chaney replies, "You heard him, Joe, he'll be looking for this scar!" With that, he heads off to work.

No other biography of a Hollywood star has influenced a larger group of young viewers. For many, it has provided an introduction to the magic and wonders of greasepaint and helped ignite a desire to follow in the footsteps of one of Hollywood's greatest make-up artists. Because of this movie, one former Ringling Bros.–Barnum and Bailey circus clown was inspired to learn sign language so that he could communicate with those in his audience who couldn't hear the laughter.

Despite its inaccuracies and the lack of scenes showcasing Chaney's great acting talent, *Man of a Thousand Faces* is a gratifying movie, and it continues to introduce the legend of Lon Chaney to a new generation of moviegoers.

ilming a scene for *Man of a Thousand Faces* (1957). James Cagney (in clown make-up) stands in ack of wagon. Director Joseph Pevney (left, in rain hat and coat) watches.

Recreating the whipping scene from *The Hunchback of Notre Dame* on the original, but slightly altered, set. Director Joseph Pevney (right) stands on a ladder.

A scene cut from the final print. Cleva (Dorothy Malone) walks into Lon's dressing room to see her son, Creighton (Dennis Rush), before attempting suicide onstage.

The scene that best captures the unique make-up talent of Lon Chaney. Lon (James Cagney), working as an extra, gives his name to the assistance director (George Mather)

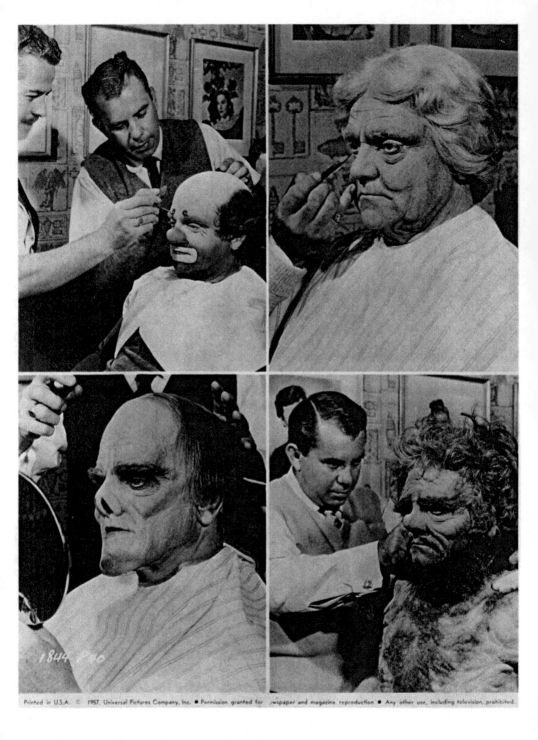

The various faces of James Cagney. Upper left: Cagney sits patiently for make-up artists Bud Westmore and Jack Kevan (left) as they apply finishing touches for the clown make-up. Upper right: Cagney is transformed into Mrs. O'Grady of *The Unholy Three*. Unlike Chaney, who used his own features, the lower half of Cagney's face was buried in foam rubber. Lower left: a pale imitation of Chaney's *Phantom of the Opera*. Lower right: Bud Westmore makes final adjustments on what is supposed to be Chaney as *The Hunchback of Notre Dame*.

In 1929, artist Al Herschfeld conceived this artwork for the pressbook of *Where East is East*. Lupe Velez (left) and Estelle Taylor (right) are featured with Chaney.

In 1994, Lon Chaney was immortalized on a United States postage stamp, along with other silent screen legends. Sixty-five years later, Al Herschfeld was once again commissioned to capture Chaney's visage. (Courtesy of the United States Postal Service)

Academy of Motion Picture Arts and Sciences tribute to Lon Chaney on June 27, 1983. Left to right: Ray Bradbury, Jackie Coogan, Lon Ralph Chaney, Patsy Ruth Miller, Dana Kalionzes (great-granddaughter of Lon Chaney), Connie Chaney, and Nicholas Kalionzes (great great grandson).

APPENDIX

Lon Chaney's Highest Grossing Pictures at M-G-M

The figures combine both domestic and foreign grosses. *The Monster* (1925) is not listed because it was a negative pick-up for the studio.

Tell It to the Marines (1927) $1,658,000
Laugh, Clown, Laugh (1928) $1,102,000
Mr. Wu (1927) $1,068,000
While the City Sleeps (1928) $1,035,000
Thunder (1929) $1,018,000
London After Midnight (1927) $1,004,00
The Unholy Three (1930) $988,000
West of Zanzibar (1928) $921,000
Where East Is East (1929) $920,000
He Who Gets Slapped (1924) $881,000
The Unknown (1927) $847,000
The Big City (1928) $833,000
Mockery (1927) $751,000
The Road To Mandalay (1926) $724,000
The Unholy Three (1925) $704,000
The Blackbird (1926) $656,000
Tower of Lies (1925) $653,000

Lon Chaney's Theatrical Appearances

This list of Chaney's theatrical appearances is by no means a complete one. As were his earliest screen appearances, much of his theatrical work was often uncredited in newspaper reviews at the time. However, this list indicates the scope of his stage roles and the plays in which he performed. Wherever possible, I have also included in parentheses the character Chaney portrayed in a play.

1902
Performed at the Colorado Springs Opera House:
The Little Tycoon (the Valet)

1903
Performed with the Casino Opera Company at the Opera House
    in Colorado Springs :
Said Pasha (Nockey)

Performed with the Columbia Comic Opera Company at the
    Opera House in Colorado Springs:
Chimes of Normandy (Assessor)

1906
Performed with the Columbia Comic Opera Company at the
    Delmar Gardens Theatre in Oklahoma City:
The Beggar Prince
Olivette
Said Pasha
Fra Diavolo
Pinafore
Girofle-Girofla
La Mascotte

1906 (Continued)

Ermine or the Two Vagabonds

The Bohemian Girl

1907

Performed at the Delmar Gardens Theatre in Oklahoma City:

La Mascotte

1909

This production originated out of Chicago and toured the
    Midwest to West Coast, performing at the Tabor Grand
    Theatre in Denver and the Opera House in Colorado
    Springs:

The Royal Chef (Lord Mito)

1911

Performed with the Charles Alphin Amusement Company at the
    Olympic Theatre in Los Angeles:

Peck's Bad Boy

A Dark Horse

Heinz in Ireland

The Aviator

The Speculators

It Happened in Reno

The Insurrectors

The Devil's Picnic

The Unkissed Man

Are You a Moose?

Three of a Kind

Who's the Fellow?

A Happy Thought

A Thousand Faces

1911 (Continued)

Performed with the Ferris Hartman Company at the Grand
  Opera House in Los Angeles:

The Girl Question (the Reporter and the Author)

The Broken Idol (J. Ely Muddleford)

The Gingerbread Man (the Gingerbread Man)

Jack and the Beanstalk (Sir Harry Haitewurk and Marquis De
  Corbas)

The Show Girl

The Time, The Place and The Girl

Performed with the Max Dill Company at the Savoy Theatre in
  San Francisco and the Majestic Theatre in Los Angeles:

The Rich Mr. Hoggenheimer

1912

Performed with Fischer's Follies at the Lyceum Theatre in Los
  Angeles:

The Hen Pecks (Ravioli)

The Song Birds

When Johnny Come Marching Home (Felix Graham)

Tillie's Nightmare

The Man Who Owns Broadway (Theatrical Man)

The Chaperons (Schnitzel)

The Yankee Prince (Steve Daly)

An American Idea (Count DeSouchet)

I.O.U.

Summer Flirts (Bubbles, a blackface role)

Adolph and Oscar

The Kissing Bugs

The Military Maids (Ezra Tuttle)

1913

Performed with the Kolb and Dill Company at the Savoy Theatre
    in San Francisco and the Majestic Theatre in Los Angeles:

Algeria (Ishi)

Peck O' Pickles

In Dutch

The Motor Girl (Adolphus)

Hoity-Toity

Serving only as a choreographer, Alcazar Theatre in San
    Francisco:

The Talk of The Town

Lon and his famous make-up case.

Lon Chaney and Joseph Dowling in the healing scene from *The Miracle Man* (1919).

This picture shows that Lon did not use egg membranes in his eyes to play the blind Pew in *Treasure Island* (1920). Instead he simply rolled his eyes up into his head for the duration of the scene. Lon is pictured here with director Maurice Tourneur and actess Shirly Mason, who played Jim Hawkins.

WARNING!

THIS IS NO
SUMMONS

You have not been arrested! But you ought to be if you pass up the chance of seeing the greatest American Melodrama ever shown on the screen

"OUTSIDE THE LAW"

STARRING

LON CHANEY

with PRISCILLA DEAN - RALPH LEWIS

You May Park in the

MAJESTIC Theatre, Elmira,

Space for About 1500 People

Thur.-Fri.-Sat., MAY 6-7-8

Keller Bros. & Miller, Printers, 221 Franklin St.,

Theatres developed many ways of advertising their product. This catchy gimmick was used to promote the 1926 re-release of *Outside the Law*. Note that Chaney is given star billing, compared to the "supported by" credit he received when the film was originally released in 1921. The change in billing reflected Chaney's growing popularity.

Universal's trade weekly advertising Chaney's upcoming picture. The title would be changed to *The Trap* prior to its release in May, 1922.

A Tom Forman Production
Presented by B. P. Schulberg

SHADOWS

featuring

Lon Chaney
Marguerite De La Motte
Harrison Ford
John Sainpolis
Buddy Messenger
Walter Long
Priscilla Bonner
Frances Raymond .

ACCLAIMED the best picture of the year by America's leading critics! A picture you will never forget! Chaney's performance is a milestone in the advancement of the photoplay art. Playing to smashing business everywhere.

It's a Preferred Picture

Poster for *While Paris Sleeps*, which was made under the title, *Glory of Love*.

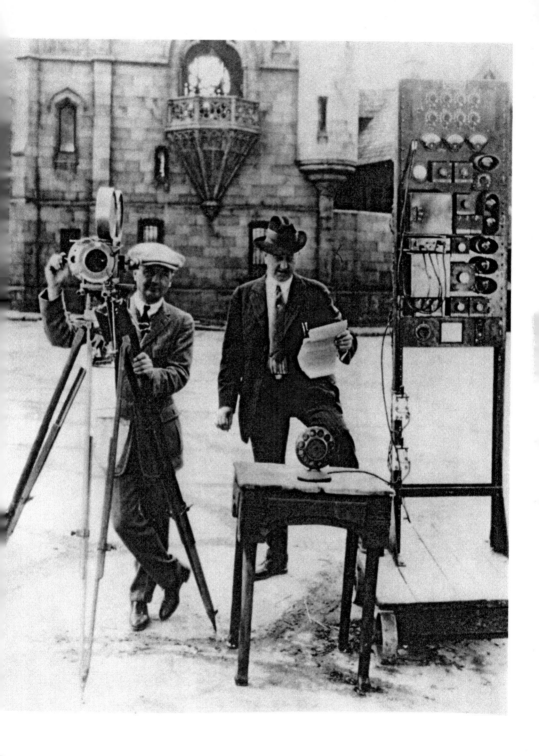

On the set of *The Hunchback of Notre Dame*, Wallace Worsley stands next to the public address system. Robert Newhard, A.S.C. stands behind the Bell & Howell camera.

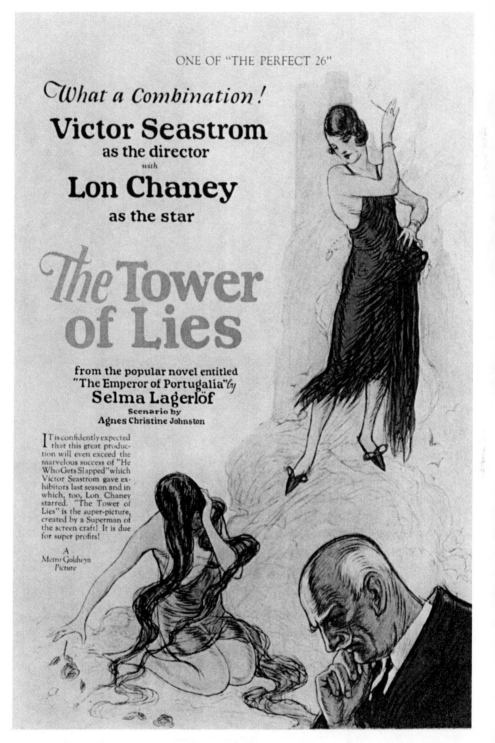
An ad from M-G-M's exhibitor's book advertising the upcoming release of *Tower of Lies*. The exhibitor books were sent to various theatre owners from every studio, advertising their future pictures.

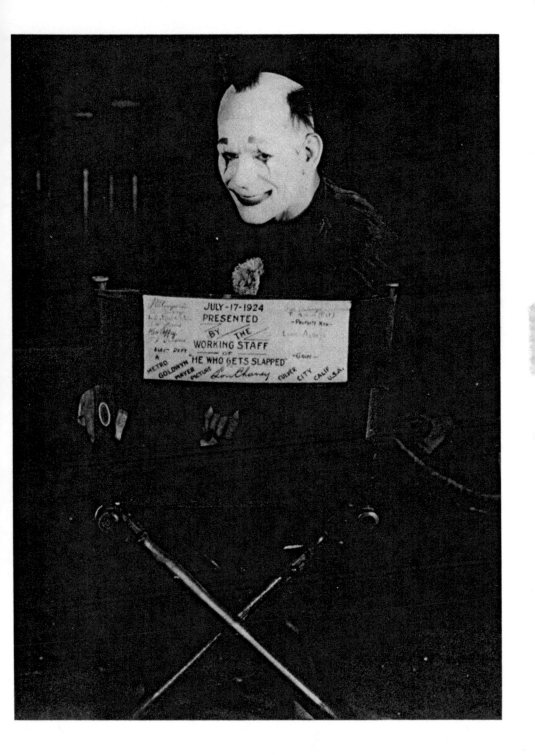

Lon poses with the chair given to him by the crew of *He Who Gets Slapped* (1924).

MELODRAMA!

IN which the sinister hand of a villain enmeshes a girl and her lover and a fortune in a web of intrigue and crime. Across the span of life fall tears; and tragedy follows romance, but Love raises its triumphant head at the thrilling end.

SPAN *of* LIFE

The Famous Stage Play *by* Sutton Vane *with*

LON CHANEY

RENEE ADOREE

No wonder this famous stage play achieved fame and fortune for its producers. It is the stuff of which the truly great success is made. And the picture, with Lon Chaney more forcefully picturesque than ever, is an attraction of which you can safely say: "Here is real money!"

A Metro-Goldwyn Picture

Lon had signed a contract with Louis B. Mayer Productions in 1923 to make this picture. The project was brought to M-G-M when Mayer's company became part of the merger. It became one of several projects planned for the actor that never materialized.

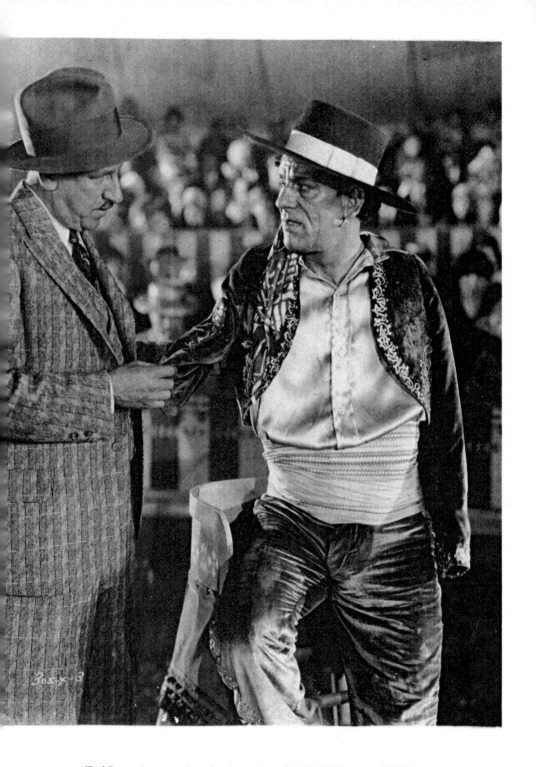

Tod Browning examines Lon's costume for *The Unknown* (1927).

LON
CHANEY *in*

TOD BROWNING'S *Production*
WEST OF ZANZIBAR

Endnotes

1. *Theatre Magazine*, October 1927.
2. *Colorado Springs Telegraph*, January 1, 1922.
3. *Motion Picture Magazine*, August 1927.
4. *Monsterscene*, March 1995.
5. Lon Ralph Chaney to the author, August 1983.
6. Aside from his height, Creighton's overall physical build and lack of his father's fluid and graceful body movements limited him to certain types of roles.
7. Vincent Price to the author, September 1979.
8. Hazel Chaney notes to Alfred Grasso, August 1932. From the Alfred Grasso family collection.
9. Ibid.
10. Ibid.
11. *Twinkle, Twinkle, Movie Star!* (New York: E. P. Dutton & Co., 1930).
12. Patrick Wood to the author, March 1985.
13. "There's Always Carpet Laying," *Motion Picture Classic*, March 1929.
14. *Colorado Springs Gazette*, April 20, 1902.
15. *Daily Oklahoman*, April 27, 1907.
16. A "flyman" is the stagehand who helps to shift the various backdrops during a stage play, moving them by means of a rope and pulley into the upper area of the stage known as "the flies."
17. Takashi Teshigawara to the author, July 1994.
18. *Los Angeles Times*, July 1, 1912.
19. *San Francisco Chronicle*, November 12, 1912. An interesting bit of obscure trivia relative to this review is that the critic, Waldemar Young, would later write the screenplay for *The Unholy Three* as well as those for several other successful Chaney-Browning pictures while under contract to M-G-M.
20. Stella George to the author, January 1984.

21. Ron Chaney, Jr. to the author, March 1990.
22. *The Big U*, (New York: A. S. Barnes & Co., 1977).
23. Ibid.
24. Ibid.
25. *The Universal Story*, (New York: Crown Publishers, 1983).
26. Ibid.
27. *Los Angeles Examiner*, March 16, 1915.
28. Ibid.
29. Ibid.
30. This unique idea was popular for some time, but when the constant public disruptions began to delay shooting, the tours were discontinued. They were reinstated in 1964 and to this day remain a very popular attraction.
31. *The Universal Story*, (New York: Crown Publishers, 1983).
32. Ibid.
33. Harvey Perry to the author, July 1974.
34. *The Universal Weekly*, December 6, 1913.
35. Ibid.
36. Betty Felch-Griffin to the author, January 1993.
37. Hazel Chaney notes to Alfred Grasso, August 1932. From the Alfred Grasso family collection.
38. Ibid.
39. Ibid.
40. Ibid.
41. Ibid.
42. Ibid.
43. Ibid.
44. Ibid.
45. Ibid.
46. Ibid.
47. Ibid.
48. Ibid.

49. "The True Life Story of Lon Chaney," *Photoplay*, January 1928.
50. Bob Birchard to the author, August 1988.
51. Hazel Chaney notes to Alfred Grasso, August 1932. From the Alfred Grasso family collection.
52. Ibid.
53. *Exhibitors Trade Review*, August 9, 1919.
54. Ibid.
55. Hazel Chaney notes to Alfred Grasso, August 1932. From the Alfred Grasso family collection.
56. Ibid.
57. Ibid.
58. Cutting continuity from the Alfred Grasso family collection.
59. Two other film versions were based on the Conrad novel, *Dangerous Paradise* (1930) and *Victory* (1940).
60. This was the second film in which Lon portrayed a dual role; the first one was *The Flashlight* (1917), in which he played half-brothers.
61. Walt Disney Productions made *Nikki, Wild Dog of the North* (1961), based on the Curwood novel; however, the plots of *Nomads of the North* and the Disney picture are not similar.
62. This sequence does not exist in any surviving prints. Hazel Chaney notes to Alfred Grasso, August 1932. From the Alfred Grasso family collection.
63. Ibid.
64. *The Penalty* was acquired by M-G-M during the 1924 merger. The studio rereleased the picture in 1926.
65. M-G-M Collection, USC Cinema and Television Library, Los Angeles.
66. A picture of this event was taken by a photographer which makes one suspect the validity of the arrest. It's possible that

it might have been staged for publicity purposes. The picture
is in Lon's personal photo album.

67. Exhibitors Trade Review, August 13, 1921.
68. Telegram to Herbert Brenon, August 20, 1921. From the Alfred Grasso family collection.
69. Telegram to Herbert Brenon, August 25, 1921. From the Alfred Grasso family collection.
70. From the Alfred Grasso family collection.
71. Ibid.
72. During this period, banks were not quick to write a loan to finance a film.
73. Zanuck and Chaney never collaborated on this or any other project. Letter from Alfred Grasso family collection.
74. The original name of the character was Radovitch. M-G-M Collection, USC Cinema and Television Library.
75. Ibid.
76. Ibid.
77. Interoffice memorandum. Author's collection.
78. Lobby cards came in a set of eight, each card measuring 11" x 14." One, called the title card, contained the title of the movie and either a picture of the principal players or some form of artwork. The other seven cards, referred to as scene cards, displayed artwork borders and a photograph of a scene from the picture. These cards were displayed in theatre lobbies as a form of advertisement, sometimes a few days or a week before the engagement.
79. M-G-M Collection, USC Cinema and Television Library.
80. Cutting continuity. Ibid.
81. His disguise as the cripple is similar to Chaney's Bishop character in *The Blackbird*.
82. Letter from Alfred Grasso family collection.

83. B. P. Schulberg was the producer of the film *Ching, Ching, Chinaman*, retitled *Shadows* on its release. In replying to Grasso's telegram, Lon stated that he would return on Monday, but wouldn't start until Wednesday, June 26.

84. The film was originally tinted in various hues. Day sequences featured either amber or sepia tones; night scenes were tinted in a blue tone.

85 Vance Pollock to the author, March, 1995.

86. *Door to Revelation*, (North Carolina: Pelley Publishers, 1939).

87. Ibid.

88. Ibid.

89. Ibid.

90. Priscilla Bonner to James Curtis, August 1992.

91. Hazel Chaney notes to Alfred Grasso, August 1932. From the Alfred Grasso family collection.

92. *Behind the Mask of Innocence*, (New York: Alfred A. Knopf, 1990).

93. *Wid's Film Daily*, December 8, 1922.

94. The role of Jude was played by George Cooper.

95. Jackie Coogan to the author, June 1983.

96. Chaney was not the first actor to essay the role as the novel was filmed three times prior to the 1922 version. "Acting Is Masquerade," *Motion Picture*, December, 1922.

97. Jackie Coogan to the author, June 1983.

98. Ibid.

99. Ibid.

100. "Dumps" was a term used when referring to second-and third-run movie theaters, which ran films after they had completed their engagements at all the first-run theaters.

101. "Cleared itself" refers to a film earning back its costs. After a film had recouped its initial expenses, the box office earnings became a profit.
102. Letter from the Alfred Grasso family collection.
103 "Gunsmoke" was one of the few popular television series to survive this problem. The half-hour episodes were sold to syndication, under the title "Marshal Dillon," while the one-hour series was still running on the CBS network.
104. Cutting continuity. M-G-M Collection, USC Cinema and Television Library.
105. *A Blind Bargain*, (New Jersey: MagicImage Filmbooks, 1988).
106. The original print was six reels, but after the necessary cuts, the picture length came to five reels. Cutting continuity. USC Cinema and Television Library.
107. *A Blind Bargain* Pressbook. Author's collection.
108. The reference to Thalberg's extending the starting date refers to *The Hunchback of Notre Dame*.
109. *San Francisco Examiner*, September 24, 1922.
110. *American Cinematographer*, November 1922.
111. Ibid.
112. They were residing in Room 836.
113. At this time, they were living next door to the property at 7152 Sunset Boulevard. The new home stood at 7166 Sunset Boulevard, but it no longer exists.
114. Chaney was referring to Malcolm McGregor, who played Joel Shore in the picture.
115. Chaney was referring to Billie Dove, who played Priscilla Holt in the picture.
116. The mine disaster was in the city of Jackson, in Amador County, California.

117. Hazel Chaney notes to Alfred Grasso, August 1932. From the Alfred Grasso family collection.

118. *Garbo*, (New York: Alfred A. Knopf, 1995).

119. Lon Ralph Chaney to the author, August 1983.

120. Although Tucker had been dead for more than a year, his name still carried influence within the industry.

121. As in the previous attempts, the deal with Associated First National failed to come to fruition for reasons that remain unknown. Letter from the Alfred Grasso family collection.

122. William Dudley Pelley claimed that after the success of *The Shock*, Carl Laemmle said Lon could choose his next project for Universal. When Lon said that he wanted to do *The Hunchback of Notre Dame*, Laemmle thought that the actor wanted to make a football picture. *Door to Revelation*, (North Carolina: Pelley Publishers, 1939).

123. March 14, 1921, telegram. From the Alfred Grasso family collection.

124. The entire set of Monte Carlo was built on the back lot of Universal, not far from where the Hunchback set stood. The large set, along with von Stroheim's extravagant spending, drove the budget to extra-ordinary heights.

125. "Ex-fur scrapers" refers to some of the studio heads who had started as fur dealers, hat and glove makers, or scrap dealers before entering motion pictures as producers.

126. Lawlor's quote, "produce nothing that can pass the four leading Broadway houses," refers to the top four movie theaters on Broadway. For a film not to play one of these top theaters signified that the movie was a typical programmer and not a major production.

127. Letter from Alfred Grasso family collection.

128. It has since been proved that Arbuckle was framed by
an ambitious district attorney and other politicians. At
his third trial, the jury issued a statement that they felt
the comedian had been unjustly accused and absolved
him of any crime. But it was too late for Arbuckle.
His friend Buster Keaton kept him on his company
payroll, and Arbuckle eventually directed films under
the name Will B. Good.

129. The National Association of the Motion Picture Industry
was formed by industry executives in 1916 in an attempt
to control censorship of their product, but it had
little success. The MPPDA was often referred to as the
Hays Office. *Behind the Mask of Innocence*, Alfred A.
Knopf, 1990, New York.

130. From the 1925 contract between Chaney and
M-G-M. Author's collection.

131. The starring vehicle mentioned in the letter
remains unknown.

132. This dispels the legend that Chaney originally was
offered but refused $1,500 a week. Supposedly
Universal contacted Lon again and his price went up
to $2,000 a week. Again Universal declined, and when
they eventually came back, they found Lon's asking price
had increased to $2,500 a week. He advised the studio
that his salary would increase $500 every time they
contacted him. Another unsubstantiated tale, also false,
is that cameraman Virgil Miller had stated that Lon
received $2,035 a week as revenge for having been
denied a $35 a week raise in his early days at Universal.

133. It was not until the 1950s, when the collapse of the
studio system had begun, that actors began to receive
a percentage of a film's profits.

134. Goldwyn Pictures began the film, as well as another picture that caused a headache for M-G-M, von Stroheim's *Greed*. The two pictures, along with others, became part of M-G-M when the film companies of Metro, Goldwyn, and Mayer merged in 1924.
135. *Motion Picture News*, September 3, 1922.
136. Hazel Chaney notes to Alfred Grasso, August 1932. From the Alfred Grasso family collection.
137. Chaney was in Del Monte, California working on *Shadows*.
138. Letter from the Alfred Grasso family collection.
139. David J. Skal to the author, January 1995.
140. Betty Compson co-starred with Lon in *The Miracle Man*.
141. Marguerite De La Motte had appeared with Chaney in *Shadows*.
142. Patsy Ruth Miller to the author, July 1988.
143. Letter from the Alfred Grasso family collection.
144. Ibid.
145. *My Hollywood — When Both of Us Were Young*, (New Jersey: O'Raghailligh Ltd. Publishers, 1988).
146. Ibid.
147. Letter from the Alfred Grasso family collection.
148. Ibid.
149. The cathedral set, which was destroyed in a 1967 fire, was located where the Earthquake attraction of the studio tour now stands on the back lot.
150. *American Cinematographer*, February 1923.
151. Ibid.
152. Ibid.
153. More than 4,500 players and 2,500 extras were costumed for the picture.
154. *American Cinematographer*, October 1923.
155. Ibid.

156. Charles Van Enger, A.S.C., to the author, March 1973.

157. Carla Laemmle to the author, June, 1995

158. *American Cinematographer*, October 1923.

159. Ibid.

160. Ibid.

161. *Lon Chaney: The Man Behind the Thousand Faces*, (New York: The Vestal Press, 1993).

162. From the Alfred Grasso family collection.

163. "Roscoe" was renamed "Sandy" when the Chaneys took ownership of the dog.

164. The Chaneys bought another dog from Moffett when they could not acquire "Roscoe." Letter from the Alfred Grasso family collection.

165. The coal mine venture turned out to be a huge loss for Dempsey. There is no evidence that Lon took advantage of Dempsey's offer to buy stock in the company. Letter dated April 26, 1923. From the Alfred Grasso family collection.

166. George was one of three sons who worked in the industry. Frank was an electrician and Keith was a cameraman, as was George. Their father was John Chaney, Lon's older brother.

167. "Discoveries About Myself," *Motion Picture*, July 1930.

168. George Chaney to the author, October 1973.

169. Telegram dated June 24, 1923. From the Alfred Grasso family collection.

170. Dr. John Webster became Lon's personal physician shortly after this telegram.

171. Lon's father was suffering from Bright's disease, which affects the kidneys.

172. This would have been the production Lon alluded to in his letter to cousin Hugh Harbert. *Lon Chaney: The Man Behind the Thousand Faces*, (New York: The Vestal Press, 1993).

173. The picture was still in the process of being edited, and no doubt Chaney's input extended to this part of the production as well.

174. "Strongly represented all cities" referrs to the theaters with whom Universal did regular business; the cross-country appearances would benefit not only *Hunchback* but also other Universal films.

175. The film was in the final stages of editing.

176. Alfred Grasso's personal notes. From the Alfred Grasso family collection.

177. Ibid.

178. *Moving Picture World*, September 8, 1923.

179. *Exhibitors Trade Review*, September 1, 1923.

180. *The Cleveland News*, August 23, 1923.

181. Letter from the Alfred Grasso family collection.

182. Ibid.

183. George Chaney to the author, October, 1973.

184. *Exhibitors Trade Review*, September 8, 1923.

185. *Moving Picture World*, September 8, 1923.

186. Alfred Grasso's personal notes. From the Alfred Grasso family collection.

187. *Moving Picture World*, September 15, 1923.

188. In addition to *The Hunchback of Notre Dame*, two other 1923 pictures were imposing productions: DeMille's *The Ten Commandments* and James Cruze's *The Covered Wagon*. These pictures were the precursors to Hollywood's epic films.

189. *Film Daily*, September 16, 1923.

190. *Behind the Mask of Innocence*, (New York: Alfred A. Knopf, 1990).
191. *American Cinematographer*, February 1923.
192. The only positive aspect of Lon's involvement with this film was that his salary jumped to $2,750 a week. Contract from the Alfred Grasso family collection.
193. Telegram from the Alfred Grasson family collection.
194. Telegram dated January 2, 1924. Ibid.
195. The Chaneys stayed at the Commodore Hotel at 42nd Street and Lexington Avenue.
196. Apparently, the deal with Carl Anderson Company had fallen apart very quickly, before this letter was written.
197. The Italian story was *The Sacrifice*. The reference to Cohn remains unknown at this time.
198. It finished its 20-week engagement at the Astor Theatre on January 20, 1924.
199. The announcement was made during the studio's New York sales conference. *American Cinematographer*, September 1989.
200. Hazel Chaney notes to Alfred Grasso, August 1932. From the Alfred Grasso family collection.
201. The dissolves were done, not in a post-production lab, but right in the camera. An accurate footage count was taken, the film was rewound to a specific number, and the second scene would then be shot. When developed, the overlap would appear as a dissolve from one shot to another.
202. Lon's son, Creighton, considered this role to be his father's finest performance. Creighton Chaney to Tom Etheridge, September 1970.
203. Richard Scheffield to the author, May 1995.

204. Hazel Chaney notes to Alfred Grasso, August 1932. From the Alfred Grasso family collection.
205. *American Cinematographer*, September 1989.
206. Ibid.
207. Ibid.
208. Charles van Enger, A.S.C. to the author, March 1973.
209. Before this stage was built, all stages were constructed of wood and glass.
210. The stage is now known as Stage 28, or simply the Phantom Stage.
211. Charles van Enger, A.S.C. to the author, March 1973.
212. Carla Laemmle to the author, June 1995.
213. *American Cinematographer*, October 1989.
214. Ibid.
215. Scott MacQueen to the author, September 1992.
216. *Moving Picture World*, September 19, 1925.
217. *The Los Angeles Record*, October 9, 1925.
218. Ann Wright to the author, March 1985.
219. *The Hollywood Reporter*, October 29, 1993.
220. Scott MacQueen to the author, September 1992.
221. *Moving Picture World*, February 14, 1925.
222. An unsubstantiated story claims that Lon shot all of his scenes for this picture in one day. Although his time on screen is limited, it's highly unlikely that all of his work could have been completed that quickly.
223. Lon's contract was signed on January 6, 1925, but did not take effect until February 15, 1925. The primary reason for the six week difference was that Lon signed the contract while making *The Unholy Three*, and had the contract taken effect immediately, that film could have been counted as one of the four pictures per contract year he would be required to make.

224. A "dolly shot," or tracking shot, is one in which the camera is mounted on a device with four wheels, enabling the camera to be moved on a track similar to train tracks.
225. Script from author's collection.
226. M-G-M Collection, USC Cinema and Television Library.
227. Ibid.
228. Script dated October 7, 1925. Ibid.
229. Ibid.
230. Letters from author's collection.
231. The 9.5mm print came from a French "show-at-home" version. In the 1920s condensed versions of movies were sold to collectors in Europe, similar to the 8mm and Super 8mm prints distributed to the American collectors' market in the 1960s and 1970s. Enlarging a 9.5mm to a 16mm print tends to produce a fuzzy or soft image compared with 16mm printed from an original camera negative or from a sharp 35mm print.
232. Report dated March 3, 1926. M-G-M Collection, USC Cinema and Television Library.
233. Ibid.
234. The scenes featuring Chaney as the younger Joe were cut from the final release print.
235. *Nova*, PBS Television, March 1994.
236. Lon Ralph Chaney to the author, August 1983.
237. Ibid.
238. Ibid.
239. The picture earned an worldwide gross of $6.1 million.
240. M-G-M Collection, USC Cinema and Television Library.
241. Charles Ray and Claire Windsor were originally announced as co-stars.
242. M-G-M Collection, USC Cinema and Television Library.

243. Ibid.

244. The term "two-dollar picture" refers to the highest
ticket price being charged at that time for a movie.
As it turned out, *Tell It to the Marines* became a
two-dollar picture when it opened.

245. M-G-M Collection, USC Cinema and Television Library.

246. This group of retakes included: Madden (Eddie
Gribbon) standing up and clubbing the rushing
bandits before going down. The bandit leader
(Warner Oland) crawling over the barricade and attempting
to knife O'Hara, but Skeet (William Haines) kills him. At
that point, the bandits would point off camera and run-
away. It was originally planned to have the Chinese
troops enter the scene, but that was cut and replaced
with the Marine airplanes flying in and dropping bombs.
The scene would have ended with Madden emerging
from underneath the pile of dead bandits with an
exasperated look. Ibid.

247. Part of the ending in the final draft, that was filmed but
later deleted, included a scene where Skeet runs into his
former fellow Marine, Harry (Maurice Kains). He introduces
Skeet to his father, General Wilcox, who happens to be the
same man Skeet had met in the train washroom at the
beginning of the picture. This is the man (dressed in
civilian attire) in whom Skeet confided that he had no plans
of serving in the Marine Corps. When the two men meet
in the conclusion, the General recognizes Skeet, who
grins sheepishly. M-G-M Collection, USC Cinema and
Television Library.

248. *The Film Daily*, February 3, 1926.

249. Joseph Newman to the author, December 1994.

250. Ibid.

251. During the Marines' heroic stand on the bridge, the viewer can observe Eddie Gribbon uttering colorful expletives as he fires his rifle!

252. Hazel Chaney notes to Alfred Grasso, August 1932. From the Alfred Grasso family collection.

253. The worldwide gross for *Mr. Wu* was $1,068,000, making it Chaney's second-highest grossing picture for M-G-M.

254. Willard Sheldon to the author, November 1994.

255. *Variety*, December 29, 1926.

256. *Photoplay*, February 1928.

257. *Motion Picture Classic*, March 1928.

258. In some reviews, Joan Crawford's character is listed as Estrillita.

259. Dismuki later toured with the Al G. Barnes Circus and Sideshow, billed as *The Man Who Doubled Lon Chaney's Feet in The Unknown*.

260. It's very possible that the studio insisted on the happy ending because they did the same thing with Chaney's *Laugh, Clown, Laugh* and King Vidor's *The Crowd*. Both of these pictures shot alternative endings.

261. M-G-M Collection, USC Cinema and Television Library.

262. Ibid.

263. Ibid.

264. Valentino's high ranking is partially attributed to the released of his last picture, *Son of the Sheik*, and his untimely death.

265. *Film Spectator*, October 29, 1927.

266. A pressbook was sent to all theatre owners running the film and illustrated publicity stories, ads, posters and promotional ideas. Pressbook from author's collection.
267. Pressbooks from author's collection.
268. Cardwell Higgins to Roger Hurlburt, 1988.
269. *The Jazz Singer* is not an all-talking picture. It contains two sequences with Jolson singing; the remainder of the movie is accompanied by a synchronized musical score. The first all-talking picture was *Lights of New York*, released the following year.
270. The worldwide gross for *London After Midnight* was $1,004,000. It was Chaney's sixth-highest grossing picture at M-G-M and the highest grossing Chaney-Browning picture.
271. Other than the 1922 German version of *Nosferatu*, this movie was the first major film to incorporate the subject of vampires into the central theme of a picture.
272. David J. Skal to the author, August 1994.
273. *London After Midnight*, (New York: Cornwall Books, 1985).
274. Ibid.
275. Ibid.
276. Bob McChesney to the author, January 1995.
277. Ibid.
278. *Photoplay*, February 1928.
279. *London After Midnight*, (New York: Cornwall Books, 1985).
280. Joseph Newman to the author, December 1994.
281. Leonard Schrader to the author, May 1994.
282. *New York Daily News*, January 1928.
283. MPPDA censor notes, Margaret Herrick Library, Academy of Motion Picture Arts and Sciences, Los Angeles.

284. Ibid.

285. Ibid.

286. *The Big City* daily production report. Author's collection.

287. Undated clipping from the scrapbook of Lamar D. Tabb.

288. Ibid.

289. Ibid.

290. *Film Spectator*, June 29, 1929.

291. George Chaney to the author, October 1973.

292. Lamar D. Tabb to the author, July 1987.

293. "It Might Be Pagliacci," *Motion Picture Classic*, May 1928.

294. Willard Sheldon to the author, November 1994.

295. Joseph Newman to the author, December 1994.

296. Herbert Voight to the author, July 1985.

297. Willard Sheldon to the author, November 1994.

298. Penny Singleton to the author, January 1995.

299. Harry Carey, Jr., to the author, January 1995.

300. Malcolm Sabiston to the author, November 1994.

301. *Door to Revelation*, (North Carolina: Pelley Publishers, 1939).

302. Eckels was an M-G-M publicist who formed a public relations business with Pelley that wasn't very successful. Ibid.

303. Pelley's last meeting with Chaney took place during the making of *The Unknown*. He claimed that a blood vessel had broken in Chaney's arm from the tightly-laced straightjacket, forming a clot that worked its way through the actor's body, stopping in his throat! Pelley's contention is completely lacking credence, not to mention that it would have been a physical impossibility. He also claims that Chaney died

on an operating table in a New York Hospital, which is so glaringly false that it makes one doubt the validity of any of Pelley's recollections regarding Chaney. Ibid.

304. Alfred Grasso notes, August 1932.

305. Hazel Chaney notes to Alfred Grasso, August 1932. From the Alfred Grasso family collection.

306. Report dated April 10, 1925. M-G-M Collection. USC Cinema and Television Library.

307. Willard Sheldon to author, November 1994.

308. Ibid.

309. The worldwide gross for the picture was $1,102,000.

310. MPPDA censor notes, Margaret Herrick Library, Academy of Motion Picture Arts and Sciences.

311. M-G-M Collection, USC Cinema and Television Library.

312. It would be another two or three years before the genre of gangster films reached their peak of popularity, with movies such as *Scarface*, *Little Caesar*, and *Public Enemy* making their mark.

313. *Lon Chaney: The Man Behind the Thousand Faces*, (New York: The Vestal Press, 1993).

314. *While the City Sleeps* was made under the working title *Easy Money*.

315. *New York Times*, June 3, 1928.

316. M-G-M Collection. USC Cinema and Television Library.

317. *Lon Chaney: The Man Behind the Thousand Faces*, (New York: The Vestal Press, 1993).

318. Cutting continuity for silent version. M-G-M Collection. USC Cinema and Television Library.

319. Cutting continuity for sound version. Ibid.

320. Daily production report. Ibid.

321. *While the City Sleeps* earned a worldwide gross of $1,035,000.

322. *Photoplay*, August 1928.

323. Ibid.

324. Interoffice memorandum from author's collection. Dated May 22, 1928.

325. *West of Zanzibar* was started under the second option of his 1926 contract.

326. In the June 7, 1928, script, Lon's character is described as "a cheap, fakery magician, in a Caligary-like make-up." Script from author's collection.

327. Bret Wood to the author, May 1995.

328. This scene was also contained in the June 7, 1928 version but it never appears in the film.

329. Script from author's collection.

330. Johnson was the original name for the character of Crane. Ibid.

331. The role of Doc eventually went to Warner Baxter, and Constantine Romanoff's part went to Roscoe Ward.

332. The studio had three additional backlots that housed various street sets, ranging from Western streets to European palaces. Lot Two was the studio's last remaining back lot. The others were sold off in the late 1960s; M-G-M's Lot Two met the wrecking ball in the late 1970s. Today, a housing tract sits on the site where some of M-G-M's greatest pictures were filmed.

333. Vincent D'Onofrio to the author, September 1994.

334. Waldemar Young adapted the story by Browning and Harry Sinclair Drago. Young was also responsible for the scenarios for *The Unholy Three*, *The Blackbird*, *The Unknown*, *London After Midnight*, and *The Big City*. E. Richard Schayer, the screenwriter for *Tell It to the Marines*, was credited with the scenario for this movie.

335. *Twinkle, Twinkle, Movie Star!*, (New York: E. P. Dutton & Co., 1930).

336. Daily production report. M-G-M Collection. USC Cinema and Television Library.

337. They are, in order, *Tell It To The Marines, Laugh, Clown, Laugh, Mr. Wu, While the City Sleeps, Thunder, London After Midnight, The Unholy Three* (1930 version), *West of Zanzibar, Where East Is East*, and *He Who Gets Slapped. London After Midnight* was Browning's biggest money-maker when he was at M-G-M during this period.

338. Browning's father died in 1922, and his mother died in late 1927. David J. Skal to the author, November 1994.

339. Joseph Newman to the author, December 1994.

340. Willard Sheldon to the author, November 1994.

341. Cutting continuity. Author's collection.

342. M-G-M Collection. USC Cinema and Television Library.

343. Ibid.

344. Ibid.

345. Telegram dated February 28, 1929. Ibid.

346. Alfred Grasso notes. From the Alfred Grasso family collection.

347. Daily production report. M-G-M Collection. USC Cinema and Television Library.

348. Willard Sheldon to the author, November 1994.

349. Daily production report. M-G-M Collection. USC Cinema and Television Library.

350. Ibid.

351. Ibid.

352. Ibid.

353. Murray died tragically a few years later; his body was found floating in a river in New York City. Willard Sheldon to the author, November 1994.

354. MPPDA censor notes, Margaret Herrick Library, Academy of Motion Picture Arts and Sciences.

355. Interoffice memorandum from author's collection.

356. Undated clipping from the scrapbook of Lamar D. Tabb.

357. *Lon Chaney: The Man Behind the Thousand Faces*, (New York: The Vestal Press, 1993).

358. Undated clipping from the scrapbook of Lamar D. Tabb.

359. The 1941 version has nothing to do with the French Foreign Legion.

360. MPPDA censor notes, Margaret Herrick Library, Academy of Motion Picture Arts and Sciences.

361. Ibid.

362. Letter dated March 1, 1929. Ibid.

363. Ibid.

364. Synopsis from author's collection.

365. Script from author's collection.

366. *Hollywood Filmograph*, July 20, 1929.

367. As in the case of *Tell It to the Marines*, the footage shot was probably background material, more commonly known as stock footage. This would probably include shots of the desert, Legionnaires on the march, etc., These scenes would later be cut into the film. *Hollywood Filmograph*, August 10, 1929.

368. *Hollywood Filmograph*, August 24, 1929.

369. Scott MacQueen to the author, August 1994.

370. The 1929 reissue of *Phantom of the Opera* is the version found on most videotapes and laser discs. Some scenes from the 1925 version were deleted and others were moved to help the flow of the picture.

371. *Phantom of the Opera* movie herald from author's collection.

372. The March 15, 1930 issue of *Universal Weekly* states that Browning will direct *The Scarlet Triangle*. There is no mention of *The Yellow Sin* or any other future project, including *Dracula*. Browning wound up directing a remake of *Outside The Law*.

373. Nothing in any of Chaney's contracts granted him veto power regarding choice of directors.

374. David J. Skal to the author, January 1995.

375. Ibid.

376. After completing *The Unknown*, Browning planned to feature Chaney and Harry Earles in a production of *Spurs*, the novel which *Freaks* was based upon. Ibid.

377. M-G-M was competing with Universal, Paramount, Pathe, and Columbia to buy the film rights. Universal obtained the rights in June 1930. Ibid.

378. *The Sea Bat* was put into production in early January 1930, with Wesley Ruggles directing and featuring Charles Bickford and Raquel Torres. The story now centered around a Mexican fisherman's daughter whose lover is killed by a giant sting-ray. She offers to marry the man who will capture the beast.

379. *Hollywood Gothic*, (New York: W.W. Norton & Co., 1990).

380. Chaney's fourth and final option on his 1926 contract would have expired on April 14, 1931. The studio picked up his third option on March 9, 1929, to expire on April 14, 1930.

381. *Lon Chaney: The Man Behind the Thousand Faces*, (New York: The Vestal Press, 1993).

382. No evidence indicates this project would feature any star other than Chaney. Undated clipping from the scrapbook of Lamar D. Tabb.

383. Letter courtesy of David J. Skal.

384. David J. Skal to the author, January, 1995.

385. Letter courtesy of David J. Skal.

386. Author's collection.

387. *Hollywood Gothic*, (New York: W.W. Norton & Co., 1990).

388. M-G-M Collection. USC Cinema and Television Library.

389. Scenario credits from author's collection.

390. Charlie Gamora played the role of the gorilla; he gained a reputation for playing such characters. He also played the gorilla in *Where East Is East*. Later he became a make up artist and was one of the finest make-up lab technicians in the industry.

391. The laser disc (released by M-G-M Home Video) not only provides one of the best prints available but also reproduces Chaney's voice clearly, as well as the voice of Harry Earles, the German midget who played Tweedledee.

392. Script from author's collection.

393. Jack Latham to the author, May 1995.

394. Echo holds up his handcuffed wrist, emphasizing his point.

395. "Movietone" was an early term used for sound pictures. Undated clipping from the scrapbook of Lamar D. Tabb.

396. Ibid.

397. *The Unholy Three* pressbook. Author's collection.

398. *Hollywood Filmograph*, May 31, 1930.

399. The date of his suspension was June 23, 1930.

400. Mary Bourne to Jim Peers III, November 1994.

401. "Lon Chaney: A Portrait of a Man Behind a Thousand Faces", *Liberty Magazine*, May 30, 1931.

402. *Los Angeles Times*, July 4, 1930.

403. Mary Bourne to Jim Peers III, November 1994.

404. Undated clipping from the scrapbook of Lamar D. Tabb.

405. Harry Earles to the author, February 1985.

406. Studio time sheet. Author's collection.

407. Ron Chaney, Jr. to the author, March 1990.

408. Lon Ralph Chaney to the author, August 1983.

409. Dr. Burton J. Lee, III to the author, August 1992.

410. Hazel Chaney notes to Alfred Grasso, August 1932. From the Alfred Grasso family collection.

411. *Variety*, August 28, 1930.

412. Hazel Chaney notes to Alfred Grasso, August 1932. From the Alfred Grasso family collection.

413. Ibid.

414. Willard Sheldon to the author, November 1994.

415. Joseph Newman to the author, December 1994.

416. *Screen Book Magazine*, November 1930.

417. Lon Ralph Chaney to the author, August 1983.

418. *The Hollywood Reporter*, April 5, 1956.

419. *Los Angeles Times*, October 28, 1956.

420. Universal Collection. USC Cinema and Television Library.

421. *Mirror-News*, August 15, 1957.

422. *The Kid Stays in the Picture*, (New York:Hyperion, 1994).

423. Ibid.

424. Hank Mann appeared in *Quincy Adams Sawyer* with Chaney in 1922. John George, who appeared in several Tod Browning pictures with Chaney, including *The Unknown* and *Outside the Law*, can briefly be seen as an extra in the bullpen sequence in which Cagney makes himself up as the East Indian sailor.

425. Kolb received an additional $1,000 to play himself in the picture.

426. Daily production report. Universal Collection. USC
Cinema and Television Library.

427. Budget reports. Ibid.

428. Production report. Ibid.

429. Ibid.

430. Ibid.

431. Ibid.

432. The difference amounted to $50,900. Budget report. Ibid.

433. Preview notes. Ibid.

434. Joseph Pevney to the author, January 1995.

435. Preview notes. Universal collection. USC Cinema
and Television Library.

436. This comment is particularly interesting because
Lon Chaney, Jr. was still active in the film and
television industry at the time of this preview. Ibid.

437. Script from author's collection.

438. Ibid.

439. *Cagney by Cagney*, *(New York: Doubleday, 1976).

440. Joseph Pevney to the author, January 1995.

441. It was called El Capitan Theatre when it opened in
1926. Originally a legitimate theatre, it was converted
for motion pictures and renamed the Paramount Theatre
in 1942. The architecture has recently been restored to
its original beauty, and the theatre has been rechristened
El Capitan and serves as a motion picture palace.

442. Universal Collection. USC Cinema and Television Library.

443. *Variety*, August 19, 1957.

444. Universal Collection. USC Cinema and Television Library.

445. *Designing Women* won the Oscar for best screenplay
that year.

446. *Man of a Thousand Faces* was re-released in 1964.

447. Unfortunately, the scar lacked Chaney's realistic touch.

Photo opposite: This picture, shot in the M-G-M photo gallery, of Lloyd Hughes (left) and Lon (holding unidentified woman doubling for Lupe Velez) was used by artists as a model in creating artwork for movie posters. Note that Chaney is not wearing the collodion scars for this photo shoot.

One of the posters for *Where East Is East*. Compare this picture to the posed photo that appears on the preceding page. Lon is now shown holding the stool (still minus his facial scars), whle Lloyd Hughes saves the young woman.

Bibliography

Books and Magazines

Ackerman, Forrest J. *Lon of a Thousand Faces*. Morrison, California: Raven Hill Co., 1983.

"Acting Is Masquerade." *Motion Picture,* December 1922.

American Film Institute Catalogue. *Feature Films 1911-1920.* University of California Press, 1988.

American Film Institute Catalogue. *Feature Films 1921-1930.* New York: R. R. Bowker Co., 1971.

Anderson, Robert G. *Faces, Forms, Films: The Artistry of Lon Chaney.* New York: A.S.Barnes & Co., 1971.

Blake, Michael F. *Lon Chaney: The Man Behind the Thousand Faces.* New York: The Vestal Press, 1993.

Brundidge, Harry T. *Twinkle, Twinkle Movie Star!,* New York: E.P. Dutton & Co., 1930.

Bodeen, DeWitt. "Lon Chaney: Man of a Thousand Faces." *Focus On Film,* May-August 1970.

Braff, Richard E. "A Lon Chaney Index." *Films In Review,* April 1970.

Brown, Harry D. "Electrical Problems on World's Largest Set." *American Cinematographer,* October 1923.

Brownlow, Kevin. *Behind the Mask of Innocence.* New York: Alfred A. Knopf, 1990.

Brownlow, Kevin. *The Parade's Gone By.* New York: Alfred A. Knopf, 1968.

Cagney, James. *Cagney By Cagney.* New York: Doubleday, 1976.

"Cagney to Star In Chaney-Life at U-I." *The Hollywood Reporter,* April 5, 1956.

Chaney, Lon (as told to Gladys Hall). "Discoveries About Myself," *Motion Picture,* July 1930.

A Thousand Faces

Chaney, Lon (as told to Maude Cheatham). "The Darkest Hour."
Motion Picture Classic, September 1922.

Chaney, Lon (possibly ghostwritten). "My Own Story." *Movie
Magazine*. Part I (September 1925): pp. 42-44, 108-110. Part
II (October 1925): pp. 55-57, 86-89. Part III (November
1925): pp. 55-56, 74-75.

"Chaney Comes to New York for Premiere of "The Hunchback."
Moving Picture World, September 8, 1923.

"Chaney Honor Guest At Reception." *Exhibitors Trade Review*,
September 9, 1923.

"Chelsea Pictures Corp. Claim It Will Produce 20 Features With
Big Stars and Directors." *Moving Picture World,* April 29,
1922.

Crowther, Bosley. *The Lion's Share*. New York: E.P. Dutton &
Co., 1957.

Eames, John Douglas. *The MGM Story*. New York: Crown
Publishers, Inc., 1975.

I.G. Edmonds. *The Big U*, New York: A.S.Barnes & Co., 1977.

"First Night Audience Breaks Into Spontaneous Applause
Following Showing of The Miracle Man." *Exhibitors Trade
Review,* August 6, 1919.

Hagerman, Arthur Q. "Costuming A Super-production."
American Cinematographer, February 1923.

Hirschhorn, Clive. *The Universal Story*. New York: Crown
Publishers, Inc., 1983.

Howe, Herbert. "A Miracle Man of Make-up." *Picture Play*
(March 1920): pp. 37-39, 96-97.

"Hunchback of Notre Dame Gets Big Reception at World
Premiere." *Moving Picture World,* September 15, 1923.

"Hunchback of Notre Dame Started." *Exhibitors Trade Review* ,
January 13, 1923.

"Hunting Whales With Cameras." *American Cinematographer,* November 1922.

"Lon Chaney Is Signed as New Universal Star." *Exhibitors Trade Review,* September 17, 1921.

"Lon Chaney Has Been Raised to Stardom; Will Play Chief Role in Wolf Breed." *Moving Picture World,* September 17, 1921.

Martin, Quinn, "The Passing of Lon Chaney." *New York World,* August 31, 1930.

Marx, Samuel. *Mayer and Thalberg-Make-Believe Saints.* New York: Random House, 1975.

Miller, Patsy Ruth. *My Hollywood: When Both of Us Were Young.* New Jersey: O'Raghailligh Ltd. Publishers, 1988.

"Miracle Man, Famous Players-Lasky Production, Wins Admiration and Praise of Sing Inmates." *Exhibitors Trade Review,* August 9, 1919.

Pelley, William Dudley. *Door to Revelation.* North Carolina: Pelley Publishing, 1939.

"Phantom Hits JumboTron." *The Hollywood Reporter,* October 29, 1993.

Riley, Philip J. *London After Midnight.* New York: Cornwall Books, 1985.

Riley, Philip J. *A Blind Bargain.* New Jersey: MagicImage Filmbooks, 1988.

Rosenthal, Stuart. *The Hollywood Professionals-Tod Browning.* New York: A.S. Barnes & Co., 1975.

Skal, David J. *Hollywood Gothic.* New York: W.W. Norton & Co., 1990.

Smith, Frederick James. "Amateur Movies." *Photoplay,* August 1928.

St. Johns, Adela Rogers. "Lon Chaney, A Portrait of the Man Behind a Thousand Faces", *Liberty.* Part I (May 2, 1931): pp. 16-20,22, 24-25. Part II (May 9, 1931): pp. 28-36. Part III

(May 16, 1931): pp. 28-34. Part IV (May 23, 1931): pp. 36-37, 40-44. Part V (May 30, 1931): pp. 39-44.

Steele, Joseph Henry. "It Might Be Pagliacci." *Motion Picture Classic,* May 1928.

"Two-Person Prologue for The Trap." *Exhibitors Trade Review*, May 20, 1922.

Turner, George. "A Silent Giant: The Hunchback of Notre Dame." *American Cinematographer,* June 1985.

Waterbury, Ruth. "The True Life Story of Lon Chaney." *Photoplay.* Part I (December 1927): pp. 32-33, 110-114. Part II (January 1928): pp. 36-37, 119-121. Part III (February 1928): pp. 56-57, 94, 112-113.

Newspaper Articles

"Lon Chaney 'Is Regular Fellow." *The Cleveland News,* (August 23, 1923).

"Lon Chaney Visitor Here; Rests From Filming Hunchback." *Colorado Springs Evening Telegraph,* (June 20, 1923).

"Lon Chaney Visits Boyhood Scenes on Visit to Springs." *Colorado Springs Evening Telegraph,* (June 12, 1928).

"Chaney Must Keep His Face Unknown; Movie Star Back To Boyhood Scenes." *Colorado Springs Evening Telegraph*, (January 1, 1922).

"Stage Employees to Essay the Role of Thespians." *Colorado Springs Gazette,* (December 19, 1902).

"The Little Tycoon" (Stage Review). *Colorado Springs Gazette* (April 20, 1902).

"Said Pasha Given Splendid Presentation By Good Company" (Stage Review). *Colorado Springs Gazette,* (June 9, 1903).

"Local Entertainers Who Will Contribute to Summer Gaiety." *Colorado Springs Gazette,* (July 12, 1903).

"Universal City Marvel in Design Says Earl Cox." Colorado Springs Gazette (May 8, 1915).

"Chaney Comes To Colorado To Restore Broken Health." *Colorado Springs Gazette,* (June 20, 1923).

"La Mascotte" (Stage Review). *Daily Oklahoman,* (April 27, 1907).

"Cleva Creighton, Famous Singing Soubrette Sings At Brink's." *Los Angeles Evening Herald,* (April 29, 1913).

"Cabaret Singer Near Death From Poison." *Los Angeles Evening Herald,* (May 1, 1913).

"10,000 Cheer as Universal City is Opened." *Los Angeles Evening Herald,* (March 15, 1915).

"New Film City Put on Map." *Los Angeles Examiner,* (March 16, 1915).

"Return Engagement Of Popular Singer." *Los Angeles Express,* (April 29, 1913).

"Stage Manager's Wife Tries To End Life." *Los Angeles Express,* (May 1, 1913).

"A New Ragtime Singer to make her Debut at Brink's is Cleva Creighton." *Los Angeles Daily Times,* (August 28, 1912).

"Drinks Poison Behind Scenes." *Los Angeles Daily Times* (May 1, 1913).

"The Yankee Prince" (Stage Review). *Los Angeles Daily Times,* (July, 1, 1912).

"Cagney, as Chaney, Will Be Man of Thousand Faces." *Los Angeles Times,* (October 28, 1956).

"Lon Chaney Visits Springs First Time In Several Years." *Rocky Mountain News,* (June 12, 1928).

"In Dutch" (Stage Review). *San Francisco Chronicle,* (November 12, 1912).

"Around the Lobbies" (column). *San Francisco Examiner,* (September 24, 1922).

Front cover for the herard of the 1929 re-issue of *Phantom of the Opera*. Note how Chaney's face was blocked out, even after the film's original release four years earlier. At the bottom, the fine print states that Chaney's performance is silent.

Index

Academy of Motion Picture Arts and
  Sciences 330
Ace of Hearts 63-66, 75, *95*, 340*n*
"Adam-12" (television series) 249, 317
Adams, Claire 54
Adolph and Oscar 334
Adoree, Renee 174, 188, *215*
Aitken, Spottiswoode 38
Algeria 335
All The Brothers Were Valiant 81-85,
  100, 117
  Lon's letters from location on 83-84
Almost An Actress 27
American Legion's Veterans Camp
  129-130
An American Idea 18, 334
Anderson Company, Carl 150-152,
  348*n*
Anderson, Mary *38*
Andreyev, Leonid 153
Antlers Hotel *12*, 15
Arbuckle, Roscoe "Fatty" 17, 110-
  111, 343-344*n*
Are You a Moose? 333
Arthur, Johnny 166
Arthur, Robert 311, 318-319
Associated First National Studios 59,
  85
Assorted Nuts 57
Asther, Nils 240, *292*
Astor Theatre 129, 131, 134, 160
Austin, George *209*
Australia, Country of 206, 267
Aviator, The 333
Away All Boats 317

Backus, Jim 316, 323
Bailey, Mettie E. 232
Bancroft, George 233
Barnes Circus, Al G. 352*n*
Barrymore, John 198, 233
Barrymore, Lionel 239, 251, 257
Barthelmess, Richard 233
Bat, The 166
Batman 156
Baxter, Warner 255, 298, 356*n*
Beaton, K.C. *140*

Beaton, Welford 85, 198
Beau Geste 269
Bedford, Barbara 195
Beery, Noah 69
Beery, Wallace 6-7, 9, 49, *89*, 249,
  269,-271
Beggar Prince, The 332
Belcher, Ernest 158
Bell, Digby 28
Ben-Hur 113
Berg, H. A. 61-63, 70, 109-110
Benjamin, Joe 125
Bentley and Jenicek Finance 70
Bentley, C. E. 70
Berkeley, California, City of 30
Berley Hills, California, City of 234
Beverly Hills Hotel 312
Beverly-Wilshire Hotel 287
Bickford, Charles 359*n*
Big Boy comedy series 236
Big City, The 205-206, 228, 331,
  356*n*
Big House, The 6
Birth of a Nation 25
Bits of Life 59, 94
Blackbird, The 169, 173-177, 179,
  215-217, 331, 340*n*, 356*n*
Blind Bargain, A 80, *99, 100*
Bloodhounds of the North 27
Blonde Captive, The 57
Blondeau Tavern 23
Blondie film series 235
Blythe, Betty 52, *89*
Boardman, Eleanor 183, *219*
Bobbs-Merrill Company, The 150
Bohemian Girl, The 333
Boston, Massachusetts, City of 131
Bourne, Mary 284-285
Bonner, Priscilla 75
Bonomo, Joe 122
Borzage, Frank 114
Bow, Clara 272
Bowers, John 64, 78
Bradbury, Ray 9, *330*
Brandt, Joe 176-177
Brenon, Herbert 60, 241, *291*
Brink's Cafe 19

A Thousand Faces

Broadbent, Lillian 57
Broadway Theater 314
Brockwell, Gladys 97
Broken Idol, The 334
Brother Officers 274
Brown, Clarence 26, 72-73
Brown, Harry D. 121-122
Browning, Tod 26, 36, *38*, 42,
    57-58, *93*, 115, 167-170, 173, 175,
    177-179, 191-194, 202-206, *211*,
    215, 218, 228, 250-251, 253-254,
    258-262, 272-273, 300, 347, 337*n*,
    356*n*, 358*n*, 361*n*
Brulatour, Jules 72, 74
Bryson, James V. 128-129, 131, 165
Bugle Sounds, The 246, 268-271,
    274, 277, 283, *305*, 358*n*
Bugle Sounds, The (1941) 269, 357*n*
Burns International Detective Agency
Burns, William J. *93*
Busch, Mae 171, 278
Bush, Pauline 28
Buster Keaton Story, The 322
Butler, U.S.M.C., General Smedley D.
    219
Butler, Thomas *219*
By The Sun's Rays 31-32

Cagney, James ix, 118, 311-315, 317-319,
    321-323, *325-328*
Campbell, R. Wright 311
Canada, Country of 267
Canter, Eddie 311
Capitol Theatre 151
Capone, Al 205, 243
Carnegie Hall 129-130
Carewe, Arthur Edmund 161, *213*
Carey, Harry 26, 236
Carey, Harry Jr. 236
Cattolica, Italy, City of 290
Central Theatre 68
Chaney, Caroline ("Carrie") (sister) 14,
    30
Chaney, Cleva
    (first wife; also see Cleva Creighton)
    17-20, 30, 317
Chaney, Connie x, *330*

Chaney, Creighton Tull
    (son; also see Lon Chaney, Jr.) 3, 7-8,
    30, 127, 130, *144*, 180-181, 287, 289,
    317, 337*n*, 348*n*
Chaney, Emma (mother) 13-14
Chaney, Frank (father) 13, 15, 236, 288
Chaney, Frank (nephew) 346*n*
Chaney, George (brother) 14, 17
Chaney, George (nephew) 126, 346*n*
Chaney, Hazel
    (second wife; also see Hazel Hastings)
    13-14, 30-31, 35-36, 46, 53, 57, 73-74,
    81-83, 113, 124, 126-127, 130, 134,
    143, 150, 153, 155, 164-165, 187,
    230, 234, 238, 249-250, 283, 287-288
Chaney, John (Jonathan) Orange
    (brother) 15, 17, 130, 346*n*
Chaney, Keith (nephew) 346*n*
Chaney, Lon *ii, iv, vi, vii,* ix-xii, *2,* 2-10,
    10, 12, 12-20, *22,* 22-23, 26-36, *36-38,*
    40, 41-46, 49-88, *89-102, 104,* 105-
    137, *138-140, 142-146, 148,* 149-159,
    161-171, 173-181, 184-196, 198-206,
    207-228, 230, 231-262, 264-290, *291-*
    308, 337-350
    birth of 13
    birth name of 13
    birth of son of 16
    cabin of 287
    cooking 73
    death of 288, 306
    debut as an actor 16
    directing films 22
    dislike of attention 83-84, 126, 233-
        234
    discussions regarding formation of
        production unit 61-63, 70
    divorce from Cleva 19
    feelings about making talking
        pictures 246, 268-269
    first exposure to make-up 28
    first known screen credit 28-29
    funeral of 288, 306
    home movies of 250, 296
    hobby of fly fishing 14-15
    honorary membership in

Brotherhood of Locomotive Engineers 264
honorary membership in United States Marine Corps 187
illness during Thunder 265-266
make-up case of 96, *102*, 124, *148*
make-up for a role 96, *102*, 124
marriage to Cleva 16
marriage to Hazel 30
popularity at the box office 231-234, 299
proposed biography book by Hazel Chaney about 57
son wanting to be an actor 7-8
start as a carpet layer 14-15
start as a prop boy 15-16
tourist guide at Pike's Peak 14
tributes after death of 288-289, 307-308
trips to Colorado Springs 126-127, 250
trip to New York City (1924) 150-151
trip to New York City (1928) 249-250, 295
United States Postal Stamp of 290, 329
Chaney, Lon Jr.
   (son; also see Creighton Chaney) 3, 7, 316, 362*n*
Chaney, Lon Ralph (grandson) 84, 180-181, 287, *330*
Chaperones, The 334
Chaplin, Charles 30, 41, 59, 128, 198
Charles Alphin Amusement Com-pany 17, 333
Chataud, Emile 114
Chelsea Pictures Corporation 112
Chestnut Street Opera House 132
Cheri-Bibi 277, 283
Cheyenne, Wyoming, City of 263
Chicago, Illinois, City of 129, 205, 264-265
Chicago-Northwestern Railroad 264
Chimes of Normandy, The 16, 332
Ching, Ching, Chinaman 75-76, 98, 293, 340*n*

Christensen, Benjamin *223-225*
Clark, Harvey *209*
Clark, Mary x, 57
Clawson, Elliott 156, 203
Cleveland News, The 131
Cleveland, Ohio, City of 130-131
Clown, The 177
Co-Artists Productions 168
Cochrane, George 108
Cody, Buffalo Bill 26
Cohan, George M. 43
Cohn, J.J. 263-264
Colorado School for the Deaf 13, 165
Colorado Springs, Colorado, City of 12, 13, 15-16, 75, 124, 126-127, 165, 234, 250
Colorado Springs Gazette 16
Colorado Springs Opera House 15-16, 332-333
Columbia Comic Opera Company 16, 332
Columbia Pictures 176-177, 359*n*
Compson, Betty 56, 59, 115-116, 345*n*
Compson Productions, Betty 57, 59
Conklin, Chester 159
Conrad, Joseph 49
Conway, Jack 26, 248-249, 280, *295*, *303*
Coogan, Jackie 77, 128, *330*
Cook, Clyde *209*
Coolidge, President Calvin 184
Cooper, George 341*n*
Copley Symphony Hall 290
Cortez, Ricardo 195
Covered Wagon, The 347*n*
Crane, Violet 211
Crawford, Joan 192, 352*n*
Creighton, Cleva
   (first wife; maiden and stage name) 16, 19, 84,
   attempted suicide of 19, 30
   divorce from Lon 19
   marriage to Lon 16
   birth of son 16
Crosland, Alan 112
Crowd, The 242, 352*n*
Cruze, James 347*n*

A Thousand Faces

Culver City, California, City of 264
Curran Theatre 159-160, 214
Curwood, James Oliver 52

D'Anza Theatre 315
D'Onofrio, Vincent 258
Daily Oklahoman, The 16
Dallas, Texas, City of 76
Daly, Jacqueline 251
Damon and Phythias 25, 29
Dane, Karl 271
Dark Horse, A 333
Davis, Marc 178
Day, Marceline 199, 205
Del Monte, California, City of 76
de Bergerac, Cyrano, Character of 239
De La Motte, Margaret 116, 345*n*
DeMille, Cecil B. 23, 134, 195
De Grasse, Joseph vi, 28, 33-34
Dean, Priscilla *38*, 42, 58-59, 108, 115
Deely, Ben 49
Defiant Ones, The 8
Delmar Gardens 16, 332-333
Dempsey, Jack 124-125, 346*n*
Denver, Colorado, City of 129, 263, 333
Department of Health, Education, and Welfare 322
Designing Women 362n
Devon, George 232
Devil's Picnic, The 333
Dill, Max 17, 312, 334
Dinner at Eight 7
Dismuki 193, 352n
Disney, Walt 52, 178
Disneyland 178
    Pirates of the Caribbean attraction at 178
Doctor, The 57
Donahue, Troy 312, 317
Dove, Billie 83, 342*n*
Dowling, Joseph *337*
Dracula 155, 203, 273-274, 276
Dracula vs. Frankenstein 8
"Dragnet" (television series) 249
Drago, Harry Sinclair 356n

Dresser, Louise 188
Dressler, Marie 249
Dunphy, William 230, 306
Dunphy, Mabel 230
Dyer, U.S.M.C.,
    Lieutenant–Commander H.S. *306*
Dwan, Allan 26-27

Earles, Harry 170, *210-211*, 278, 286
    359-360*n*
Easy Money
    (also see *While The City Sleeps*) 355n
Eckels, Eddy 238, 354*n*
Educational Pictures 236
Elendale, California, City of 23
Edison, Thomas A. 26
Edwards, Snitz 161
Eisenstadt, Herman 131-132, *146*
El Capitan Theatre 362*n*
Elephant On His Hands, An 27
Emanuel, Jay 177
Emperor of Portugallia
    (see *Tower of Lies*) 173
Empty Gun, The 58-59
England, Country of 267
Epstein, Phil 306
Ermine or *The Two Vagabonds* 333
Evans, Robert J. 105, 312, 315, 319, 321, 323
Exhibitors Trade Review 44, 60, 68, 133, 149

Fairbanks, Douglas 128, 198
False Faces 42-43
Farnum, Franklyn *37*
Farnum, Joseph 256
Father and The Boys 27-28, *36*
Fazenda, Louise 78
Feinberg, Jack *221*
Felch, Edward S. 28
Felix on the Job 27
Ferris Hartman Company 17, 30, 152, 334
Film Daily 86, 134-135
Film Forum 290
Film Spectator 198, 232-233
Fischer's Follies 17-18, 334

Fitzgerald, Cissy 291
Fitzroy, Emily 197
Flashlight, The 339n
Flesh and Blood 68-70, *96*
Fly & Co., H.K. 106-107
Foolish Wives 107
Footlight Parade 118
For Those We Love 59
Forbes, Ralph 188
Ford, John 26
Forman, Tom *97*
Fox Film Corp. 108, 184
Fox West Coast Theatre 315
Fra Diavolo 332
Frankenstein 192
Freaks 359n
Full Metal Jacket 258

Gamora, Charlie 359-360n
Garbo, Greta 84, 198
Garden of the Gods, Colorado 127
George, John 193, 205-206, 361n
Gerstad, Merritt *225*
Gibson, Hoot 159
Gift Supreme, The 51-52
Gilbert, John 167, 198, 243
Gilded Spider, The 27
Gillespie, Arnold 203-204
Gingerbread Man, The 17, 334
Girl Question, The 333
Girofle-Girofla 332
Glenwood Springs, Colordo , City of
   126-127
Glory of Love (see *While Paris Sleeps*)
   85, *342*
God's Lightning 62, 85
Godowsky, Dagmar 67
Goff, Ivan 311, 318
Goldberg, Whoopi 9
Goldwyn Pictures 44, 53, 56, 59, 63-64,
   68, 80, 344n
Goldwyn, Samuel 66
Gone With The Wind 116
Gothic Pictures 168
Gowland, Gibson 161
Grand Central Station 131, 146
Grand Hotel 6-7

Grand Opera House 334
Grasso, Alfred 56-57, 60-63, 70-71, 76,
   78, 81, 83-85, *92*, 106-107, 109-111,
   113-117, 119, 124, 126-127, 129-130,
   134-135, *145*, 150-152, 238, 264
Great Western Coal Mine Company
   124-125
Greed 344n
Green Bay, Wisconsin, City of 264-265
Greenwood, M.E. 269
Greer, Jane 321
Greer, Julian 107
Gribbon, Eddie 182, 186, *222, 296,*
   351n
Griffith, D. W. 24-25, 234
Grip Of Jealousy, The 27
"Gunsmoke" (television series) 342n

Haines, William 182, 186, *220, 222, 296,*
   351n
Hale, Alan 67
Hamlet, Character of 239
Hampton, Hope 71-72, 74, *97*
Happy Thought, A 333
Harbert, Hugh 234, 346n
Harbert, Loren (grandson) 10
Harelip, The (also see *Mockery*) 196
Harlacher, L.A.P.D., Lt. Roy *295*
Harlan, Kenneth 54
Hart, William S. 35-36, *37*, 41-42
Hartman, Sigfried 276
Hastings, Hazel
   (second wife; maiden name; also see
   Hazel Chaeny) 30
Hawaiian Love 57
Hays Office, The (also see MPPDA) 55
Hays, Will 111
Heart of A Wolf 340
He Who Gets Slapped 80, 149, 153-155,
   199, *208*, 239, 331, *344*, 356n
Heinz in Ireland 333
Hen Pecks, The 334
Henley, Hobart 114
Her Escape 27
Her Grave Mistake 27
Her Life's Story 27
Herron, F.L. 269-270

A Thousand Faces

Herschfeld, Al 290, *329*
Hersholt, Jean 26
Higgins, Cardwell 200-201
High Noon 8
Hill, George 183, 186, *220*, 270-271, *296*
Hillbillies in a Haunted House 8
Hillyer, Lambert
Hinckley, R.L. *306*
Hitler, Adolph 72
Hoffman, Milton 119
Hoity-Toity 335
Holland, Cecil 189
Hollywood, California, City of 23-24,
   135, 137
Hollywood Filmograph 258
Hollywood Magazine 258
Holt, Jack 49
Holubar, Allen 114
Honor Of The Mounted, The 27
Hopkins, Robert 277
Hopple, U.S.M.C., Sgt. H.H. *296*
Horsley, David 23
Hotel Astor 133
House of Wax, The 85
Howard, James L. D.D.S. 122-123
Howe, James Wong 241-242, *291*
Hubbard, Lucien 66
Hughes, Harry 127
Hughes, Lloyd 259
Hugo, Victor 106, 109, 112, 135-136
Humberstone Kennels 124
Hunchback Illuminator, The 122
Hunchback of Notre Dame, The xi, 3-4,
   62, 73-74, 76, 78, 80-81, 84, 88, 105-
   137, *138-146*, 151-154, 157, 159, 167,
   195, *213*, 289-290, 313, 315, 317, 320,
   328, 343*n*, 346-347*n*
   financing for independent
      production of 106-107, 109-112
   make-up for 122-123, 135-136
   première of 128-134, 137
   salary for 112, *138-139*, 344*n*
Hymer, John B. 277
Hypnotist, The 202, 226

I.O. U. 334

If My Country Should Call 27
In Dutch 19, 335
Independent Film Exchange 176
Independent Motion Picture Film
   Company (IMP)
Indiana Jones 43
Ingelwood, California, City of 266
Insurrectors, The 333
International Mystery Film Festival 290
It Happened in Reno 333
Iverson's Ranch 221

Jack and the Beanstalk 334
Jacobs, Louis S. 61
Jahnke's Tavern 30
Jannings, Emil 233
Jazz Singer, The 201, 204, 352*n*
Jeske, John 127, 234, *306*
Jiggs, U.S.M.C., Sgt. (U.S. Marine Crops
   mascot) 185
Johnson, Julian 17-18
Johnson, Edith 37
Jolson Story, The 311
Joy Jason 267, 269-270
Joy, Leatrice 64
Julian, Rupert 156-157, 161-162, *212*
Jurassic Park 134

Kains, Maurice *219*, 351*n*
Kalionzes, Dana (great-granddaughter of
   Lon Chaney) *330*
Kalionzes, Nicholas (great-great-grandson
   of Lon Chaney) *330*
Kane, Bob 156
Kansas City, Kansas, City of 129
Karloff, Boris 6-7, 9, 321
Kaufman, Edward 182
Kearns, "Doc" 125
Keaton, Buster 59, 159, 198, 311, 344*n*
Keith, Ian 172
Kent, Leon *37*
Kenyon, Charles 53
Kerry, Norman *140*, 160-161, 193, 272
Kevan, Jack 318, *328*
King, Claude *223*
King, Joseph 28
King, Ruth 154

Kino Video 165
Kissing Bugs, The 334
Koenig, William 128-129
Kolb, Clarence 312, 361*n*
Kolb and Dill 19, 30, 312, 335
Kongo 251
Kortman, Robert *100*
Kubrick, Stanley 258

La Marr, Barbara 78
La Mascotte 16, 332-333
Laemmle, Carl 24-26, 105-106, 108-109,
    129, *140*, 165, 343*n*
Laemmle, Carl, Jr. 275-276
Laemmle, Carla 121, 158
Lamont, Charles 237
Lang, Matheson 187
Last Command, The 195
Last of the Mohicans 86
Latham, Jack 280-281
Laugh, Clown, Laugh 7, 239-243, *291-*
    292, 331, 354*n*, 356*n*
    happy ending for 242-243, 292, 352*n*
    title song for 242, *293*
Lawlor, J. Hoey 107-109
Lawrence, Ludwin *223*
Layton, Hal 61, 110
Lebedeff, Ivan 271
Lee, Dr. Burton J. 283
Lee Mercantile Co., H.D. 267
Lee, Lila 278, 280, *303-304*
Lehr, Abe *100*
Lejuene, U.S.M.C., Major-General John A.
    184
Leonard, Robert Z. 17
Leroux, Gaston 150, 152, 272
Lesser, Sol 76-77
Levin, Charles 263
Levy, Bernard 112
Lewis, Ralph 69
Leyser, Billy 131
Liberty Theatre 165
Light In The Dark, The 71-74, 97, 111
Light of Faith, The (also see *Light In The
    Dark, The*) 72
Lights of New York 352*n*
Lincoln, Elmo 78

Linow, Ivan 278
Lissner, Ray 241
Little Caesar 355*n*
Little Church Around The Corner 76
Little Tycoon, The 16, 332
Lloyd, Doris 175
Lloyd, Harold 198
Locan, Clarence 258
Lockheed Company 57
Loeb, Edwin 276
Loeb, Walker and Loeb, Law Offices of
    275
Loew, Arthur 223
Loew's Theatre Chain 153
Lohman, Willie, Character of 239
*Lon Chaney: The Man Behind the
    Thousand Faces* x, 180
*Lon Chaney's Gonna Get You, If You
    Don't Watch Out* (song) *299*
London After Midnight 199, 202-204,
    224-227, 331, 353*n*, 356*n*
London Film Company 44
Lonergan, Philip 53
Long Beach, California, City of 315
Loring, Hope 97
Los Angeles, California, City of 17, 19-20,
    23, 30, 76, 129-130, 250, 264
Los Angeles Examiner 152
Los Angeles Record 164
Los Angeles Times 17
Lost Patrol, The 7
Louis B. Mayer Productions 152
Lovsky, Celia 322
Lowe, Jr., Edward T. 113
Lugosi, Bela 155
Lyceum Theatre 334
Lyle, Clinton 306
Lynch, Robert 176-177

MacDermott, Marc 154
MacQuerrie , Murdock 32
Mack, Mr. and Mrs. Willard 277
Mackaill, Dorothy 207
Majestic Theatre 19, 334
Malone, Dorothy 316, 319, 321-323,
    327

A Thousand Faces

Manitoc, Wisconsin, City of 263

Man of a Thousand Faces (film biography) 3, 105, 289, *310*, 311-324

Man Who Laughs, The 156

Man Who Owns Broadway, The 334

Mann, Hank 78, 99, 312, 319, 361n

Mansfield, Richard 15

Marion, Frances 183

Marshal Dillon (television series) 342*n*

Marshall, Charles 263-264

Mason, James 55

Mason, Shirley 338

Mather, Geroge *327*

Mayer, Jerry (brother) 263-264, 266

Mayer, Louis B. 115, 127-128, 149, 176 186, 263, 265, 277

Mayo Brothers Hospital 286

McAvoy, May 116

McChesney, Bob 203-204

McConville, Bernard 156

McCormick, John 84-85

McDonald, Francis 52

McGee, Col. Gordon 119

McGregor, Malcolm 82-83, *100*, 342*n*

McKee, Raymond *99*

McKim, Robert 83, *101*

McLaglen, Victor 169, *211*

Measure of A Man, The 27

Meighan, Thomas 45

Memorial Hospital 283-284, 286

Menace to Carlotta, The 156-157

Menjou, Adolph 233

Merry-Go-Round, The 156-157

Messenger, Fred 271

Metro-Goldwyn-Mayer Studios (M-G-M) ix, 4, 6, 52, 55, 58, 79, 84, *92*, 112, 149, 1520-153, 159, 166-167, 171, 176-177, 186-189, 199-201, *208*, 234, 238-239, 242-243, 246, 249-250, 256, 262, 264, 267-269, 272-276, 280, 283, 286-287, 359*n*

   contracts with Chaney 153, 167, 176, 243-244, 274, 276-277, 344*n*, 349*n*, 358-359*n*

   contract suspension between Chaney and 274, 276, 283

   Lot Two of 220, 257, 266, 356*n*

   merger of 152-153,, 344-345*n*

Metro Pictures 71, 81-82, 108, 152, 173

Midnight Story, The 317

Military Maids, The 334

Miller, Virgil 344*n*

Miller, Patsy Ruth 116-117, 121, *330*

Miracle Man, The 36, 40, 43-46, 56, 59-60, 85

   cutting continuity of 46-49

Mr. Wu (1914) 187

Mr. Wu (1927) 7, 187-191, 222-223, 331, 356*n*

   make-up for 189-190

Mockery 169, 195-198, 223-225, 331

Mockingbird, The (see *The Blackbird*)

Mong, William V. 56, 83, 101

Monster, The 152, 166-167, 209, 331, 349*n*

Montana, Bull 49

Montgomery, Robert 271

Moore, Matt 171, 278

Moore, Owen 174, 215

Moran, Eddie 197

Moran, Lois 263

Moran, Polly *215*, 246, 249, *293*

Moran of the Lady Letty 82

Morgan, Ira 186, *220*, 271

Morris, Governeur 53, 63, 85, 93, 150

Mother's Atonement, A 27, 33-34

Motion Picutre News 112-113

Motion Picture Producers Distributors Association (MPPDA) 111

   censor notes of 205-206, 242, 267, 269-270, 344*n*

Motion Picture Theatre Owners of America 150

Motion Picture World 112

Motor Girl, The 335

Moving Picture World 29, 133, 163

Mt. Lowe, California 27

Mulhall, Jack 69, 96

"Munsters, The" (television series) 317

Murphy, Joe 125-126
Murray, James 266-267, 357*n*
Myers, Carmel 186

National Association of the Motion
  Picture Industry 344*n*
Natural History Museum of Los Angeles,
  California 124
Neilan, Marshall 59
Nestor Film Company 23-24
Never Say Can't 57
New York Morning Telegraph 150
New York, New York, City of 74, 124,
  128-131, 137, 150, 206, 249-250, 283,
  290, 321
Newhard, Robert A.S.C. 343
Newark, New Jersey, City of 76
Newman, Joseph 186, 262, 288
Next Corner, The 149, 207, 347*n*
Niblo, Fred 115, 274
Nigh, William 190, *223*, 264-267, *302*
Night Rose, The (also see V*oices of the
  City*) 68
Nikki, Wild Dog of the North 339*n*
Nolan, Mary 251, 253
Nomads of the North 52-53, *89*
Nosferatu 353*n*
Novarro, Ramon 167, 198
Nugent, Elliott 277-278
Nugent, J.C. 277
Nye, Carroll 244

Oakley, Laura 26
Oakman, Wheeler 58, 244
Octave of Claudius, The (see *A Blind
  Bargain*)
Odeon Theatre 321
Of Mice and Men 8
Oklahoma City, Oklahoma, City of 16,
  332-333
Oland, Warner 351*n*
Oliver Twist 70, 76-77, *97*
Olivette 332
Olympic Theatre 17, 19, 333
Omaha, Nebraska, City of 129, 263

One Clear Call 57
Oral Hygiene 122
Oubliette, The 32-33
Outside The Law 57-60, 74, 87, 93,
  339, 361*n*
Owen, Selena 49

Packard, Frank L. 43
Page, Anita 244, 249
Paramount Pictures 44, 110, 149, 195,
  312, 359*n*
Paramount Theatre 321, 362*n*
Park Ida May vi, 33
Parker, Claude I. *306*
Parry, Harry 97
Pasadena, California, City of 59
Pasha, Kalla *38*, 252, 257, *297*
Pathe Pictures 359*n*
Pearl Harbor 187
Peck's Bad Boy 333
Peck O' Pickles 335
Pelley, Adelaide (daughter) 74
Pelley, Marion (wife) 73-74
Pelley, William Dudley 72-74, 237-238,
  343*n*, 354*n*
Penalty, The 5, 53-56, 30, 63-64, 75, *90-
  93*, 150, 339*n*
Perry, Harvey 27
Pevney, Joseph 311-312, 317-321, *325-
  326*
Phantom of the Opera ix, 3-4, 32,*148*
  149-153, 155-166, *207, 212-214*,
  275, 289-290, 313, 319-320, 328
  153, 155-166, 207, 212-214, 275, 289-
  290, 313, 319-320, *328*
    London *première of* 165-166
    Los Angeles *première of* 164-165
    Los Angeles sneak *preview of* 159
    make-up for 148, 155-156, 158
    New York City *première of* 160,
      163-164
    re-release of (1929) 272, 358*n*
    San Francisco *première of* 159-
      160, 214
    sequel to 272
    stage built for 212-213, 303-314,

348-349n
Phantom of the Opera (musical version) 160
Philadelphia, Pennsylvania, City of 76, 130, 132
Philbin, Mary 32, 157-158, 160-161, 272
Photoplay 232, 274, 282
Pickford, Mary 26, 41, 128, 198
Picture Play 58
Pierce, Jack 313
Pike's Peak 14, 127, *143*
Pinafore 332
Pit of the Golden Dragon, The 74
Pitt Theatre 132
Pittsburgh, Pennsylvania, City of 130, 132
Place Beyond the Winds 27
Pollard, Snub 312, 319
Portland, Oregon, City of 30, 58
Poor Jake's Demise 27
Prince William of Sweden *296*
Prince Erick of Denmark *296*
Printzlau, Olga 76
Pryor, Charles 17
Public Enemy 355n
Puffy, Charles 195, *223*

Quasimodo, Character of 101, 134-137
Quick, Dr. 284-285
Quincy Adams Sawyer 71, 77-79, 99, 117

Rainey, Tina x
Ranch Romance, A 27
Rambeau, Marjorie 316
Ramsey, Marion 320
Rapf, Harry 189
Rasch, Albertina 164
Ray, Charles 59, 181, 350n
Raymond Theatre 59
Red Margaret, Moonshiner 27
Remember Mary Magdalen 27
Return Good For Evil 85
Return of the Phantom 272
Rialto Theatre 164
Rich Mr. Hogginheimer 17, 334
Richelieu 27

Riddle Gawne 35-36, 37, 42
Ringling Bros.–Barnum and Bailey Circus 324
Riverside, California, City of 315
Riviera Theatre 58
Rivoli Theatre 58
RKO Palace Theatre 321
Road To Mandalay, The 168, 177-180, 203, *218*, 253, 255, 331, 350n
Roberts, Ben 311, 318
Roberts, Edith 69, *96*
Rochester, New York, City of 204
Rogers, Buddy 233
Rogers, Will 311
Rogers St. Johns, Adela 20, 286
Romanoff, Constantine 257, 356n
Ross, Milton 55
Rosson, Arthur 27
Royal Chef, The 333
Roxie Theatre 290
Ruggles, Wesley 359n
Rush, Dennis 320, 327

Sabiston, Malcolm 236-237
Sacrifice, The 61-62, 348n
Said Pasha 16, 332
Salkow, Lester 311
Salt Lake City, Utah, City of 265
San Bernadino, California, City of 265
San Francisco, California, City of 17, 19, 30, 53, 58, 71, 81-84, 124, 159-160, 234, 290
San Francisco Chronicle 19
San Francisco Examiner 81
San Diego, California, City of 290
Sandy (Chaney's dog) *102,* 124, 346n
Santa Ana, California, City of 30, 314
Santa Fe Train Station 264
Savage, Henry W. 56
Savages 57
Savoy Theatre 334-335
Sawyer, Arthur H. 78-79, 117-118
Scar, The 112
Scarface 355n
Scarlet Car, The 34-35, 37
Schayer, E. Richard 182, 356n
Schulberg, B.P. 71, 75, *97,* 151, 340n

Index

Screen Book Magazine 288-289
Scott, Randolph 184
Sea Bat, The 273
Sea Hawk, The 82
Sea Urchin, The 27
Seattle, Washington, City of 234
Seastrom, Victor 153, 171
Sedgwick, Edward 159, 161
Seigel, Bernard 239, *291-292*
Sekely, Bella 175-176
Sergeant Bull 268
Seven Falls, Colorado 127
Shadows, ix, 74-76, 81, *98, 101*, 115, 118, *336, 341*, 340n, 345n
Shearer, Norma 154, 167, 171, 312, 319
Sheehan, Perley Poore 61-63, 113-114, 119
Sheldon, Willard 189-190, 235, 241-242, 265-267, 288, *291*
Sherwood, Robert E. 76
Shipman, Samuel 277
Shock, The 70, 74, 86-87, 102, 343n
Shooting of Dan McGrew, The 117-118
Show Girl, The 334
Sierra Nevada Mountains, Eastern 234, 287
Simon Louvier 150
Silent Movie Theatre 290
Sing Sing Penitentiary 44
Singleton, Penny 235
Sistrom, William 35
Skal, David J. 262, 273
Skinner, Frank 322
Smith, Roger 319, 322
Son of the Skiek 352n
Song Birds, The 334
Sony JumboTron screen 165
South Carolina, State of 59
Span of Life, The 127-128, *346*
Spearing, James 156
Speculators, The 333
Spurs (also see *Freaks*) 359n
St. Francis Hotel 71, 81-83
St. Louis, Missouri, City of 129
St. Vincent's Hospital 287
Stahl, John 57
Stallings, Laurence 269

Stammers, Frank 30
Star of the Sea 27
"Star Trek" (television series) 317
"state rights" 62
Steck, Olga 19
Sterling, Ford 30, *209*
Stern, Abe 61
Stern, Julius 61
Stern, Walter 275
Stevenson, Robert Louis 51
Stoker, Bram 203
Stone, Lewis 26, 52, *89*
Stuckel, Elliott 131
Summer Flirts, The 334
Suspense 29
Swain, Mack 196-197
Sweet, Blanche 78

Tabor, Grand Theatre 333
Taggert, Errol 204, 262
Talk of the Town 335
Tammy and the Bachelor 317-318
Taylor, Estelle 259, 261, 329
Tec–Art 152, 166
Tell It To The Marines 2, 4, 6, 9, 80, 169, 181-187, 191, 200, *219-222, 296*, 331, 350-51n, 356n, 358n
Ten Commandments, The 347n
Terminator 2 62
Terror (also see *Mockery*) 197
Terry, Ethel Grey 54
Thalberg, Irving G. 6-7, 57, 66, 81, 105-106, 1008, 111, 114-115, 118-119, 127-128, *138-139*, 149, 152-153, 167-168, 175, 182-183, 201, *210*, 233, 250, 273, 277, *303*, 311-312, 314-315, 319, 323
These Wilder Years 311
Thirteenth Chair, The 272-273
Thornby, Robert 66
Three of a Kind 333
Thug, The 112
Thunder 262-267, 286, *302*, 331, 356n
Thurston (magician) 164
Tillie's Nightmare 334
Time, The Place and The Girl, The 334
Toledo, Ohio, City of 130

A Thousand Faces

Tower of Lies 171-173, 215, 331, *345,*
Torrance, Ernest 271
Torres, Raquel 359n
Tourneur, Maurice 49, 51, 86, *338*
Trader Horn 236
Traffic in Souls 44
Tragedy of Whispering Creek 27
Trap, The (1922) 60, 66-68, *95,* 118
Treasure Island 51, 86, *338*
Tremont Temple Theatre 131
Twelve Miles Out 243
20th Century-Fox Studios 63
Tucker, George Loane 44, 46, 56-57,
    62-63, 85

Unconquered, The 7
United States Marine Corps 181-187
United States Marine Corps Recruit
    Depot 183, *219*
Universal Film Manufacturing Company
    24
Universal-International Studios (see
    Universal Studios) 311
Universal Studios 3, 8, *22,* 24-26, 28-29,
    31, 35-36, 41-42, 57, 60-61, 70, 87-88,
    92, 105-109, 111-115, 118-121, 127-
    131, 149-153, 156-157, 159-161, 165,
    168, 238, 272-276, 359n
    dedication of 24
    Jaws studio tour attraction 314
    Pollard Lake location 314
Universal Weekly 22, 28-29, 113
Underworld 243
Unholy Three, The (1925, silent version)
    80, 159, 167-171, 176, 200, *210-211,*
    275, 277, 331, 337n, 349n, 356n
Unholy Three, The (1930, sound version)
    200, 277-283, 286, *303-305, 328,* 331,
    356n
Unkissed Man, The 333
Unknown, The xii, 168-169, 191-194,
    203, 224, 250, 331, *347,* 354n, 356n,
    359n, 361n
Unlawful Trade, The 27
USS California 186

Valentino, Rudolph 198, 352n
Valentino (film biography) 82
Valli, Virginia 86, *102*
Van Enger, Charles 157-158
Variety 311
Veidt, Conrad 156, 274
Velez, Lupe 258, 261, *300,* 329
Victory 49-51, 86, 89, 339n
Vidor, King 352n
Viola (Chaney Family cook) 234
Violin Maker, The 27
Viva Villa 6-7
Volga Boatman, The 195
Voices of the City (also see *The Night
    Rose*) 68, 96
Von Sternberg, Josef 243
Von Stroheim, Eric 107, 114, 156-157,
    343n, 344n

Walker, Jimmy 249-250
Walt Disney Productions 339n
Walthall, Henry B. *38, 218*
Walsh, Raoul 114
Ward, Patricia 231
Ward, Roscoe *297,* 356n
Warner Bros. 76
Warner, Jack 76
Warren, E.A. 58
Washington, D.C. 76
Wayne, John xi, 184
Weber's Bread 289-290
Weber, Lois 29
Webb, Jack 184
Webber, Andrew Lloyd 160
Webster, Dr. John C. 127
West of Zanzibar 168-169, 179-180,
    199, 250-260, 331, *349,* 355-356n
West, Roland 166
West Productions, Roland 152, 166
Western Welcome, A 57
Westmore, Bud 3133, 318, 328
What Price Glory? 184
Wheelright, Ralph 311
When Johnny Comes Marching Home
    334
Where East Is East 258-262, 273, *300,*
    329, 331, 350, *375-376* 356n, 360n

Index

Where's Haggerty 112
While Paris Sleeps 85-86, *342*
While The City Sleeps 4, 5, 9, 169, 244-250, 293-295, 331, *355n*
White Faith 72
White, Pearl 311
Who's The Fellow? 333
Who Won In the First? 29
Wicked Darling, The *38*, 42
Willat, Irvin 81-82
Williams, Ben Ames 82
Willis and Ingles (Chaney's first motion picture agent) 35, 46
Wilson, Millard K. (also known as M. K. Wilson) *220*
Windsor, Claire *350n*
Withey, Chet 114

Wolf Breed (also see *The Trap*, 1922) 60
Wolf Man, The 192
Woman's Folly, A 29
Worsley, Wallace 53, 55-56, 64, 68, 80, *95*, 115-117, 119, 121, *140*, *343*
Written on the Wind 319

Yankee Prince, The 334
Ye Alpine Tavern 27
Yellow Sin, The 273
Young Loretta 239-241, *292*
Young, Waldemar 203, 228, 337n, 356n

Zan (Chaney's wigmaker) 83
Zanuck, Darryl F. 63

WEST COAST UPTOWN
WESTERN at TENTH
Newsette

| VOL. II | FRIDAY, MARCH 23, 1928 | NO. 19 |

Lon Chaney in "The Big City"

Lon Chaney in "The Big City" Starting Friday March 30th

A glimpse into the "Invisible City" within New York; that strange manifestation of life known as "the underworld," is afforded in a graphic and enthralling way in Lon Chaney's latest Metro-Goldwyn-Mayer picture, "The Big City," which opens a week's run at the Uptown next Friday.

In the picture Chaney again gives a masterful demonstration of his versatility. He has given the screen many strange characters, but in "The Big City" he invades the present, and plays a New York gangster leader of modern times, in a compelling characterization.

The story teems with thrills and mystery, interspersed with a delightful romance. Chaney and his gang, in conflict with a rival gang; a sensational holdup of a popular night club, battles with the police and duels of wits with the detectives; these are all breathlessly exciting backgrounds for the charming love idyll of a boy and girl — parts played by pretty Marceline Day, and James Murray.

Betty Compson is also in the cast and is convincing in her role of the gangster's feminine accomplice. This is the first time incidentally, that Miss Compson and Chaney have appeared together since "The Miracle Man," in which both were launch-

Some theatres printed their own heralds in lieu of the studio-released heralds. Many of these heralds included ads for near-by businesses as well.

About the Author

Michael F. Blake is acknowledged as the leading historian on the life and career of Lon Chaney. Critics have called his recent biography, *Lon Chaney: The Man Behind the Thousand Faces,* the definitive work on the famous actor. In the summer of 1994, he appeared as a guest speaker during a film tribute to Lon Chaney at the International Mystery Film Festival in Italy.

Michael was responsible for the 1986 renaming of a theatre in

A Thousand Faces

Chaney's honor in his hometown of Colorado Springs, Colorado. The author was also instrumental in the Hollywood Make-up Union posthumously honoring Chaney's achievements in motion picture make-up, by presenting the award to the actor's grandson, Lon Ralph Chaney, during a film retrospective at UCLA in 1983. Michael recently became the first make-up artist to be allowed to examine Chaney's make-up case at the Natural History Museum in Los Angeles, as part of a story for the French Television show, "Hollywood."

He has lectured extensively and authored many articles pertaining to Chaney for such publications as *Filmfax*, *Performing Arts*, *Fangoria* and *Leatherneck*: the Magazine of the Marines. Michael's collection of Lon Chaney memorabilia is considered to be the most extensive in the world, containing 120 lobby cards, 10 posters, over 1,900 photographs and 4 autograph pictures.

For the past 16 years, Michael has worked as a professional make-up artist on such productions as *Star Trek VI*, *Sister Act I & II*, *Soapdish*, *Tough Guys*, "Magnum, P.I.," "Happy Days," and the recently released *Strange Days*. Before that, he worked as a child actor appearing in "The Munsters," "Adam-12," "Bonanza," "The Lucy Show," "Bewitched," and "Marcus Welby, M.D." He has also performed several times as a guest clown with the Blue Unit of Ringling Bros.–Barnum and Bailey Circus.

Between make-up assignments, Michael is writing *The Films of Lon Chaney* and *Greasepaint to Prosthetics: The History of Motion Picture Make-up*. He lives with his wife, Linda, and dog, Tara, in Los Angeles, California.